Unruly Domestication

The publication of this book was made possible by the generous support of the Louann Atkins Temple Women & Culture Endowment.

« KRISTIN SKRABUT »

Unruly Domestication

POVERTY, FAMILY, AND STATECRAFT IN URBAN PERU

University of Texas Press AUSTIN

The Louann Atkins Temple Women & Culture Endowment is supported by Allison, Doug, Taylor, and Andy Bacon; Margaret, Lawrence, Will, John, and Annie Temple; Larry Temple; the Temple-Inland Foundation; and the National Endowment for the Humanities.

First edition, 2024

Portions of chapters 3 and 6 were previously published in "Residency Counts and Housing Rights: Conflicting Enactments of Property in Lima's Central Margins," *Current Anthropology* 59, no. 6: 691–715. DOI: 10.1086/700758

All photographs, images, and maps are courtesy of the author.

♾ The paper used in this book meets the minimum requirements of ANSI/NISO Z39.48-1992 (R1997) (Permanence of Paper).

Library of Congress Cataloging-in-Publication Data

Names: Skrabut, Kristin, author.
Title: Unruly domestication : poverty, family, and statecraft in urban Peru / Kristin Skrabut.
Description: First edition. | Austin : University of Texas Press, 2024. | Includes bibliographical references and index.
Identifiers: LCCN 2023029857 (print) | LCCN 2023029858 (ebook)
ISBN 978-1-4773-2909-2 (hardcover)
ISBN 978-1-4773-2910-8 (paperback)
ISBN 978-1-4773-2911-5 (pdf)
ISBN 978-1-4773-2912-2 (epub)
Subjects: LCSH: Poverty—Social aspects—Peru—Lima. | Poor—Peru—Lima. | Poverty—Government policy—Peru—Lima. | Bureaucracy—Peru—Lima. | Single mothers—Peru—Lima—Social conditions. | Squatter settlements—Social aspects—Peru—Lima. | Squatters—Peru—Lima—Social conditions.
Classification: LCC HC228.L56 S58 2024 (print) | LCC HC228.L56 (ebook) | DDC 362.50985/255—dc23/eng/20231128
LC record available at https://lccn.loc.gov/2023029857
LC ebook record available at https://lccn.loc.gov/2023029858

doi:10.7560/329092

For my families,
for my girls.

Contents

Illustrations

Acknowledgments

This book would not have been possible without the generous support of many individuals and institutions in Peru and the United States. First and foremost, I am indebted to my friends, mentors, and interlocutors in Pachacútec for their generous support of this project and for inviting me into their homes and lives. Though I will not use their real names here to preserve their anonymity, they above all made this book possible. The people I call Pablo, William, and Ismael supported this project from the very start, and their influence critically shaped the evolution of this book and my own trajectory as a thinker and scholar. In the everyday, the women I name Marisa, Anita, and Milagros made this research possible, inviting me into their homes and confidences and teaching me how to make a life. Their lessons inform the core of this writing. There were also many others in Pachacútec and Ventanilla, *dirigentes* and *mujeres luchadoras* too numerous to name here, whose insights and camaraderie shaped this work. I am in awe of their savvy and strength, infinitely grateful for their friendship, and aspire to repay the many kindnesses they have shown me. I must also thank the employees at the municipalities of Ventanilla, Pisco, and Tupac Amaru Inca and the agents from the INEI, SISFOH, COFOPRI, FONCODES, RENIEC, and GRIAS who tolerated my endless questions with astonishing grace.

For the fieldwork upon which this book is based, I gratefully acknowledge the financial support of the Wenner-Gren Foundation, the National Science Foundation, and the Population Studies and Training Center and Graduate School at Brown University. Over the years, I have had the opportunity to refine the ideas presented in this book through conversations, collaborations, and additional research trips that were funded and facilitated by a number of institutions, including the Cities and Development Cluster in the Department of Geography at the London School of Economics; the Department of Social Studies at Harvard University; and at Tufts University, the Mellon Sawyer Seminar on the Politics of Kinship, the Center for the Humanities, the Faculty Research Awards and Grants-in-Aid program, and the Departments of Urban and Environmental Policy and Planning and of Anthropology.

At Brown University, I had the privilege of working with an array of brilliant scholars. I am especially grateful to my adviser, Kay Warren, for her inspiration and advocacy and to my mentors Jessaca Leinaweaver and Daniel Jordan Smith, whose support, responsiveness, easy brilliance, and sage advice have been invaluable to me throughout my career. I was also surrounded by peers who enriched my life and work with their empathy and insight. Rebecca Peters, Katie Rhine, Maya Judd, Andrea Maldonado, Jennifer Ashley, Kathleen Millar, and Rebecca Galemba graciously advised me as I moved through each stage of this project. Susan Ellison, Sohini Kar, Stacey Vanderhurst, and Maya Mesola inspired me with their enthusiasm and intellect. Inna Leykin, Yagmur Nuhrat, and Kendra Fehrer went through everything alongside me, teaching me about the diverse gifts every scholar brings to the table.

I received valuable feedback on earlier iterations of this text from Linda Seligmann, Sylvia Chant, Daniella Gandolfo, Clara Han, Krista Van Vleet, and Sarah Pinto and from colleagues at the Contemporary Latin American Anthropology Working Group at the David Rockefeller Center for Latin American Studies. I am grateful to all of these scholars for their generous readings and constructive advice. Some of the material presented in chapter 3 appeared in "Documents, Law, and the State in the Andes" in the 2018 volume *The Andean World*, edited by Linda Seligmann and Kathleen Fine-Dare. Some of the research presented in chapter 6 has appeared in "Residency Counts and Housing Rights: Conflicting Enactments of Property in Lima's Central Margins," *Current Anthropology* 59, no. 6: 691–715; "Housing the Contingent Life Course: Aspiration and Extreme Poverty in Peru's Urban Periphery," *City and Society* 30, no. 2: 263–288; and the chapter "Recognizing (Dis)Order: Topographies of Power and Property in Lima's Periphery," in the 2014 volume *The Housing Question*, edited by Edward Murphy and Najib Hourani. I am grateful to the editors and to the many anonymous and named reviewers of those pieces for their support as I developed these ideas and to the two anonymous reviewers through the University of Texas Press for their suggestions about how to make this book speak to a wider array of students and scholars. I must also thank my editor at the University of Texas Press, Casey Kittrell, for believing in this project, Robert Kimzey for seeing this book through its final stages, and my research assistant, Louisa Winchell, for her keen eye and timely editing support.

I also want to acknowledge the people whose love and support for me and this project extended across borders. My mother, Lucy, and brother Paul provided steady assurances and frequent phone calls. My grandparents Freida and Will did not live to see the end of this project, but I felt their love and encouragement throughout. My Peruvian family facilitated every aspect of this research and, though I still have far to go, have made me a gentler, more patient, and more grounded person in the process. No tengo las palabras suficientes para expresar cuanto amor y gratitud siento para ustedes. Les extraño y les quiero para siempre.

Finally, I must express my gratitude to a few very special individuals. To Pat, whose wisdom, humor, and generosity have helped me learn to get out of my own way. To Adam, who makes everything possible. And to Mira and Risa, who taught me to love in ways I never imagined.

Introduction

EXTREME LIVES

In Pachacútec, poverty and development are inscribed in the landscape and can be felt in your joints, your muscles, your lungs. In 2010, this twenty-square-kilometer settlement marked the northwestern edge of metropolitan Lima-Callao. Marisa and I had been traversing the giant sand dune all morning. We began at 7:30 a.m., tumbling down from Marisa's house on the sandy hillside through an open-air market already thick with street vendors trying to catch buyers on their way to the main avenue where the asphalt, installed with great fanfare only a year earlier, was already wearing thin. Buses and passenger vans spewed exhaust and kicked up dust, creating a world in sepia that prematurely aged the concrete exteriors of franchise restaurants and pharmacies that lined this strip of prime real estate.

At the avenue we turned right. As we walked along the undulating hills of rutted, packed dirt on the side of the road, Marisa and I spotted new houses edging toward the dune's summit. Overnight, people had dragged *esteras* (straw mats) and plywood panels up the sand dune,[1] fashioning these materials into makeshift structures that they could use to lay claim to an apparently vacant stretch of littoral desert. My mind flashed to a recent conversation with a woman named Laura in which she described her first few nights in Pachacútec. She and her husband laid down some cardboard and blankets, precariously enclosed the small area with straw mats and, in the cold damp of winter, slept one on top of the other for warmth "como sapos," like toads, she explained.

Marisa dialed Pablo's number, then hung up after a single ring to avoid being charged for the call. He called back immediately, and she told him about the new *invasión* (invasion, illegal land occupation) we had just identified on the periphery of the neighborhood known as sector K.

Pablo said he already knew. Marisa was the third person to call him that morning. It sounded like a complaint, but I knew Pablo was proud that he was so many people's first call and was thus kept apprised of large gatherings, invasions, and any other site where politics might happen. While he awaited instructions from higher-ups about how to handle the new settlement, Marisa was to continue with the district mayor's latest business formalization campaign, encouraging people to register their businesses with the municipality and to reap whatever rewards and suffer whatever consequences might come with this new political visibility.

We turned left and walked briefly along the creamy black pavement that led to the governmental center of Pachacútec, the settlement's first three concrete buildings, before spilling farther down the sand dune to the lower residential groups. This was Marisa's zone; it was the area where she, as a "promoter" for the municipality, was responsible for spreading the word about various district government campaigns, building relationships with residents, and otherwise expanding the mayor's political network. We passed women sweeping morning dust out of brightly painted plywood homes and took turns picking up small rocks and hissing "¡Tss tss, fuera!" (Get out!) to intimidate rogue dogs that barked and lunged at us as we walked by. Upon reaching a house along Pachacútec's lower avenue, we dropped off a birthday card from the mayor. These cards were part of an ongoing project his administration used to construct personal relations with residents while simultaneously keeping tabs on who was actively inhabiting and participating in the community. We then wended our way back up the dune, stopping at any home that seemed to double as a store or restaurant to tell proprietors about the mayor's latest one-time formalization campaign: "Act now, and a single payment will formalize your business for life!" Paying the fee would render it a politically visible and proper enterprise. Most people regarded us with suspicion, took a flyer, and sent us away.

By 2 p.m. we were tired and hungry, on edge from the barking dogs, and dizzy from the fog that had swirled about us for most of the morning. We made our way to an unassuming restaurant frequented by promoters like Marisa because the owner let them eat on credit and pay for their meals at the end of the month or whenever the municipality got around to paying them. Other promoters—Elisabet, Oscar, Julia, and Irma—were already sipping warm chicken soup when we arrived. We sat and chatted absently about the work of formalization until the television screen glowing on the counter grabbed our attention.

"Next time on *Vidas Extremas*!" a booming voice overlay a tinny guitar playing minor progressions as a montage of crumbled adobe, barren deserts, and piles of garbage eventually led to a Peruvian celebrity huddled in a dark corner giving a tearful testimonial about the day's hardships. From 2008 to 2012, this popular reality TV show, *Extreme Lives*, sought out the poorest of the poor, those living in the direst circumstances, and sent Peruvian celebrities to live among them for three days. Pornographic displays of everyday suffering, followed by charitable donations and a dash of celebrity gossip, proved a winning formula. When I asked my companions if they watched the show, their collective and unequivocal response was "Every Saturday night." Their opinions of the program, however, were mixed, and my inquiry incited a full roundtable discussion. Elisabet responded,

> It has various messages, good and bad. You know, they [the celebrities] also make money from this. . . . I was naïve at first, but a friend of mine who works at the channel told me. . . . But I did admire Viviana Rivasplata [Miss Peru 2001] as a participant because she committed herself to that family and still helps them. She has come down here [to Pachacútec] and given that woman rice and sugar. She put up their storefront, and she keeps helping them. . . . She's even paying for one of the daughters to get a technical degree.

Marisa chimed in, "Sure, she was good, but I hated the one from sector D4, the one that Tula went to." Sighs of disgust erupted around the table. I remembered the episode well. Tula Rodriguez, a Peruvian showgirl turned actress, came to Pachacútec to experience the "extreme lives" of a shoeshine boy and his mother. The episode was originally meant to feature the boy's father, who, the episode insinuated, had died suddenly of AIDS. Making the best of the situation, the show's producers began the episode with footage of the father's burial in Pachacútec's clandestine cemetery and followed thirteen-year-old Pedrito as he struggled to learn his father's shoeshine trade and support his impoverished family. During her three days with them, Tula shined shoes and tried to teach timid Pedrito how to attract customers and compete with the hundreds of other children struggling to make a living on the street just as he was. In accordance with the show's formula, the three-hour episode ended with a tearful reunion between Tula and the family, followed by donations to the family on behalf of local politicians and the show's corporate sponsors. These gifts, which spoke volumes about how poverty and appropriate poverty relief were conceptualized, included: a certificate of property possession from the regional government that would support the widow's efforts to obtain legal title to her land; a wooden modular home with a tin roof to replace the house of straw and plastic sheeting that allowed Pachacútec's thick winter fog to collect in bulging overhead pools and spill onto the dirt floor; a street cart and vendor's license so the widow could sell *mazamora morada* (sweetened purple corn gelatin) nearby and earn a living while remaining close to home; and scholarships to technical institutes for Pedrito and his sister. "Yes, I hated that one," Marisa continued, "because that woman they helped didn't deserve it. . . . That woman never loved her kids, and she never loved that man."

Elisabet agreed. "She never loved that man, and he was the one who worked his fingers to the bone. She had already left him and was pregnant with another man's baby. . . . I know the woman, only by sight, but I know her."

I asked if they were suggesting that the woman wasn't "truly needy," drawing on a phrase often used in Peruvian media to critique poorly targeted assistance programs. Marisa corrected me. "Of course she's needy. We're all needy here. But it's a shame that a similar case didn't . . ." She trailed off and decided to explain the issue a different way.

> I'll give you an example. You've got your partner, and he's needy. But you left him. You went off with another man. Then he [the former partner] dies, and you come back to cry about it, 'Oh my husband is dead.' The television program discovers you, and you go on TV with Tula to shine shoes, pretending you're this poor little thing that's really needy. Your partner was the one who really needed the help, but he's dead, and you're *más viva* [livelier, craftier], and so they give all the benefits to you, and you run off to spend it with another man. But who knows about this? No one except us who live here in Pachacútec. We know and it's infuriating. That's why Elisabet says that there are good and bad messages. . . . That woman is going to get everything when she never really loved her kids or that man.

When I suggested that the show must attend to real cases too, Marisa corrected me again:

> They are all real cases, Kris. They are all real cases. But there are cases that need stuff just like there are cases that have gone from needing to not needing. But as I say, they make you pity them and from this pity they grab you, "Oh, poor little thing, she's poor," when she doesn't have

> anything to do with the man who died. . . . And the woman doesn't even love her kids because she left them and went off alone with another man. . . . And you know what? After the show she left again. . . . I think now her kids are staying with some relative.

All told, I spent almost a decade (2007–2017)[2] exploring how Peru's ongoing *lucha contra la pobreza* (war on poverty) played out in Pachacútec and other officially designated "extreme poverty zones." Up until the Covid-19 pandemic hit Peru in March 2020, the country had experienced one of the largest and most sustained poverty declines in Latin America, with official poverty rates plummeting from approximately 58 percent of the population in 2004 to just over 20 percent in 2019 (World Bank 2020). Critics, meanwhile, countered these sunny statistics; they argued that the stats were being rigged, that help wasn't getting to the "truly needy," and that the poor didn't feel any less poor than they had a year before.

Yet for all the time I spent scrutinizing statistics, poring over news reports, interviewing officials, shadowing program promoters, attending community meetings, and cooking alongside participants in community-managed food assistance organizations like *comedores populares* (dining halls serving low-cost lunches) and Vaso de Leche branches (Glass of Milk, a low-cost breakfast program that targets children), I consistently returned to this moment as one that crystallized the complex dynamics surrounding Peru's perpetual war on poverty. For my interlocutors who lived and worked in Pachacútec, it seemed that true need was ubiquitous and yet hidden behind its own prevalence. These interlocutors described poverty as something they could see; it was embedded in the landscape and reflected in the news and reality TV programs that caricatured their lives, yet they also cautioned that looks can be deceiving. In these frameworks, poverty was clearly spatial and aesthetic and thus could be attributed to everyone who lived in Pachacútec, including the promoters themselves. However, through the language of the truly needy, "los que verdaderamente necesitan," and the exceptional claims that such a language makes on others, poverty was also tied to time, to circumstance, and critically, to the supposedly private realms of family, intimacy, and affect. It is in part because of these entanglements—between the static spaces and fleeting times of poverty, between faith in poverty's self-evidence and a pervasive mistrust of appearances, between poverty's public politics and its manifestations in private life—that I describe the phenomena presented in this book as the unruly domestication of poverty.

Poverty's multidimensional and multivalent domestication was evident in the various ways the Peruvian state endeavored to understand and control poverty through individual households. Poverty was measured through household surveys and officially associated with specific features of the house and home, including building materials, infrastructural connections, number of rooms and occupants, number of children, and the gender and marital status of the household head. Poverty relief was likewise targeted to specific households and often took the form of efforts to shore up household boundaries and regulate their internal dynamics through property formalization, marriage campaigns, and education initiatives to teach women "proper" household governance strategies. Official and popular discourses also identified "precarious," "broken," and "disintegrating" households as the source of Peru's intractable poverty. Like "culture of poverty" discourses in the United States,[3] this framework tended to obscure poverty's origins in global and local relations of inequality and encouraged people, especially women, to turn inward, identifying themselves as the source of Peru's poverty problem and the site of any potential solutions.

Beyond this, efforts to fight poverty through housing since the mid-twentieth century have entangled the concept and experience of poverty with failing to obtain normative, state-sanctioned ideals of domestic life. Through public discourse, school curricula, tax code, and myriad mundane administrative policies and practices, the Peruvian state has generated a master narrative of the life course and encouraged individuals to map their identities and experiences onto that narrative (Creed 2000). These basic story lines help produce patterns of belonging that "form the basis for feeling . . . at home, in one place and not another," while individual divergences from the prescribed narrative can prompt experiences of inadequacy, marginality, and out-of-placeness even when one is otherwise at home (Borneman 1992, 287). Moreover, Peru's precedent-setting "progressive" and "self-help" housing policies, in which the state allows Peruvians to build homes on vacant land progressively as their means permit, have helped to spatialize and aestheticize these domestic life-course aspirations, refracting them onto landscapes where they can be photographed, mapped, and transformed into the purportedly objective criteria by which poverty is assessed, managed, and frequently misread.

The various ways Peruvian officials have sought to pin down poverty and fight it in and through domestic spaces have had unruly consequences that extend far outside the home, challenging the ordering capacities of the state and shaping everyday life in Peru's urban settlements in paradoxical ways. Peru's war on poverty has perpetuated and remade forms of moral precariousness and discrimination, created troubling disjunctures between expectations of technocratic development and the profoundly political ways development programs have been implemented in practice, enabled illicit livelihood strategies, and reproduced landscapes of poverty in the urban periphery. Paradoxically, it seemed that the more closely poverty was scrutinized, the harder it was to get a handle on; the more it was documented and defined, the harder those documents were to trust; and the more it was identified with the home, the more it spilled out onto the landscape, undermining official narratives of Peruvian economic development even as it refracted Peruvians' pursuits of state-sanctioned development ideals.

Understanding how Peru's war on poverty shapes lives and relationships within extreme poverty zones like Pachacútec requires several analytic moves. First, we need to unsettle conventional, universalizing definitions of poverty in order to think more critically about how poverty is assembled and experienced in specific contexts. Second, we must adopt an experience-near understanding of the state, scrutinizing how it is constituted in and through its ostensibly excluded margins and how state poverty-fighting technologies like formalization reproduce and recode long-standing race and class inequalities. Finally, we need to overcome hegemonic, modernist assumptions about neat divisions between personal and political spheres to explore the myriad ways politics are entangled with ideals of family, realities of kinship, and the intimate aspirations and insecurities that find physical expression in Peru's urban peripheries. Together, these moves provide ways of thinking about the situated rollout of development policy that transcend this specific context and can inform analyses of how official policy frameworks might both misunderstand and shape social life in other sites.

RETHINKING POVERTY

Although poverty has been a perennial concern of policy makers since the dawn of the modern era,[4] in the 1990s and early 2000s, attention to "global poverty" became especially acute (Gupta 2011; Roy and Shaw-Crane 2015). At that time, the consequences of economic structural adjustment programs that prioritized economic growth over social well-being had become starkly apparent, with many in the international development community arguing that the short-term costs of increased mortality, malnutrition, and unemployment were simply too high a price to pay for the promise of eventual capitalist prosperity (M. Davis 2006; Portes and Roberts 2005). Scholars and policy makers began seeking new ways to conceptualize poverty and development that might provide a better baseline than GDP for assessing and improving quality of life, particularly for the world's poor. Global development organizations, along with interdisciplinary consortia at elite universities, began to develop multidimensional definitions of poverty as well as composite numerical indicators—such as the Human Development Index and the Multidimensional Poverty Index—that took health, education, and the possession and distribution of various assets into account when evaluating the poverty and development of different nations (Green 2006; Merry 2016; World Bank 2000). Economists worked to move beyond conflations of GDP with quality of life by focusing on particular aspects of the poverty experience and using randomized control trials to test the effectiveness of specific interventions (Banerjee and Duflo 2020; Cookson 2018). Finance scholars began looking more closely at the complex financial lives of the poor in order to better integrate them into global markets (Collins et al. 2009). Meanwhile, development sociologists endeavored to combine qualitative and quantitative approaches in a way that preserved local definitions of poverty while still facilitating cross-national comparisons (Kanbur and Shaffer 2007).

Much of this scholarship is innovative and thoughtful, and taken together, these initiatives have prompted important debates about how best to conceptualize the poor and the most effective and ethical forms of assistance.[5] Nonetheless, I am wary of the political and ideological implications of many of these poverty identification and assessment practices. While there are arguably good reasons for global development practitioners to compare levels of poverty over time and across space, the fixation on universally applicable definitions and measures ultimately serves to reify poverty; it constructs poverty as an objective thing that exists "out there" rather than recognizing it as an effect of ongoing relations of inequality at multiple levels (Green 2006). Anthropologist Akhil Gupta (2011, 7) argues that defining poverty in a way that allows for global comparisons inevitably favors a "contextually thin" understanding of poverty likely to inspire universalistic solutions that cannot possibly take seriously the current development "mantras of decentralization, participation and empowerment." More perniciously still, the fixation on defining "the poor" as a single global class united by some intrinsic quality—such as their meager earnings, low caloric intakes, or some quantifiable lack of opportunity—distances us from the very features most responsible for whatever we might understand as poverty on a global scale, "namely historically grounded inequalities [and] asymmetries of power" (Gupta 2011, 8).

Additionally, as a cultural anthropologist I believe that context and meaning are critical to understanding any aspect of human experience. Veena Das and Shalini Randeria (2015, S4) argue that there is "no Archimedean point from which the diverse, subtle, and often imperceptible forms of social marginalization and discrimination . . . can be reduced to measurable categories of absolute or relative poverty." Grasping what poverty means for people requires exploring its tight alignment with other conditions of life in specific contexts, such as "the possibility of democratic participation, the erosion of infrastructure, the denial of citizenship . . . [or] the effect of race and policies of incarceration" (Das and Randeria 2015, S4). While poverty is often depicted as a force that reduces human concerns to basic needs and mere survival, anthropological research on topics as seemingly primal as famine and motherhood challenges the notion that any aspect of human experience is so vital, so close to naked biological life as to be beyond meaning (De Waal 2005; Gupta 2011; Scheper-Hughes 1992). Experiences of suffering are always social and contextual. They are governed by specific articulations of political-economic structures and historic inequalities that unevenly distribute life chances, informed by collective cultural models of how to undergo life struggles, and shaped by intersubjective interactions that affirm, deny, reinterpret, exacerbate, or ameliorate experiences of suffering (Farmer 2003; Kleinman and Kleinman 1996).

With these anthropological frameworks in mind, in this book I approach poverty in a way that will make it feel strange to most readers. I intentionally seek to *estrange* poverty from anxious imaginaries that alternately spur spastic reactivity and political paralysis,[6] so that we might better appreciate the multidimensional lives and life projects of people too often flatly depicted as "the poor" while also gaining a better understanding of the work that the concept of poverty does in particular contexts. Thus, rather than beginning with a preformed understanding of poverty and fleshing out its meaning, I explore how the idea of poverty emerges and comes to have force in everyday life. I investigate poverty as a cultural construct, a category of administration, a language of politics, a site for everyday negotiations of entitlements, and an identity that fades in and out of view in the face of the many other networks and relations in which the urban poor necessarily participate (Das and Randeria 2015; Green 2006; Roy 2003).

I am certainly not the first to take such a critically distant approach to the analysis of poverty. Some of the oldest traditions of theorizing poverty have explained it not as some essential experience or identity but as a social and administrative category that establishes particular relations between those who give and those who receive assistance. In the early 1900s, sociologist Georg Simmel argued that being poor does not automatically place someone in the specific social category of "the poor." Rather, Simmel contends, "it is only from the moment that they are assisted that they become part of a group characterized by poverty" (1965 [1908], 122); they become a group united by the collective attitude that society adopts toward them as recipients of ameliorative assistance. In the modern Europe that Simmel describes, the poor were given assistance not because they were entitled to it as rights-bearing citizens but to prevent them from becoming "dangerous enemies of society" (121). Poverty assistance was thus an "application of public means to public ends" (123). In this context, "the poor man as a person and the perception of his position in his own mind" were as irrelevant to public administration as they were "to the giver who gives alms for the salvation of his own soul" (121).

When the poverty concept began to be applied globally in the wake of World War II,[7] it remained a category defined by the purveyors of assistance and helped to perpetuate long-standing hierarchies between the "developed" nations that gave assistance and the "underdeveloped" nations that received it (Escobar 1995). As donating institutions with different priorities proliferated over the course of the twentieth century, poverty emerged in different sites as a composite category forged by the diverse charitable organizations and statelike actors operating in a given context (Das and Randeria 2015, S11).

The specific ways the poverty idea is assembled in different times and places results from the ways diverse political technologies (such as surveys, maps, legal systems, and political discourses) and modes of representation come together in particular circumstances (Ong and Collier 2005; Roy and Shaw-Crane 2015). The general tendency among scholars and the discerning public is to treat statistics and narratives as opposing forms of representation. Statistics are depicted as cold, objective, aggregating, and flattening, while narratives are viewed as humanizing and individualizing but perhaps also partial and emotionally manipulative. Conversely, I find that these two forms of representation work in tandem to generate Peru's "total poverty fact."[8] This total poverty fact is a contextually specific construct that is *produced* as mass-mediated numbers, maps, and dramatic testimonies mingle with the low-level buzz of individual poverty stories and suspicions. This production links the sensational to the sensory, creating a generic intimacy and a visceral common sense about the nature of Peruvian poverty and the country's national reality.[9] In a special irony, the naming, measurement, and mediation of a grandiose and impossibly precise "extreme poverty" in Peru enhance poverty's unruly domestication. The extreme poverty imaginary radically limits the number of people who may make claims on the state, prompts a fixation on familial dimensions of poverty that distract from poverty's political and economic causes, and encourages a deep mistrust of any specific poverty claim.

The definition and boundaries of the poverty category, which we may also interpret as the boundaries of the "deserving poor,"[10] or to invoke the Peruvian category "los que verdaderamente necesitan," are likewise asserted and maintained by those involved in the everyday work of poverty assistance and by anyone who engages in quotidian conversations about the distance between those who receive assistance and those who *should* receive assistance. In this way, the politics of poverty play out in routine negotiations over "entitlements," that "complex system of claims . . . embedded within the social relations and practices that govern possession, distribution and use in society" (Kabeer 1994, 140). It is through these everyday discourses and practices that we see how understandings of poverty and the politics of need become linked to aesthetics, space, time, circumstance, and moral judgments about kin relations and intimate behaviors.

Importantly, to focus on poverty as a construct, a category, a discourse, or a politic does not deny the real experiences of human suffering that occur around the world or ignore the structural violence that unequally distributes life chances in different contexts. Rather, this ethnographic view of poverty, which "shifts attention from need to the discourse over needs . . . [and] from poverty to the politics of poverty" (Roy 2003, 74), helps us establish a critical distance from conventional poverty imaginaries that simultaneously trouble and comfort us in their familiarity (Fassin 2007; Roy 2011). In the process, this ethnographic view makes space for understanding the lived experiences of people conventionally categorized as poor while attuning us to the complex effects of being both subject to this category and engaged in its production. To appropriate a phrase from Michael Taussig's 1984 analysis of the "culture of terror," my goal in analyzing poverty this way is to "penetrate the veil while retaining its hallucinatory quality" (471), that is, to see past or through powerful imaginaries of poverty in a way that gets closer to people's lived experiences while still attending to the real-world effects of these imaginaries.

STATECRAFT AND FORMS OF MARGINALITY

An analysis of Peru's war on poverty requires critical engagement with the state, not only because the state implements antipoverty policy but because the state plays a critical role in shaping how poverty is conceptualized and experienced. Since the 1990s, Peru's war on poverty has largely taken the form of formalization initiatives that promote inclusion for those at the margins of society.[11] This suggests that Peruvian officials conceptualize poverty as a kind of sociopolitical exclusion or invisibility that prohibits people from engaging with dominant social institutions, such as banks and education systems, or participating in democratic decision-making about the direction their societies should take.

At first blush, formalization, conceptualized as a two-part process of inscription in official state registries and the distribution of documents to certify this inscription, is a sensible if not ingeniously simple solution to poverty. Most Peruvians I spoke with saw formalization as a process of making oneself visible to the state and thus a necessary precursor to inclusion in any state-sponsored development or assistance program. They also described formalization as a good in itself, part and parcel of becoming a developed nation composed of engaged and governable citizens. Yet efforts to fight poverty through formalization misunderstand the identity of the state and its relation to poverty in Peru.

From an empirical standpoint, the presumption that poverty stems from political invisibility ignores the very real ways the Peruvian state has helped to produce its supposedly excluded margins for the past five hundred years. History shows that documents and formalization procedures were critical tools of colonial domination (Arguedas 2002 [1941]; Comaroff 2001); that poor, indigenous, and other minoritized populations were included in Peruvian legal systems as particular types of juridical persons with special rights and obligations (Milton 2007; Thurner 1997; Walker 1999); and that these populations sought rights within Peru's legal system under those terms (de la Cadena 2015; Seligmann 1995). Anthropologists have further shown how the state's ostensibly excluded margins are in fact integral to its legitimacy, such that the state's margins are often characterized by an excess of statelike practices (Appadurai 1996; Aretxaga 2005). Das and Poole (2004) explain that because the state is rhetorically all about order, it "must constantly be spoken of—and imagined—through an invocation of the wilderness, lawlessness, and savagery that not only lies outside its jurisdiction but also threatens it from within" (7). States also tend to reserve their most invasive practices, including household-level surveillance and intervention, for their social margins, where state rule is a visibly unfinished project or occupants are positioned far enough outside the political community that their claims to privacy or autonomy might be ignored (Appadurai 1996; Balibar 2007; Caldeira 2000). Moreover, in an age of global interconnection and decentralized governance, visibly promoting an antipoverty agenda can bolster political legitimacy. In this context, the poor can become a precious commodity, with different political actors competing to be seen as active on their behalf (Corbridge et al. 2005). The challenge of resolving poverty, then, involves not simply overcoming exclusion from the state, but understanding how it is that, despite their inclusion, people are still poor (Gupta 2011). As I show in this book, documentation and formalization procedures ironically play an important role in generating the experiences of exclusion, insecurity, subordination, and inadequacy that constitute poverty in urban Peru.

Although official formalization discourse depicts the state as a coherent entity with a singular, rational, and rationalizing intention, when examined ethnographically, this fiction falls apart, revealing the state to be not a fact but a claim, "at most a message of domination—an ideological artifact attributing unity, morality and independence to the disunited, amoral and dependent workings of the practice of government" (Abrams 1988, 81). Anthropologists thus prefer to explore how the imaginary of the state is produced through discourse, practice, and everyday interactions with the individuals and documents that operate in its name (Das 2007; Poole 2004; Sharma and Gupta 2006). When investigated this way, it is easier to see that who or what constitutes the state, the degree to which it is associated with particular economic interests or structures of authority, and how it aligns with the mediators who enforce its rule are all empirical questions that depend on local and historical contexts.

Ethnographic examinations of the state in Peru highlight the ways bureaucratic processes and physical documents may be both racializing and politically partisan. As part of Peru's colonial inheritance, the formal worlds of government, national culture, and capitalist exchange are associated with a masculine whiteness, while informality and economies based on reciprocity are associated with feminine indigeneity (de la Cadena 1995; Degregori and Sandoval 2008). Though these racial ideologies and associations remain constant, the racial category an individual occupies is shifting, contextual, relational, and influenced by education, class, appearance, behavior, and one's capacity to assume a dominant position in exchange relations (de la Cadena 1995; Wade 2008; Weismantel 2001). Bureaucratic exchanges that put some in a position of authority (whiteness) and others in the position of supplicants (indigenousness) reproduce colonial hierarchies. As the media of official communication, documents can likewise be raced and racializing and have the capacity to whiten their bearers (Weismantel 2001).

In contemporary Peru, purportedly neutral technocratic state documents can also be politically partisan and imply membership in specific political or clientelist networks. In urban settlements, streetscapes are littered with billboards and banners that bombard onlookers with images of larger-than-life politicians proclaiming their good works. As these portraits look down on dusty, trash-lined streets, they encourage Peruvians to think of the state as a collection of individual power holders who exist in and manage a level of reality above their own (Ferguson and Gupta 2002). Thus, while dominant discourse in Peru suggests that the state is supposed to be an orderly governing body and power holders gain legitimacy by taking on technocratic projects of mapping, surveying, and documenting, Peruvians also understand the state to be rife with politics. The word *política* in Peru means both policy and politics, and every government action is Janus-faced, a high-level plan that deploys accepted procedures in pursuit of broadly embraced social goals and a manipulative act of self-interested subterfuge in the ongoing contest for power and privilege. Although my interlocutors occasionally spoke of their rights vis-à-vis the state, they readily slipped into descriptions of the interests, actions, and im/moral engagements of particular politicians. As a result, formalization processes and the documents that are integral to them can become tools for producing partisan political networks; the identity of a newly formalized individual or organization is interwoven with the political administration that recognized it.

In many instances, documentary recognitions are duplicative; being recognized by one organization breeds subsequent recognitions by others. However, in places where there are multiple governing bodies, it is possible to be recognized by one entity and not by another or for entities to disagree about how an individual or organization should be recognized. Although documents are prized for their ability to fix meanings, their value and significance are in fact context-dependent; it can therefore be hard to discern whether being documented in a particular way will guarantee or threaten someone's rights vis-à-vis different power holders. Deborah Poole (2004) suggests this is the essence of state marginality, not geographic or social peripheralization, but the uneasy suspension between "threat" and "guarantee," when it is unclear whether a document will protect or expose one to the arbitrary power of the state (36). Matthew Hull notes that these "messy and excessive potentialities" can make documents a source of "fear, panic, insecurity, nervousness, and tentativeness," even as they are also highly sought after as evidence of proper, law-abiding citizenship (2012, 255).

The manner and frequency with which a person engages documents also have powerful moral connotations that can inform how they are perceived by neighbors and their capacity to access state benefits. Documents play an important role in the social production of "formality" as the performance of a particular, racially inflected "disposition to following the rules" and as an expression of transparency and a willingness to "fix" values and promise their permanence through time (McFarlane and Waibel 2016).[12] Meanwhile, being either under- or overdocumented can make someone morally suspect. People who are underdocumented or whose documents are out of date are accused of being *dejado*, careless, apathetic, and lacking the entrepreneurial spirit to exit poverty. By contrast, people who are overdocumented or who seem to be too good at navigating bureaucratic and documentary worlds, are accused of being *vivos*, wily, crafty, and untrustworthy.

Finally, formalization procedures and the documents that are integral to them reinforce normative social orders. They communicate the categories through which identity and social status are interpreted and governed and help to constitute individual subjectivities and socialities (Hull 2012). Even seemingly straightforward identity information like name, address, and civil status plays an important role in constructing the bearer by connecting her to other people and places and situating her on a map of the nation that is imbued with racial, political, and socioeconomic meaning (Jeganathan 2004). The official categories people occupy, and the specific dissonances between an individual's documented and lived social identity, have practical implications for their ability to access state benefits and inform their experiences of marginalization and (non)belonging in the Peruvian nation.

DOMESTIC POLITICS

The role that documents play in mediating social life and shaping experiences of self and belonging brings me to a broader set of arguments about the ways personal and political spheres mutually produce and interpenetrate one another. Scholars of gender and kinship have a long history of troubling the modern myths of neat divisions between personal and political spheres while also illustrating how ideals of properly modern relations between these spheres shape social life (McKinnon and Cannell 2013). These scholars have shown how states rely on and reproduce normative kinship ideals (Borneman 1992; Butler 2008; Lambek 2013); how vital events (e.g., birth, death, marriage, migration, household formation) and demographic identities (e.g., family size, number of spouses, age at first birth) become important "objects of interpretation" through which "people identify themselves with particular groups and contrast their behavior to others" (Kreager 1986, 152); and how pursuing particular kin formations and life-course trajectories has become central to the intimate ways people seek to constitute themselves as modern individuals, national citizens, and gendered beings (Thornton 2001; Johnson-Hanks 2002; Hirsch 2003).

In describing relations between kinship and the state, Michael Lambek argues that kinship "is part and parcel of what the state is and means. The state is constituted in and through such acts as making citizens, providing birth and death certificates, registering property, taxing households, and more generally producing and authorizing the means by which people are related to one another as parents, offspring, spouses, siblings and the like" (2013, 257). John Borneman (1992, 33) likewise draws attention to the importance of the domestic life course, that is, the enactment of kinship and changing relational identities over time, in constituting state, nation, and subjective experiences of belonging. He explains that the state, through a variety of discourses, documents, laws, and institutions, proposes for citizens a single master narrative of the life course. The extent to which individuals map their lives onto that state-sanctioned narrative is an important measure of the state's success in producing a nation, a group of people who feel themselves to be of the same ilk because their lives and "the hold life has on them," to appropriate Bronislaw Malinowski's phrase,[13] can be understood in the same terms. Relatedly, the extent to which one's life experience corresponds to the state's aesthetic and ideational framework affects one's sense of belonging in the nation.

Marriage and ideals of companionate love play an especially important role in linking the state to kinship, life course, and intimate experiences of self in the age of modernity. Although marriage has always been an important site for regulating the external structure of social groups and disciplining the internal behavior of members, especially women, a paradoxical feature of modernity, which is largely characterized by the rise of rationality and predictability, has been the insertion of an individuated and irrational love into the marriage mix (Hirsch 2003; Povinelli

2006). According to Borneman (1992, 303), love created a new type of family, "built around neither exchange nor control, but romantic affective ties. . . . In this design for life, the centrality and meanings of marriage, sandwiched in the life course between birth and death, were the generative motor of the plot."

In urban Peru, fulfilling state-prescribed life-course ideals plays an important role in women's constructions of themselves as full social persons and modern citizens, and failure to attain these ideals becomes central to profoundly gendered experiences of poverty and marginality. Anthropologists have long argued that personhood is a socially ascribed status and that what it means to be a full social person varies by context (Harris 1980; Scheper-Hughes 1992; Van Vleet 2008). For instance, early ethnographic studies of Andean societies demonstrated that in these contexts, young people were not considered full social persons until they married. Thus, the couple, rather than the individual, was the foundational unit of society (Bolton and Mayer 1977; Carter 1977). Blending Andean dualistic cosmologies with Catholic moralities and modern ideals of companionate marriage, in present-day Peru, romantic partnerships and new family formation are similarly important for attaining full social personhood.

However, the effects of failing in this pursuit play out differently for men and women due to the social scripts available to each and the different ways gendered identities are performed in relation to kinship. Though romantic liaisons and responsible fatherhood can be important sites for the performance of masculinity, the onus of converting romantic love into responsible parenthood falls largely to women, and women are systematically instructed that love, home, and family should be central to their aspirations and enactments of citizenship in ways that boys and men are not. In this model, fathering is an achievement, while mothering is an obligation (Coutin 2003). Men who exist apart or parted from family contexts are viewed primarily as sources of danger and delinquency and disappear almost entirely from poverty conversations except, perhaps, as a cause of it. By contrast, the loss of companionate love and the corresponding disintegration of the ideal family is central to discourses of female poverty, emerging with particular force in the figure of the impoverished single mother.

On the one hand, everything from popular media to women's internal monologues to disjunctures on their ID cards suggests that single mothers are a special variety of social person; though they were once whole, they have now been parted and are permanently incomplete. On the other hand, the single mother imaginary is larger than life, an extraordinary icon built up around Marianist discourses of sacrifice, modern ideals of female empowerment, and international poverty narratives surrounding female-headed households. Seen through this double lens, single mothers are the poorest of the poor and the most deserving of assistance. However, because they diverge from Peruvian ideals of modern, moral, duly constituted, and consolidated nuclear-family households, they are also a social threat and blamed for reproducing poverty across generations (Boesten 2003; Chant 2008).[14]

In contemporary Peru, where neo-Malthusian fears of overpopulation mingle with gendered Catholic moralities, having many children or having children out of wedlock or with multiple partners marks women as nonmodern, irrational, immoral, and undeserving. Moreover, any effort these women make to ameliorate their situations further undermines their identities as members of the deserving poor. Seeking out jobs, romantic partnerships, or anything else that might mitigate their experiences of material or relational deprivation introduces a level of complexity, ambiguity, and instability into their relational identities that is even more maligned than straightforward single-motherhood. The marginalization of unstable families and individuals with ambiguous relational identities links hegemonic understandings of moral families back to ideals of formality and fears of documentary duplicity.

The politics of the domestic and women's central role in these politics emerge even more explicitly in government initiatives that alternately assert and transgress normative boundaries between political and domestic spheres. As elsewhere in Latin America, in Peru, distinctions between public and private spheres are often expressed through discourses that contrast *calle* (street) and *casa* (home). The *calle* is depicted as a site of crime, danger, and moral degeneration, dominated alternately by *gente malo*, *vivos*, and *mafiosos* (bad people, tricksters, and corrupt groups) and by the cold indifference of state bureaucracies and the capitalist market (Caldeira 2000; Han 2012). By contrast, the *casa* is a site of intimacy, affect, and moral virtue where family members may be protected from these public dangers and, to use the words of my interlocutors, *formado* (formed, molded) into proper citizens.[15] Pachacutanos' use of the verb *formar* when discussing childrearing indicates that parenting in this context was not simply a matter of care but a matter of creation and subject-making; it further draws attention to understandings of the household as a container with the potential to shape and mold particular personalities.

In Peru, only certain kinds of homes are deemed adequate for molding children into proper citizens. Homes that diverge from the nuclear-family model are commonly described as "broken" or "disintegrating," incapable of protecting children from the dangers of the street and sites of corruption in their own right. Combining an extreme logic of cultural particularism with a racialized hierarchy of *educación*—meaning formal education but also upbringing, socialization, and cultural formation—homes in Peru are often described as distinct cultural territories whose interior realities are unknowable to those outside them, even as physical household structures are read as indicators of the kinds of families that might occupy them. As black boxes of cultural formation, the households charged with producing proper Peruvian citizens can just as easily forge violent subjects who endanger society. Thus, some of the most popular policies and politicians are those that promise apolitical social assistance to shore up the boundaries of households and support mothers in properly forming their children.

Despite the sociomoral weight of the idealized and clearly contained nuclear family and the important ways this imaginary informs official policy, individual aspirations, and patterns of discrimination, the realities of family and kinship in Peru have never aligned with this model. Anthropological studies of kinship in Latin America have demonstrated that, far from a static biological fact, kinship is flexible and variable and may be strengthened or attenuated over time depending on the manner and fervor with which it is performed (Han 2012; Leinaweaver 2008). Andean scholarship in particular has shown how kinship may be constructed through everyday reciprocities and constituted via the circulation of food and other substances that accumulate in people's bodies through the daily reproduction of the household, helping to connect people to places and building relationships that are simultaneously intimate and hierarchical (Van Vleet 2008; Weismantel 2001). These practices are further implicated in the construction of extended kin networks that cut across class lines, linking patrons and peons in vertical systems of reciprocity such that performances of kinship slip easily into practices of a morally maligned clientelist politics (Auyero 2000; Lazar 2008; Wolf 1966).

These two kinds of families—the discrete nuclear family and the flexible kin network—can be mapped onto distinctions between the families Peruvians live *by* and the ones they live *with*, while the interplay between the two helps to shape the ambivalent identity of the state and the practice of antipoverty politics. Political candidates gain popular support in Peru's urban settlements by promising technocratic and beneficent governance that will promote the well-being of nuclear families rather than practicing *politics*, which is understood only to benefit politicians and their inner circles. To convincingly spread this message, they enlist female kin (i.e., extended family and friends) who have broad social networks and strong sociomoral standing in the community, due largely to their ability to perform identities as devoted mothers who have been only appropriately politicized in service of their families. As a result, even though politics is conventionally associated with the public sphere and gendered masculine in Peru, quotidian political practice is largely women's work.

In exchange for their support, this extended network is implicitly promised sustained assistance in the form of jobs or social programs made more accessible due to their personal/political relations with the new administration. Those inside this network see themselves as receiving their due and rightfully benefitting from programs that support the well-being of families, while those outside the network find themselves excluded from the state in this new personalized form. In an added twist, the women who facilitate the connection between these two forms of family politics often end up in precarious sociomoral positions. Their association with either politics or paid employment outside the home can undermine their previous social standing as devoted mothers, which in turn can adversely impact their social, emotional, and economic lives. The issue here is not simply that politics and kinship interpenetrate one another but that the distance and interplay between the ideals and realities of family-state relations is productive of politics itself, contributing to everyday experiences of exclusion and to broader perceptions of a morally impoverished Peruvian state.

THE PLACE-TIME OF POVERTY AND SITES OF EXCEPTIONAL INCLUSION

The framework of unruly domestication invites a third line of exploration into how poverty has been nationalized,[16] that is, how poverty has been constituted and politicized in a way specific to Peru, even as this particularly Peruvian formulation has been made through transnational interactions over the past five hundred years. Taking a historical long view of poverty helps to denaturalize contemporary poverty frameworks and reveals how the place-time of poverty—where we locate it and the temporal ideologies we project onto it—has shifted over time, accruing additional meanings and associations.

During Peru's colonial and early republican eras, the concept of poverty was largely subsumed by racial ideologies of civility associated with distinctions between rural and urban space. With the rise of twentieth-century urbanism, poverty also came to be identified with working-class neighborhoods and homes in Lima where experts presumed poverty would be passed down across generations unless these living conditions were ameliorated through cultural-environmental interventions. As rural-to-urban migration picked up in the mid-twentieth century, poverty was relocated to the neighborhoods these settlers created in Lima's peripheries. There it was viewed as endemic until new policies began theorizing poverty as a temporary stage in the growth and development of these neighborhoods. Following a decade of national political and economic trauma, neoliberalism took hold in Peru. Under the leadership of President Alberto Fujimori, Peru's national government implemented economic austerity policies that by some measures left over half of the population living in poverty. At the same time, the government deployed new statistical and mapping technologies to circumscribe official, actionable poverty in discrete pockets (*bolsones de pobreza*) and extreme poverty zones that could be subject to exceptional interventions. It was in this context, in which inclusion in targeted social assistance programs was an exception to the rule of intentional and fiscally responsible neglect, that I began my fieldwork.

I conducted the bulk of my research in the extreme poverty zone of Pachacútec on the outskirts of metropolitan Lima. Yet as my research on poverty progressed, I found myself drawn into policy-design organizations and other extreme poverty zones in metropolitan Lima and around the country. Through this grounded but mobile research methodology, I came to understand that poverty, albeit often conceptualized spatially and aesthetically, was also a temporal phenomenon, a category in motion and a crisis-minded sociolegal production that transformed everyday hardships into something exceptional that people were moved to act on. This exceptional space-time of poverty also had household-level associations, as particular physical and kinship structures were officially believed to put children at risk, positioning them in a category of uncertain future time that threatened their lives and society writ large.

My primary research site of Pachacútec emerged as an extreme poverty zone on February 3, 2000, when as one of his last acts in office, President Fujimori relocated 25,000 squatters from private lands in the south of Lima to a sparsely populated desert several hours northwest of Lima's city center. Given the dire circumstances of these settlers now awaiting aid in the desert—a six-kilometer hike to the nearest satellite urbanization, which had been founded in the 1960s to encourage Lima's decentralization—Fujimori had the military provide them with food, water, and provisional

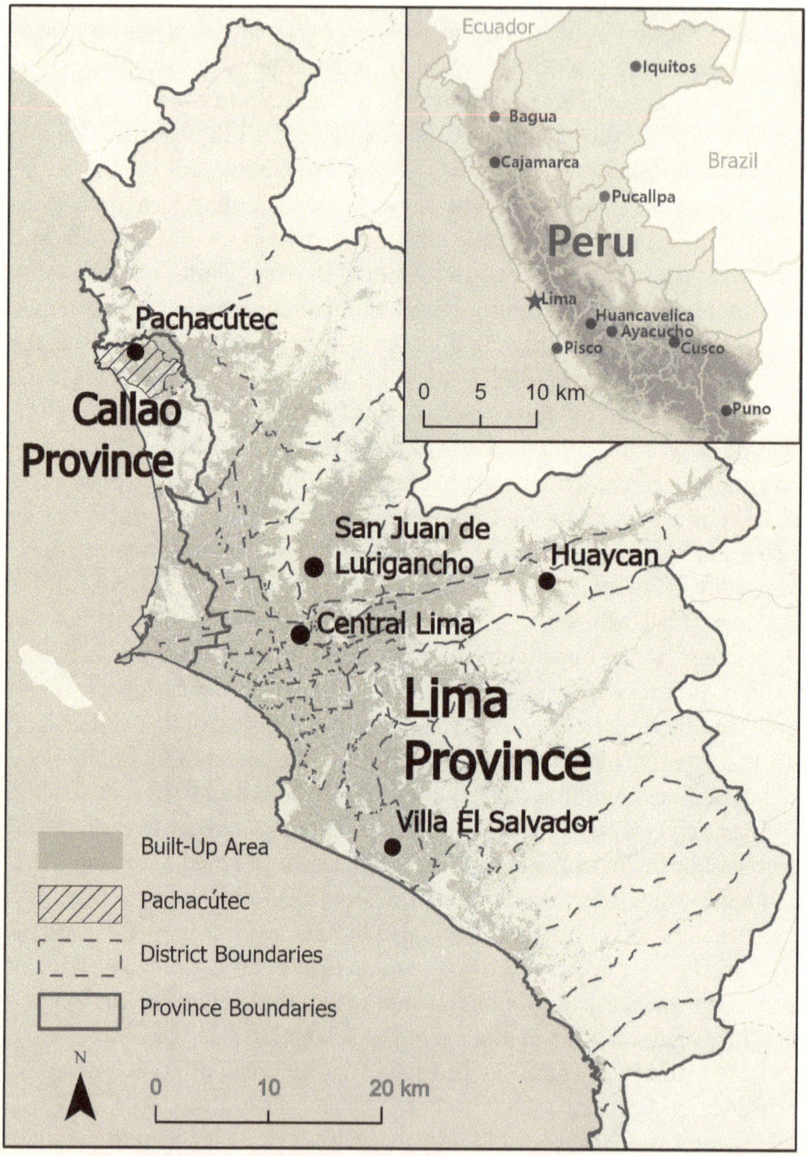

MAP 0.1. Developed area of metropolitan Lima-Callao, circa 2017. Significant peripheral settlements including Pachacútec are indicated. The inset elevation map of Peru shows additional research locations. Map by Morgane Dackiw and Kristin Skrabut.

shelter. He also promised to bypass the standard bureaucracies and make exceptions to the normal rules of property acquisition in order to deliver land titles and urban infrastructure quickly and create a model city, the Proyecto Piloto Nuevo Pachacútec (Pilot Project of New Pachacútec). However, the promise of free land in a rapidly developing area attracted thousands more settlers from across Lima to the distant desert site. This population influx, combined with the political melee that followed Fujimori's resignation, undermined the original plans for orderly and efficient development.

Ten years later, Pachacútec's population had exploded to almost 200,000. Most experts I spoke with imagined Pachacútec to be populated by migrants from impoverished Andean and Amazonian regions, fitting it into narratives about the self-help housing settlements that had formed in Lima's outskirts throughout the second half of the twentieth century as rural inhabitants were pulled into the city by economic and educational opportunities and pushed out of the countryside by extractive export industries and terrible political violence. In reality, at least 55 percent of Pachacútec's population had migrated to the area from other districts in metropolitan Lima, meaning that many were second- and third-generation rural migrants, a population that Carlos Aguirre and Charles Walker (2017) describe as "new Limeños," who saw Pachacútec as their best option for obtaining affordable housing. Only 15 percent and 9 percent of the population hailed from mountain and jungle regions, respectively (INEI 2010).[17] Yet, whatever their origin stories, when people arrived in Pachacútec they were confronted with the challenge of how to survive in extreme poverty. Beti, a member of the original cohort of *reubicados* (relocated persons) described the move as a terrible social equalizer. "Most of us had come directly from our parents' houses," she explained, and therefore knew nothing about "how to live in extreme poverty," how to organize themselves, or how to reach out to officials for assistance. "At that time, everyone was equal. . . . Everyone was in extreme poverty. . . . We were all living in *esteras* [straw huts], that's it."

Some of Pachacútec's 150 neighborhoods had improved over the years through residents' hard work, political acumen, and luck, but by 2010 most Pachacutanos still lacked sturdy housing and access to piped water and electricity, and area indices of tuberculosis and childhood malnutrition were among the highest in metropolitan Lima.[18] As a result, Pachacútec remained a place infamous for its poverty, and it continued to attract the attention of local and national politicians, international development agents, NGOs, and anyone else whose vocation or legitimacy depended on identifying and supporting the truly needy. But Pachacútec

FIGURE 0.1. East-facing landscape of Pachacútec where houses spill from Callao into Lima Province, 2016. In 2011 this mountainside was empty. Photo by the author.

is not a monolith, and residents' experiences of it are mediated by the settlement's internal political and legal structures.

Pachacútec comprises three areas with distinct institutional histories and governance structures. The Pilot Project that was established in 2000 through Fujimori's relocation is divided into five sectors, each of which is subdivided into five residential groups. In 2005, a fully serviced government housing project called Techo Propio (My Own Roof) was built adjacent to one of these sectors, and for a time, it was politically integrated into the Pilot Project.[19] The Special Project is a group of seventy distinct invasion sites represented by a coalition known as the United Front and located largely on privately owned land. The Special Project was originally founded by the national government in 1988 as part of an effort to decentralize Lima by granting area land to impoverished families. Due to the lack of government support for infrastructure, though, few families chose to live there. The area remained relatively uninhabited until 2005, when Alberto Carillos—whom Pachacutanos described as both a respected *dirigente* (community leader) and a nefarious land trafficker who sold land that did not legally belong to him—began inciting land takeovers

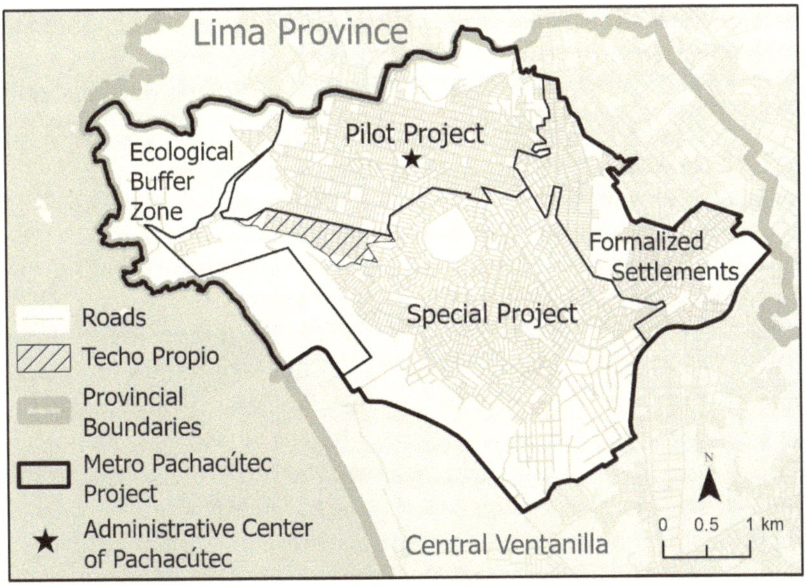

MAP 0.2. Estate types that constitute the Macro Pachacútec Project. Map by Morgane Dackiw and Kristin Skrabut. *Source*: Asociación Macro Distrito Pachacútec.

by people who claimed to have more immediate need than the absentee titleholders. Occupants of the Special Project had spent years fighting to have the land expropriated and legally redistributed to current residents. Finally, there are the Formalized Settlements, a federation of otherwise unaligned neighborhoods that were established independently and received recognition for their neighborhood land claims from different governing bodies at various times beginning in 1980 and continuing as of this writing. Together these three areas constitute Pachacútec's Macro Project, a coalition that endeavors to promote the collective interests of area residents, when representatives can agree on what those are.

I was beginning to get a handle on Pachacútec's internal political dynamics when a 7.9 magnitude earthquake struck Peru's southern coast, suddenly shifting the location of need and highlighting how the time of emergency and a particular makeshift aesthetic are critical to the production of aid-worthy poverty. It was August 15, 2007. I was standing outside the recently constructed *agencia municipal* (district government field office) when the ground began undulating beneath me. The women I was speaking with cried out for patron saints and ran home to their children, and officials who had often spoken to me of their commitment to Pachacútec's impoverished residents jumped into their cars and sped to their homes in more central districts without saying a word.

The next day, Pachacútec was relatively quiet. Several women admitted to throwing themselves in front of televisions and stereos during the earthquake to protect the appliances they had struggled to purchase or were still paying off, artifacts that represented past investments and future obligations. For the most part, though, in a place where homes were made of straw, plywood, and plastic, there wasn't much for the earthquake to damage. Pisco was a different story. This port city two hours south of Lima was older and built primarily of adobe; being at the epicenter of the earthquake, the destruction there was fierce. Moved by the graphic images of a city in ruins and the heart-wrenching tales of loss they heard on the news, Pachacutanos began taking up collections of food and clothing for Pisco's *damnificados* (earthquake victims). One Pachacutana explained to me that she and others still had problems, but now it was time to focus on the truly needy in Pisco: "They have lost everything. They are living in tents and have no water or food. Just imagine!"

Pisco had suddenly been thrust into the space-time of emergency. In a testament to the importance of poverty assistance for political legitimacy, the politicians and NGOs that had been working in Pachacútec went to Pisco to assist, and be seen assisting, in the emergency response. The INEI (Instituto Nacional de Estadística e Informática, Peru's National Institute of Statistics and Computer Technology) organized an emergency census of the area, hoping numbers would help them get a governmental handle on the problem and better target assistance. Although other areas of Peru's southern coast suffered greater numerical losses,[20] Pisco, with its crumbled buildings and concentration of displaced persons, became the symbolic center of the disaster (Cáritas 2008).

The recently reelected president, Alan García, declared a state of emergency in Pisco, suspending the normal rule of law—including building codes, customs checks, and property regulations—in the name of an urgent moral imperative to assist those in need (Bambarén 2010). This short-term state of emergency was extended seventeen times covering a period of three years, from August 2007 to July 2010, and the geographic area of the emergency was expanded four times. It wasn't until record cold temperatures hit the nation and two-thirds of the country was placed under a state of emergency to cope with the ensuing challenges that the state of emergency brought on by the earthquake officially ended.

Anthropological literature rightly critiques states of emergency and states of exception as dangerous measures that eliminate checks on official power and allow states to operate with impunity (Aretxaga 2005; Benjamin 1978). Yet it is also true that when the norm is self-help, neglect, or hostility, people often *want* to be the exception and work hard to be included in the sociolegal category of emergency. In Pisco, each state of emergency had to be formally requested by the regional government of Ica and the National Institute for Civil Defense. Though Pisco might be considered an extreme case of sudden need and emergency relief,[21] the similarities in how poverty was framed and relief efforts played out in Pisco and Pachacútec illuminate how exceptionality functions as a mode of inclusion within the everyday logics of poverty assistance.

Implicating myself in the bursts of hypervisibility that constitute much of Peru's war on poverty, I too followed poverty to Pisco, visiting for brief periods in 2007 and 2008 and for several months in 2010. Once retaining walls, which locals termed *muros de verguenza*, walls of shame, were constructed to obscure collapsed buildings from view of the city's main thoroughfares, aid agencies focused their attention on more familiar sites of poverty in Pisco's peripheries. These areas had long been populated by precarious homes but hadn't garnered much attention until Pisco's former renters, newly categorized as *damnificados*, arrived, suddenly forced by circumstance to establish the homes of their own that many had long desired. I also tracked poverty to other sites within metropolitan Lima and other regions of Peru based on news stories, poverty maps, the work of relief organizations, and interviews in which people told me that if I was interested in real poverty I should be seeking it elsewhere, in Pachacamac, Huaycán, Huancavelica, Puno. Indeed, wherever I was, it was possible to find someone who would tell me there was a worse poverty, a more real poverty elsewhere.

Though most of the stories that animate this text come from my long-term fieldwork in Pachacútec, and Pachacútec forms the center of my ethnographic theory building, putting these various sites in conversation helped me retain what Laura Nader (1994) describes as a "comparative consciousness," an awareness of other places and realities that guards against presumptions of either representativeness or uniqueness and helps to illuminate connections between sites. Pisco's earthquake created "true need" among individuals whose emergency circumstances prompted a sudden influx of attention and assistance, the rapid writing of new laws, and the creation of exceptions that allowed some to pursue long-desired living conditions. The production of an extreme poverty requiring emergency assistance was likewise evident in Fujimori's founding of Pachacútec and reappears in every subsequent invasion carefully staged by groups of settlers seeking homes of their own and demanding exceptions to conventional property rules. Moreover, in every site I visited, poverty was framed in familiar ways, associated with women and informal or fragile family forms, and subject to policies and politics focused on home and family.

ETHNOGRAPHIC PRACTICE AND MAKING RELATIONS

I originally went to Peru interested in poverty and politics, in hard-nosed battles for social justice and housing, in indigeneity, inequality, and statecraft. I certainly found many of these things, but the long-form work of ethnography also revealed the subtle everyday labor of making lives and relations in which my interlocutors were constantly engaged. I met many of the people whose lives animate this book in 2007, continued to work with them through 2011, revisited them every summer from 2016 to 2019, and remain in periodic contact with them as of this writing. I witnessed their transformations from ardent *dirigentes* to government employees and back again and saw them move in and out of these explicitly political worlds in response to diverse opportunities and obligations. Over time, I realized that their actions with or against the state, the relationships they established, and the networks they built were part and parcel of their efforts to make a life, to make ends meet, and to do something they considered meaningful while working to help themselves, their families, and their communities *salir adelante*, an oft-used colloquialism meaning to progress and overcome that fuses temporal, spatial, and social meanings, as movements through time and transformations to space are tied to efforts to climb social ladders in pursuit of middle-class urban ideals (Leinaweaver 2008; Takenaka and Pren 2010).

As an anthropologist and ethnographer, I too had been involved in the intricate and sometimes clumsy work of making relations. While conducting this research I also constructed homes and wove networks and in so doing made a life. I mean this both in the presentist sense of inhabiting and participating in place and seeking genuine human connection even as I was also always doing other things, and in the longitudinal sense as these relations compounded, setting me on different paths that have led to my writing this book in a comfortable home in Massachusetts.

Thinking back, I realize that the double valence of ethnographic relations as both genuine and instrumental was readily apparent to many of my interlocutors. They seemed to understand intuitively and better than I did that my research was a life-course phenomenon. They saw my efforts to write a thesis the same way they viewed those efforts among many young women in Peru; it was a necessary stage in my professional development that would help me earn a position of respect. As far as I could tell, they viewed this pursuit as admirable and honest, and they frequently counseled me to be savvier about creating connections and cultivating multiple income-generating opportunities for myself. The people who supported my research did so for their own reasons: because they thought it was the kind thing to do, because they were curious about me, because they were bored and I helped pass the time, or because they thought a relationship with me, like so many they established, could prove advantageous in ways not yet apparent.

In her innovative 2009 ethnography of urban renewal in Lima, Daniella Gandolfo suggests that anthropologists who describe their interlocutors as "friends" elide power relations and obscure the unbridgeable distances that divide researchers from their subjects, participants, or interlocutors. This is an important critique, and my identity as a white, female US citizen in her twenties certainly shaped my interactions and gave me access to institutions that would have been closed to many of the Peruvians I worked with. And yet, I do consider many of my interlocutors friends. The people who play the greatest role in this text are the people I felt most comfortable around, the people with whom I developed genuine personal connections, the people I would be relieved to see at parties. Moreover, "friend" was a common way my interlocutors described me to others, though they would also sometimes refer to me as a North American friend, colleague, cousin, aunt, niece, or *comadre*.

Todne Thomas (2016) suggests that in thinking through how to describe our ethnographic relations, it can help to consider how these relations might describe us. The use of kin terms to describe me in various circumstances facilitates a provocation, the notion of ethnography as kinwork. Research on kinship in Peru and the Andes has demonstrated that affective ties exist across differences of race and class, that intimacy emerges within and through hierarchies, and that these hierarchical intimacies are constructed through everyday interactions and reciprocities and may be attenuated over time or invoked and reinvigorated at particular moments (Leinaweaver 2008; Van Vleet 2008; Vincent 2000). Ethnography is an art of relation and reflection, of establishing relations and reflecting on how the sum of those relations shape what you see, how they open some doors and close others, how they create opportunities or pull you back into relations despite your better judgments. It is thus not unlike what my interlocutors, colleagues, friends, and kin in Peru did on a regular basis.

When I began my work in Peru I stayed with Vicky, the mother of an archaeologist friend of mine, who lived in an urbanized neighborhood of Ventanilla, a few kilometers from where Pachacútec juts off the main highway. Vicky's neighborhood was established in the 1980s when the national government lotteried small but expandable cement houses, complete with water, sewer, and electrical connections, to low-wage government employees. Vicky and her husband got lucky but opted to hold the house in reserve and live in a more central location until circumstances demanded otherwise. They ultimately moved into the one-bedroom, one-bathroom home with their four teenage children during the "Fujishock" of the 1990s, when Vicky's husband, like many Peruvians, suddenly found himself unemployed.

By the time I met Vicky in 2007, her husband had moved out. With funds she earned through piecework embroidery and some creative encroachment into adjacent vacant lots, she had added two small rooms to the house to better accommodate the seven-person extended and intergenerational family that now inhabited the house on a rotating basis. For a time, I was one of these rotating inhabitants, staying with Vicky for short stints when it was impractical for me to set up house elsewhere. Yet even when I was staying elsewhere—a nearby apartment in Vicky's neighborhood, a housing project in Pachacútec, a rented bedroom in Pisco's periphery, or inexpensive hotels on trips to Andean provinces—Vicky's home and family were integral to my fieldwork experience. Her house was a place I always felt welcome, a place where I could take a reasonably warm shower, watch pirated DVDs with her children and nieces, and despite the constant jackhammering of Vicky's sewing machine, get something of a reprieve from the self-conscious grind of fieldwork. In a sense, it was home. Vicky often described me to others as her niece, and her grandchildren called me Tía (Auntie). Many of my most interesting insights emerged from discussions with Vicky's family. Meanwhile, conversations with Vicky's neighbors about their life histories and moments when they found themselves squatting to obtain land in the periphery highlighted how the spaces and times of poverty intersect in people's lives and how access to particular spaces can both reinforce and ameliorate experiences of poverty in time.

In Ventanilla I began most mornings with a walk or bus ride to the administrative center of Pachacútec in the northwestern corner of the settlement. This area housed Pachacútec's first three concrete buildings: the civic center, the *agencia municipal*, and a failed model home known to some as "the matchbox." The civic center was constructed by the national government and donated to the nebulously defined community of Pachacútec in 2005. Though falling into disrepair, the civic center still housed social assistance programs like the Women's Emergency Center (Centro Emergencia Mujer), a Catholic charity soup kitchen, and the INABIF (Programa Integral Nacional para el Bienestar Familiar, National Holistic Program for Family Well-Being) after-school program for youth deemed "at risk." The civic center also hosted many temporary assistance campaigns sponsored by NGOs and the national government. The municipal field office, referred to simply as the *agencia*, was built by the district government of Ventanilla in 2007. By 2009 it housed a RENIEC (Registro Nacional de Identificación y Estado Civil, National Registry of Identification and Civil Status) branch office, a separate office for Ventanilla's civil registry,[22] DEMUNA (Defensoría Municipal del Nino y del Adolescente, Municipal Advocacy Office for Children and Adolescents), and a *mesa de partes*, a document reception desk. The third building, "the matchbox," a two-story yellow eyesore, was built by the Ministry of Housing in 2005 as an example of the kinds of houses that could be offered at a subsidized rate to impoverished residents of Pachacútec. Apparently, Pachacutanos disliked the design and refused to apply for loans to obtain the houses. The matchbox stood empty, a monument to failed state plans, until 2010, when some enterprising individuals appropriated the building for use as a photo lab to sell ID photos to people processing documents across the street. On this street the state was made manifest in concrete boxes, then spilled out into the community through agents clad in vests of various colors depending on the organization or political body they represented. Through the matchbox, the site also highlighted the ways people try to penetrate the business of the state in pursuit of their own life projects.

The civic center and *agencia* also provided meeting spaces for local community leaders, and it was in stumbling upon one of these meetings that I first found myself implicated in a complex weave of sociopolitical networks. The first person I met in Pachacútec in 2007 was Ismael, an administrator of the civic center and member of Pachacútec's Central Executive Committee. Ismael was well-educated, a Marxist and a lawyer by training who was interested in promoting an indigenous identity for Pachacútec that would encourage tourism and investment; he was therefore enthusiastic about working with a North American anthropologist. At one of our early meetings he counseled me not to work with any *dirigente* he did not introduce me to, explaining that they were part of the problem. He described them as land traffickers who were in the pockets of politicians and more interested in themselves than in Pachacútec's development.

FIGURE 0.2. The administrative center of Pachacútec, 2007. People line up outside the *agencia municipal* (*left*). Across the street are the one-story civic center and "the matchbox" model home. The photo was taken shortly after the *agencia municipal* was constructed and before the street was paved. Photo by the author.

A few weeks later I stumbled upon a meeting of some of these *dirigentes* in the *agencia*. They contended that Ismael's committee members had overstayed their terms and refused to hold elections but continued to represent themselves to outsiders as legitimate community representatives. The *dirigentes* had therefore established a parallel government to reform the electoral statute and elect new legitimate leaders. I did my best to maintain congenial relations with both groups, an effort that initially made me suspect to many, but I eventually became closer to the statute reformers, particularly William and Pablo, the two *dirigentes* spearheading the reform.

By 2009 the original executive committee had all but disappeared, and the statute reformers bemoaned the loss of their own initial unity. Some of them had been absorbed by the municipality, others left their leadership positions in the community for other opportunities or obligations, and still others had simply grown disillusioned with political work or tired of accusations that they were corrupt or incompetent. Pablo was among the *dirigentes* absorbed by the municipality and was now in charge of enhancing connections between Pachacutanos and the district government. Having known me for several years, he was comfortable with my presence at most events and meetings, and he connected me with some of his most effective promoters, including Marisa and Anita. Pablo treated me as something of a protégé, often taking the time to explain the rationale for his actions and sometimes asking my opinion of them. These relationships provided insight into local politics and statecraft that would be unavailable to me otherwise, but they also meant I was easily associated with the district government.

To help overcome this association and gain a broader understanding of social life in Pachacútec, I was deliberate about pursuing the perspectives of those less explicitly tied to the district government. I worked with women involved in community-managed food-assistance programs, I became well acquainted with the women running community child care centers, and I made it a point to investigate new settlements in Pachacútec's periphery independent of district government employees. In many of these endeavors I got lucky, meeting women like Milagros, Patricia, Charo, and others who took me under their wings.

It was largely through my conversations with Pachacutanos and my encounters in the *agencia* and civic center that I identified which organizations to include in my research on Peru's war on poverty. RENIEC and a suborganization, GRIAS (Gerencia de la Restitución de la Identidad y Apoyo Social, Administration for the Restitution of Identity and Social Assistance), operated out of Pachacútec's administrative center. Although Pachacutanos engaged with them infrequently, these organizations played an important role in facilitating access to other institutions. Organizations focused on supporting women and children like the Women's Emergency Center, DEMUNA, and INABIF likewise had a permanent presence in these buildings and also sent promoters, psychologists, and social workers to meet residents in the community. I decided to work with COFOPRI (Comisión de Formalización de la Propiedad Informal, Commission for the Formalization of Informal Property), Techo Propio, and the titling office for the regional government based on conversations I had with Pachacutanos that revealed how central these offices were to their aspirations. I also engaged with various NGOs and religious organizations that either periodically operated from these buildings or that Pachacutanos described working with in their efforts to improve their lives and community.

The primary exception to my rule of using Pachacútec to determine what organizations to examine was my work with entities that measure, locate, and assess poverty, including the INEI and its subsidiary unit ENAHO

(Encuesta Nacional del Hogar: Condiciones de Vida y Pobreza, National Household Survey: Life Conditions and Poverty), FONCODES (Fondo de Cooperación para el Desarrollo Social, Cooperative Fund for Social Development), and SISFOH (Sistema de Focalización de Hogares, System of Household Targeting). Though all these government entities sent field agents to Pachacútec or eventually established offices in Ventanilla, I chose to work with them because they grounded or sought to ground the work of other institutions by designating areas or individuals as poor to begin with.

For all of the aforementioned organizations, I interviewed the field agents I encountered in Pachacútec, observed interactions between agents and Pachacutanos over multiple days or weeks, visited their central offices in Lima to interview managers about institutional goals, operations, and challenges, and scrutinized reports, policy documents, and laws that I was told either synthesized or guided their work. Some of these agencies graciously allowed me to shadow fieldworkers or surveyors to better understand how Pachacútec fit into their broader work. I spent several weeks accompanying itinerant GRIAS agents as they went to extreme poverty zones around the country registering people for national ID cards, and a month accompanying ENAHO surveyors as they translated life conditions in Pachacútec into the categories that mattered to policy makers.

Working with these different agencies and organizations produced a messy picture of poverty assistance in which definitions shift, coverage is uneven, laws and priorities change frequently, and potential recipients are left to navigate all of this on their own. I consider this messiness an important analytic insight. While ethnographies focusing on single institutions and programs can reveal much about governance and the force of particular categories, they risk producing overly determined analyses that overestimate the power of a given institution in people's lives. By contrast, my efforts to center Pachacútec and Pachacutanos' experiences without limiting my perspective to this site provided insight into which frameworks and features are common across social spaces, which are distinctive, and how Pachacutanos experienced this broader poverty reduction regime.

Throughout these activities I took copious field notes and was playfully mocked for my tendency to write everything down. Mostly, people treated this as something between a nervous tic and evidence of my studiousness, and they seemed to have little trouble ignoring it. When the moment did not allow for notetaking, I listened attentively and jotted notes afterward. Upon returning home, I spent long hours reproducing that day's happenings as best I could from memory, spurred by the jottings in my field notebooks.

Though my jottings raised few eyebrows, cameras and voice recorders have more evidentiary, journalistic connotations and could make people nervous. I was therefore much more selective in how I used those technologies, generally taking pictures only at people's express request or when the event was intended as spectacle, and I recorded public meetings only with the permission of meeting organizers. With government officials, recorded formal interviews often preceded more sustained interactions and participant observation. With aid recipients, residents of Pachacútec, promoters, and *dirigentes*, I tended to conduct formal interviews only after several weeks of interactions, when interlocutors seemed receptive to them.

In this book I draw on field notes, meeting recordings, and interview transcripts to convey my interlocutors' voices as faithfully as possible, changing only what is necessary for the text to read smoothly to an English-speaking audience. When words and phrases have multiple potential translations or marked meaning, I also provide the Spanish-language version. Translations of Spanish documents and texts are mine unless otherwise indicated. Although I, as an anthropologist and author, am not the focus of these chapters, I do not erase myself from them and include details that provide insight into the specificity of my ethnographic vantage and instances when interlocutors disagreed with my interpretations. While a primary goal of mine in this book is to challenge dubious distinctions between the "deserving" and "undeserving" poor, if taken out of context, some of the stories from this text could compromise the sociomoral standing of my interlocutors and their ability to secure jobs or other forms of social assistance. I therefore use pseudonyms for everyone I discuss in this text. I include public figures such as government employees and elected officials in this practice, not because I think this would fool anyone with in-depth knowledge of politics in Lima-Callao but because this is not a story about any particular politician or bureaucrat. Rather it is a story about the politics of poverty writ large and how those politics shape the aspirations and experiences of Peruvians who make their lives in and through the urban peripheries.

WRITING POVERTY: ANALYTIC AND REPRESENTATIONAL CHOICES

The work of ethnography neither begins nor ends when we leave the field,[23] but rather includes the theoretical engagements that help us link microlevel phenomena to broader sociopolitical insights and the choices we make as writers endeavoring to translate socially situated logics and experiences for people outside these sociocultural milieus. Unlike fieldwork, which is largely about standing back and balancing mindful engagement with self-effacement,[24] these other aspects of ethnography require staking claims and making choices that shape the work we produce.

Ethnographers rarely discuss how they choose theory, acting as though our theoretical choices were natural outgrowths of our ethnographic encounters. Although it may indeed feel this way to the practicing anthropological ethnographer, our theoretical choices are political in their origins and their effects. They are informed by how we are situated socially and intellectually, and they assert truths the same way (re)writing history does, by acknowledging some connections and ignoring others. However, anthropological ethnography is distinct in the way it treats these theories, not as models to fit data into but as ideas that are provisionally good to think with. Our insistence on letting the ethnographic encounter speak back to theory, commitment to what is in the field, and efforts to ground-truth our ideas through dialogue and return help to ensure that theory remains responsive to context while also allowing us to draw on insights generated elsewhere.

Because in this text I am concerned with how poverty is imagined and experienced and how efforts to combat this poverty shape life in urban Peru, I've drawn primarily on three differently located bodies of theory. The first is theory on poverty and statecraft generated from diverse contexts including Peru, the United States, India, South Africa, and explicitly global locations such as the United Nations and World Bank. These global borrowings make sense given that poverty monitoring practices and the postcolonial nation-state form have transnational reach. The second is anthropological scholarship on urban poverty and politics in countries across Latin America, including Argentina, Bolivia, Brazil, and Chile, where similar articulations of global, historical, and political structures obtain and where findings resonate with phenomena I encountered in Peru. The third is scholarship on gender, marriage, and kinship in the Andes. Though potentially controversial given the rightful critiques of early anthropological quests to uncover "lo Andino" as essential cultural holdovers from a pre-Columbian past (Starn 1991), I draw on this research for several reasons. First, I believe one can draw on observations of practices and social structures from the Andes without presuming that these practices persist unchanged since pre-Columbian times. Second, Lima's earliest *barriadas* (settler-built neighborhoods) were founded by migrants from the Andes, and many of the laws and institutions established to manage them were in dialogue with Andean practices both as they existed and as they were imagined by state agents (Lloyd 1980; Lobo 1982). Finally, practices identified as Andean often align quite neatly with those deemed "informal" because of how they trouble the operations of the modern state, defying and exceeding state categories and jurisdictions (de Soto, Ghersi, and Ghibellini 1989; Matos Mar 1984). These seemingly Andes-specific insights might therefore tell us something valuable about the paradoxes, peculiarities, and unruly effects of statecraft in other contexts.

The choices we make as writers are likewise integral to the work of ethnography. One of my choices that merits attention is the way I name the site of Pachacútec. Numerous scholars have wrestled with how to name the spatializations of urban marginality in which they work, as every term has implications for how the site is interpreted and the other sites with which it is deemed comparable.[25] Terms like "slum," "shantytown," "settlement," "progressive" or "self-help housing project," "margin," "periphery," and "informal city" are in some ways interchangeable, and yet all invoke different ideas about advancement or decay, nobility or vice, apathy or entrepreneurialism, authoritarian imposition or democratic expression. Even relying exclusively on Peruvian terms leaves an array of options—including *barriada*, *pueblo joven*, *asentamiento humano*, *barrio popular*, *barrio marginal*, and *invasión*—each with its own political-legal specificities and moral connotations.

Although I avoid terms like "slum" and "site of urban relegation" (Wacquant 2008) that invoke despair and abandonment and have little purchase in sites like Pachacútec, which are inundated with state practices and alive with community development initiatives, I have generally responded to the dilemma of how to name and thus categorize and characterize Pachacútec's neighborhoods through a strategy of discriminating promiscuity that accounts for the diverse political, moral, and historical frames into which Pachacútec may be inserted. In most cases I use the term "settlement" to invoke the simultaneous realities of precariousness and possibility that characterize this largely settler-built site and capture some of the political unease that it inspires.[26] I also use terms like "extreme poverty zone" when discussing how Pachacútec is brought into view through this official designation or "shantytown" when describing how its precarious urban sprawl aligns with a particular global poverty aesthetic. I use Peruvian terms like *barriada*, *pueblo joven* (young town), or *asentamiento humano* (human settlement) when linking Pachacútec to a history of similar settlements in Lima's outskirts or to the affordances of a particular political-legal designation. I also retain the term *invasión* (invasion) in the many instances when my interlocutors applied it. Though I certainly recognize the term's problematic racial and moral connotations, the continued use of the term "invasion" by people who participate in them reveals the persistent moral and legal ambivalence surrounding this practice. Reminding readers of these connotations helps guard against tendencies to romanticize these grassroots housing initiatives by highlighting how this property system forces people into tenuous moral and legal positions in which their land rights depend on political largesse and exceptions to the official rules (Castells 1983).

I have chosen to name my interlocutors by the places to which they claimed residence, belonging, or representativeness in conversation with me, that is, as Pachacutanos or more broadly as Peruvians. I do this because despite the great internal diversity of Peru and Pachacútec, many of the dynamics I describe are functions of seeking rights to space in Pachacútec or being subject to Peruvian state forms and ideologies. In using these terms, I am also refusing to name my interlocutors "migrants" or "Indians" mostly because these terms do not apply, at least not in the essentializing, categorical ways English-speaking audiences typically understand them. Despite the frequent association of Lima's peripheral settlements with rural-urban migration, a majority of Pachacutanos were either born in Lima or lived there for many years before coming to Pachacútec. The term "migrant" describes neither their self-concepts nor lived experiences but serves merely to differentiate them from unmarked urban inhabitants and imply their subordination. Terms like "Indian," meanwhile, are almost never used as self-identifiers in Peru, and race and ethnic identities such as "Indian," "cholo," "mestizo," "criollo," and "white" are experienced as gradient and relational phenomena rather than static categories (de la Cadena 1995; Huayhua 2014).[27] People may move from one category to another, becoming more or less "Indian" depending on the amount of power they can assume in any interaction and relatedly, their capacity to inhabit positions associated with official, formal state culture. As I show in the chapters that follow, this is highly variable in Pachacútec.

CHAPTER OVERVIEW

Each chapter in this book provides a different piece of the puzzle of what poverty is in urban Peru and where skepticism of official poverty statistics comes from. I have divided the book into three parts to emphasize the central threads of this analysis: international antipoverty paradigms and metrics; the situated implementation of policies via documents and local actors; and the intimate worlds of women who are both agents and objects of these policies.

Part I, "Concepts in Situ," examines how international policies, concepts, and metrics are folded into my interlocutors' worldviews and strategies of living. In chapter 1 I explore how Peruvians living and working in "extreme poverty zones" contribute to the production of poverty statistics and imaginaries that they also mistrust. In chapter 2 I examine poverty's inverse of development. I argue that Pachacutanos' disillusionment with development results in part from the contradictory ways discourses of family and practices of kinship are implicated in the politics of development and show how women experience development as an exhausting effort to negotiate conflicting relational identities and commitments.

In part II, "Materialities of Statecraft," I scrutinize the long histories and present realities of formalization as antipoverty policy in Peru. In the process, I detail what these programs reveal about the nature of the Peruvian state and illustrate how documents, and the will to document, inform contemporary patterns of race and gender discrimination. Chapter 3 sets the stage for understanding Peruvian antipoverty policies by illustrating the moral valences of formalization campaigns that serve as precursors to and enactments of development. This chapter also highlights the many ways the documents that are integral to these campaigns do not clarify relations so much as bring new and often unruly entities into being. In chapter 4 I explore how Peru's internationally inspired efforts to fight poverty by distributing national ID cards are embedded in national projects to construct particular kinds of relations between states, citizens, and families and ultimately place the burden of national development squarely on women's shoulders.

In part III, "Intimate Expanses," I explore how antipoverty policy shapes domestic ideals, intimate experiences of marginality, and ultimately the whole of the urban landscape. In chapter 5 I examine the forces that inculcate Peruvians with particular ideals of domestic life and shape experiences of relational failure. I scrutinize how grandiose imaginaries of single mothers inform ideologies and performances of deserving poverty and describe how the "single mother" designation fails to capture the variability and elasticity of relationships in practice. In chapter 6 I link these dynamics back to the broader landscape of Peruvian poverty by describing how Peruvians' domestic aspirations, kin obligations, and intimate uncertainties intertwine with housing policies in ways that are refracted onto space, perpetuating everyday battles over land accumulation, experiences of injustice, and the precarious and pockmarked urban landscapes that Peruvians associate with poverty.

I conclude by reflecting on the central insights of this ethnography for anthropological theory and antipoverty practice.

« PART ONE »

Concepts in Situ

« ONE »

Poverty Productions

MEASUREMENT, MEDIATION, AND MISTRUST

Loreto had been chosen to statistically represent Peru's national reality, and he was not happy about it. To produce its official poverty statistics, the Peruvian government relies on the ENAHO national household survey together with a rigorous statistical methodology developed in consultation with a team of international poverty experts (INEI 2011, 2012). This methodology involves gathering survey responses from a probabilistic, stratified sample of approximately 26,000 individuals who are randomly selected from rural and urban areas of each of Peru's twenty-five political departments. To develop a robust cross-sectional and longitudinal understanding of poverty, the ENAHO divides this sample into "nonpanel" respondents, who can come from any household in the designated survey area, and "panel" respondents, who are revisited each year for three to five years. Loreto belonged to one of approximately 225 households in Callao randomly selected to repeat the four- to five-hour survey year after year. Again, he was not happy about it.

I accompanied an ENAHO surveyor as she knocked at the bars of a small store in Pachacútec where neighbors said we would be able to locate Loreto after we found his official Pachacútec residence empty. At sixty years old, with no family to speak of, Loreto apparently spent most of his time working as a shop assistant in the neighborhood store in exchange for his meals and modest pay, which he described as just a few *soles* (the Peruvian currency).[1] After three years of interviews, Loreto was familiar with what was coming and remained behind the iron bars of the storefront as the surveyor asked him one mind-numbing question after another.

"In the last two weeks, have you consumed any of the following products: common bread, wheat bread, french bread, hamburger bread, serrano bread, prepackaged bread," and so on. If Loreto was foolish enough to answer yes to any of these queries, he was condemned to another round: "How did you acquire it? With what frequency did you acquire it this way? How much did each unit weigh? How many units did you consume? How much was each unit worth?" And so on for fifty food categories before moving on to expenditures on health, education, clothing, transportation, and whatever else a team of interested social scientists could think up.

Whenever Loreto asked, "Yeah, señorita, are we almost done?" the surveyor responded, "Oh yes, yes, sir, just a few more questions." Yet as we headed into hour three of the survey, Loreto was fed up.

> Yeah, that's enough, señora! Four years you all have been asking me these questions, but what do I ever see in return?! You all benefit from us and from our information, but nothing ever happens. I answer all your questions, but . . . the big guys, they never look out for us. We support them with signatures and demonstrations, but for the people nothing. All of these questions you ask me are a waste of time.

The surveyor pleaded with him, "But sir, that is exactly why we are doing this survey, so that the government can know the needs of the people and help them." Loreto would have none of it. "No señora, no," he replied. "The problem is you don't have a way to channel resources to make things happen. Sure, I'm poor . . . but there are people who are far worse off than me. So much poverty that one sees around here. Why aren't you talking to those people?!" With that, the interview was over.

The surveyor told me she would return later with a National Institute of Statistics T-shirt as a peace offering that might allow her to finish the interview. If that didn't work, she consoled herself with the fact that she had finished the most important part of the survey. "What really matters for us are the expenses," she said. In Peru, where most labor is informal and income unpredictable, social theorists and technocrats had concluded that consumption was the most reliable indicator of poverty. As a result, Loreto's complaints about his medical expenses, monthly debt payments for his stove and stereo, even what he spent on daily bread and bathwater would be used to statistically demonstrate that he was climbing out of poverty.

Most ENAHO surveyors were women who had taken on the feminized labor of coaxing information from strangers on a contract basis as a way to make ends meet.[2] They expressed misgivings about this sunny statistical rendering of expenses, which seemed to exploit the gap between what respondents said and what they meant. A surveyor explained,

> I don't believe consumption is the best way to measure poverty, because when you need something, when you have to buy school supplies for your kids, for example, no matter what, you find a way to get it. Even if it means that you work double or that you go into debt, you find a way to do it. That doesn't mean you're not poor.

Other critiques of Peru's poverty and development metrics were grounded in alternative readings of statistics, as when public intellectuals pointed out that using a poverty line meant a few extra cents could prompt a person's reclassification as "nonpoor" without substantively improving their circumstances, or when bureaucrats argued that economic growth was driven by improvements among the middle and lower middle classes while the poorest of the poor were left behind. Yet by far the most common critiques of Peru's statistical successes were, like Loreto's, grounded in a mistrust of government and a pervasive sense that the state was incapable of properly targeting the truly needy despite poverty's omnipresence in the landscape.[3] No matter what the numbers said, people argued that they still *saw* poverty everywhere. They would point to the sprawling shantytowns and trash-lined streets, the mange-covered dogs and barefoot children and ask, "Does that *look* like development to you?" Yet, as Loreto's case demonstrates, specific manifestations of poverty were also distrusted and oddly estranged from lived experience. Real poverty, as my interlocutors understood it, had a mirage-like quality; it seemed to disappear as you got close to it.

To understand the specific contours of the Peruvian poverty construct and how poverty, as a nationally compelling concept and globally actionable object, comes into being, I draw on the ideas of assemblage, aesthetics, and production. Aiwha Ong and Stephen Collier (2005, 11) define "global assemblages" as sociocultural constructs with a "distinctive capacity for decontextualization and recontextualization, abstractability and movement" that materialize in particular contexts where their meanings are shaped and delimited by the other variables at play. "Poverty," like "democracy," "neoliberalism," and "bioscience," fits this definition well. It is a highly mobile abstraction whose ability to travel across social spheres is facilitated by bureaucratic norms and statistical technologies. At the same time, it is also always unstable, partial, and contingent, actively assembled in real time as actors draw on unique combinations of histories, experiences, and imaginaries to evaluate what real poverty is.

Beginning from the idea of poverty as a global assemblage, I explore how understandings of poverty are assembled as Peruvians draw on popular renderings of the nation's history, free-floating statistical representations of Peru's reality, and graphic poverty portrayals that permeate Peruvian media. These diverse representations of poverty combine to produce a particular aesthetic of poverty in which sociostructural and moral hierarchies are encoded visually and viscerally, and the status of a person or place as "poor" is misrecognized as obvious, even primal, rather than the product of particular political relations and projects of government (Ghertner 2015; Peattie 1992; Roy 2003).

I then examine how Peruvians living in the urban periphery are integral to the (re)production of an ideal-type poverty that they also mistrust. They collaborate with development agents, posing for pictures, articulating testimonials, contriving signatures, and generating their own statistics, in an effort to produce the imaginaries donors demand in exchange for much-needed resources. I keep alive a tension between the idea of production as a highly mediated performance and production as the manufacture of an exchange-worthy commodity, as both meanings are integral to the complex and conflicted morality of poverty assistance. Most Peruvians I encountered, rich and poor alike, were concerned that beneficiaries of antipoverty programs were faking it, selling a dissimulation and profiting from poverty while the truly needy remained at the margins. Although I maintain a critical distance from the question of deservingness, I show how beneficiaries were required to align themselves with particular administrative categories and trauma narratives in order to receive assistance. This helped to (re)produce the specific poverty imaginaries that circulated in different spheres of Peruvian society, as commodities do. Also, like commodities, these poverty imaginaries were produced by the flexible, low-wage labor of a largely female workforce, with most of the benefits accruing to the institutions, political administrations, and NGOs at the top of the supply chain, whose main contributions related to marketing and quality control over the collective product (Davis, Kingsbury, and Merry 2010). Ironically, engaging in this official image-work reinforces understandings of what "deserving poverty" looks like while also contributing to a generalized mistrust of appearances. By examining accusations of national deceits and local immoralities, I illuminate the multiple fictions that shape official and subjective understandings of poverty and reveal how the production of global knowledge about poverty perpetuates skepticism, uncertainty, and mistrust.

POVERTY'S PRESENT PAST

Understanding the different ways poverty is assembled in Peru requires reckoning with Peruvian history, not as a definitive catalogue of all poverty-shaping moments but as those events and epochs that Peruvians explicitly invoke to make sense of the current poverty moment. Though other aspects of Peru's past inform how Peruvians explain, experience, and seek to combat poverty, I limit the discussion here to what emerged as relevant during my ethnographic encounters; it is the history that my interlocutors pointed me to or that I had to learn in order to understand the policy organizations and political debates they were caught up in. This most present past of Peruvian poverty includes the country's colonial inheritance, the relocation of poverty in the mid-twentieth century, the political-economic crises of the 1980s, and the antipolitical politics that emerged in response.

I often heard Peruvians describe their country as one defined by its past glories and unrealized potentials. The adage "Peru is a beggar seated on a gold bench" was uttered by numerous Peruvian development practitioners and residents of Pachacútec.[4] It is a reference to the apparent paradox of Peru as a country rich in a diverse array of natural resources, including copper, gold, natural gas, and a substantial portion of the Amazon rainforest, and yet somehow still plagued by poverty, seeking assistance from ostensibly richer and more developed nations. Many of the most prominent public discussions about Peruvian culture, politics, and society are in conversation with this idea. In his 2010 New Year's speech, poverty-fighting president Alan García encouraged Peruvians to "burn the ghosts of pessimism past" and "do away with this idea that Peru is a country where they take everything away from us." Ten years later, President Pedro Castillo won national elections with the promise of "no more poverty in a rich country," referencing the idea that Peru's perennial poverty ran counter to what the country naturally was, or at least to what it had been before the Spanish arrival.

For many, it is hard to imagine an event more significant in the history of Peru than the Spanish conquest, both as a single event and as a period that established the hierarchies and conflicts that shaped Peruvian life for centuries to come (Orlove 1985). First through violence and then through the combined disciplinary powers of law and religion, Spanish colonists sought to reformulate every aspect of indigenous life, remaking "conceptions of time, space, work, property, marriage and the family" (Merry 1992, 363). This violent, moralistic "lawfare" laid the foundations for a country riven by racialized inequalities,[5] a single nation in which Indians and whites confront each other not as strangers but with the "lethal familiarity of estranged kin" (Weismantel 2001, 16).

During the run-up to Peru's war of independence from Spain in 1821, Peruvian-born elite criollos blamed colonial power structures for reducing the once-mighty Inca civilization to the wretched state of contemporary *indios* (de la Cadena 2000; Walker 1999). Despite promises that independence would end formal ethnic differences, the rise of the Peruvian republic brought about a second conquest of the Andes through the violent expansion of large haciendas that held domain over the indigenous communities living there (de la Cadena 2015; Degregori and Sandoval 2008, 154; Orlove 1985). Peruvian elites celebrated imagined historical Indians and ignored the possibility that contemporary Indians were fully rational subjects (de la Cadena 2000). Indigenous peoples were at once foundational to Peru's national identity and "excluded from these same identities by the sorts of disciplinary knowledge that marked them as racially or civilizationally 'other'" (Das and Poole 2004, 9). Indians represented the margins of the state, the lawlessness and irrationality against which the modern state defined itself. The raison d'être of this state could be found in its continued efforts to dominate, civilize, and uplift the individuals that the state itself had preemptively excluded from the political community (Das and Poole 2004).

These racial distinctions had an important spatial component. Throughout Peru's colonial and early republican periods (1535–1895), Lima had been the center of empire;[6] it was a city-state synonymous with whiteness, urbanity, and official national culture whose rule and civilizing influence seemed to diminish as one moved farther from the city center. Gandolfo (2009) powerfully articulates the meanings that Limeños attached to urban space and urban life more generally with her explanation of the concept of *policia*. Brought to the New World as a key metric of civilization, *policia* referred to

> the town's orderly layout, to the adornment, beauty, and harmony of its buildings as well as to the degree of politeness, civism and courtesy of its residents, to their sociability and level of instruction in the

> Christian doctrine, their composure, good upbringing, and refinement of manners, their good sexual habits and industriousness, and their clothing, especially if adorned or elegant. (77)

Urban life was thus understood, Gandolfo asserts, as "the only mode of living conducive to a properly human way of being" (76). To live outside or beyond the confines of an orderly city implied barbarism and subhuman existence. Historical records show that white Limeños could certainly exist in penury, but they had a status and degree of political entitlement that far exceeded that of Indian inhabitants, the majority of whom lived in rural spaces and whose poverty was perceived as either intrinsic to their racial designation or a rightful consequence of it (Milton 2007).

During the twentieth century, these dynamics began to shift as poverty was relocated spatially, politically, and temporally. Peru's increasing integration into a global capitalist economy, and the corresponding development of extractive export industries, pushed rural inhabitants off their land but offered few jobs to compensate (Fitzgerald 1979). This prompted unprecedented migration into Lima. Between 1940 and 2000, Lima's population ballooned from 662,000 to 7.5 million, accounting for roughly a third of the entire Peruvian population (INEI 2001, 10).

Lima's elites experienced this migrant influx as an "overflow of the popular masses."[7] During my fieldwork, Peruvian development agents often invoked this period of mass urbanization to explain poverty in Lima, describing it through naturalizing hydraulic metaphors that erase the political foundations of this phenomenon. In this framework, the first migrants "saturated" the city center, subdividing homes that had been vacated by the upper classes into ever smaller tenements known as *tugurios*. They then "spilled" into previously uninhabited riverbanks and hillsides before "flowing" outward to the north, south, and east, forming Lima's visibly impoverished *conos* (cones) through creeping expansions and overt mass land takeovers, tellingly referred to as *invasiones* (invasions) to index the apparent foreignness of settlers and the sociolegal boundaries they transgressed (Collier 1976; Gandolfo 2009). The presence of Andean migrants in the city challenged long-standing geographies of race that associated whites with urban space and Indians with rural space. The proliferation of untidy shantytowns likewise visibly challenged the ordering capacities of the Peruvian state. As "matter out of place" (Douglas 2002), migrant settlements were largely viewed as sites of dirt, disorder, and disease whose contaminating influence threatened the city (Collier 1976; Weismantel 2001).

The first efforts to control these settlements were both violent and pastoral in nature. Lima was surrounded for miles by vacant deserts, so settlements that occurred on private property, abutted upper-class neighborhoods, or otherwise upset elites were relocated to the city's periphery (Collier 1976). These new neighborhoods quickly became targets for religious and private charities and new state-run social welfare institutions that explicitly focused on the holistic development of families with particular emphasis on pre- and post-natal treatment, abandoned and neglected minors, and teaching women proper household management (Blondet and Trivelli 2004; MIMDES 2007). By 1968 these programs were expanded to include emergency and disaster relief and sharpened to focus even more intently on the "mother-child pair" (MIMDES 2007), illustrating how the gendered logics of exception and a particular temporality of deservingness were first integrated into Peru's national aid apparatus.

At the same time, another redistributive politics was taking hold in the now nominally democratic Peru as politicians sought creative ways to accommodate the growing constituency of new Limeños residing in the periphery. In 1961 Peru's congress passed Law 13517 on Marginal Settlements, then referred to as *barrios marginales* or *barriadas*. This landmark legislation specified prohibitions against land invasions while promising to help "organized settler associations" transform their existing settlements into dignified, fully serviced urbanizations and to legally recognize the individual property rights of inhabitants. However, the provision of this law prohibiting new invasions was only selectively enforced. Moreover, although legalization under Law 13517 initially depended on complying with urbanization norms, when Peru's congress realized it could not keep pace with its new obligations to finance infrastructure, it decoupled physical and legal land regularization. That change generated a pattern in which settlers illegally seized land, subsequently legalized their settlements and individual property holdings, and installed infrastructure after the fact at a pace dependent on settlers' grassroots initiative, political savvy, and capacity to garner public sympathy for their plight (Calderón Cockburn 2002; Dietz 1998; Fernández-Maldonado 2010; Stokes 1995).

The political dynamics that followed from Law 13517 ushered in a new space-time for urban poverty in Peru. Poverty was decidedly spatial; it was located in the peripheries and largely an effect of infrastructural lack (*carencias*), yet it was also invested with a particular temporality of transformation (Caldeira 2017). The poverty of the *barriadas* was still understood as dire and corrupting, but it was also expected to be temporary. Viewed through the emergent lens of progressive urbanism, *barriadas* could be conceptualized as nascent urban forms, young towns just starting their journey on the long but clearly mapped road to urban modernity (Collier 1976; Fernández-Maldonado 2007; Mangin and Turner 1968).

This physical and political relocation of poverty attained new heights on October 3, 1968, when under the leadership of leftist General Juan Velasco, Peru's military seized power to implement sweeping, pro-poor reforms. Within six days, the new Revolutionary Government of the Armed Forces nationalized foreign-owned oil wells. Within a year, it passed agrarian reform measures to transform old haciendas into peasant-owned cooperatives. The political ethos driving these changes was simultaneously pro-majoritarian and pro-poor. As Velasco articulated in a 1969 speech: "The government must be, above all else, a government for the majority and also for the most needy" (2005, 282). He went on to assert that the government's greatest challenge would be to construct "a social order where man can live with dignity, knowing that *he lives on land that is his* and in a nation that owns its destiny" (283, emphasis mine). The language of land reform and social justice helped legitimize squatters' ongoing demands for homes of their own where they could live dignified lives and properly form their children, such that housing in Lima's periphery became central to the everyday machinations of the politics of poverty.

During the decade of military rule, the Peruvian state became the main provider of infrastructure and welfare services and established programs like SINAMOS (Sistema Nacional de Apoyo a la Movilización Social, National System of Social Mobilization and Support) in an effort to enhance and harness the political power of Lima's peripheral inhabitants. These community organizations also helped limit and delegitimize alternative political formations that might oppose the military regime (Collier 1976; Fitzgerald 1979). Though women seldom held official leadership positions in these neighborhood organizations, they were nonetheless critical protagonists in community efforts to obtain land and basic services. As household managers, women were understood to have a legitimate stake in autoconstruction efforts, and their inclusion in land takeovers and neighborhood development initiatives lent moral legitimacy to controversial and often illegal political actions. By promoting the art of popular political mobilization, the military government invigorated a new politics of poverty as men and women learned to combine democratic protest and clientelist patronage to obtain government assistance for their efforts to improve their lives and communities (Collier 1976; Lloyd 1980; Stokes 1995).

Ironically, it was only after the official transition to democracy in the 1980s that the ugliest sides of Peru's expanded state apparatus appeared.

These included the state's capacity for violent abuse in the name of order and the potential for private political interest to interfere with the collective advancement of the imagined Peruvian nation. On the eve of the 1980 elections, the Maoist insurgent group Sendero Luminoso made its first appearance by burning ballot boxes in the central Andean province of Ayacucho. Sendero's goals were brutally simple: to overthrow the state capitalist system and to arrive at a classless utopia by crossing a "river of blood" (Starn 1991). Most scholars agree that Sendero's rise was related to the ways capitalist modernization had increased interconnections between Peru's city and countryside and simultaneously widened the gaps between rich and poor, urban and rural, and criollo and indigenous populations (Degregori 1997; Starn 1991). For many, this period is a reminder of what can happen if poverty and inequality are not held in check. Critically, though, Sendero Luminoso made no appeals to indigenous pride and instead visited intense violence on Andean peasants reluctant to join their cause. In this, Sendero resembled the Peruvian state, which likewise treated indigenous peasants as poor, ignorant, and irrational subjects, "alien to modernity," and thus killable (Franco 2006; Poole and Rénique 1992). Fully 75 percent of the 69,000 deaths amassed during fifteen years of war were Quechua speakers (Laplante and Theidon 2008). Many of my interlocutors had memories from this period that involved the deaths of loved ones, forced recruitment by either Sendero or the Peruvian army, or fleeing natal villages in the hopes of finding greater safety and security in Lima.

By the end of the 1980s, Peru was struggling under severe economic crisis as well. In 1985 Alan García, leader of Peru's longest-surviving political party, APRA (Alianza Popular Revolucionaria Americana, American Popular Revolutionary Alliance), won the presidency. Since the 1930s APRA had maintained a platform that was both pro-poor and pro-technocrat, promising a "scientific politics" in which experts would govern in the interests of a poor majority who had too long "remained at the margins of the business of the state" (Haya de la Torre 2005 [1931]). Nonetheless, through a combination of corruption, mismanagement, and failed gambles, García's administration exacerbated existing economic challenges, creating runaway inflation and unprecedented unemployment, and alienating the international financial community (Cameron and Mauceri 1997; Crabtree 1992). This period of scarcity and the sense that party politics were to blame for it left an indelible mark on Peruvian political consciousness. One of my most eloquent interlocutors, Felipe, recalled the hardships.

> Everyone remembers Alan's first government being difficult because it affected peoples' habits. . . . Before, there were two types of bread that were always available. . . . Then the shortage happened and suddenly there was no bread, or the price went up so much you couldn't buy it. . . . And without these basic elements, the meals just don't exist. . . . And *oouuff*, you had to wait in line all day for some of these basics. What's worse, you'd get to the front of the line and say "I want five kilos of rice," and the shopkeeper would say, "Sorry, only one kilo per person." That is, unless you were Aprista [a member of APRA].

Felipe likened APRA to a nationwide fraternity whose unifying principle was that you had to support your fellow Apristas. "That has always been the goal of APRA, to maintain people inside the public institutions. . . . When you go for a job, other Apristas are there to support you, and this creates loyalty between them." People with personal political connections were able to get by. Those without them organized other sorts of mutual aid societies that, for a time, operated outside the official state apparatus (Cameron and Mauceri 1997; Dietz 1998).

Tired of the continually deteriorating economic situation and politics as usual, in 1990 Peruvians elected Alberto Fujimori to the presidency. Fujimori was a self-proclaimed political outsider who promised to represent "the people" in their struggles against the "political elite." Fujimori's politics and policies came up regularly as I tried to understand social life in Pachacútec and the institutions from which residents sought assistance. Although Fujimori initially campaigned on a platform of economic stabilization without recession, within two weeks of his election he implemented harsh, Washington Consensus-style structural adjustments: slashing state programs, privatizing assets, and strengthening legal protections to create an environment conducive to foreign investment.[8] Inflation, which had been about 40 percent per month, shot up to 398 percent in August 1990. The number of Peruvians living in poverty rose to 54 percent, and real wages fell to 33 percent of what they had been in 1980 (Roberts 1995). Confronted with congressional opposition to this economic program, Fujimori dissolved the congress, claiming that he was enabling a more direct democracy and would not permit interference from "the political class" (in Roberts 1995).

In 1993 Fujimori justified these policies by claiming they were critical to winning Peru's long fight against poverty:

> We [implemented] a firm policy that encompasses the most basic principles of soundness, austerity, and efficiency. . . . The

> impoverishment and exploitation of millions of Peruvians throughout five centuries has accomplices known to all. That poverty has worsened in the past decade owing to misgovernment and terrorism. Let us work in an orderly and responsible fashion to eliminate that terrorism and for the first time create objective conditions to uproot the problem of poverty. (2005, 466)

Under Fujimori's neoliberalism, poverty was acknowledged as a phenomenon with deep historical and structural roots but ultimately blamed on a bloated state apparatus, government incompetence, and political corruption. In this framework, the solution was to depoliticize relief efforts, making them more technocratic, more efficient, and less expensive. Fujimori's administration sought to accomplish this by prioritizing what they termed *formalización* (formalization) and *focalización* (focalization, targeting); they created central registries of all Peruvians and their property holdings and at the same time introduced selective criteria to determine who, among the 54 percent of the population then living below the poverty line, was truly needy and deserving of the ever more limited assistance the state offered. This is where the seemingly objective neutrality of numbers and maps comes into the story of how poverty is assembled in Peru.

POVERTY BY NUMBERS

Efforts to count poverty rely on and reproduce the assumption that poverty is an objective thing and that levels of poverty can be compared over time and across space. However, poverty's apparent objectivity is not a natural fact, but the product of historically and institutionally embedded statistical practice. Moreover, how nations and international organizations define and measure poverty has shifted over time to reflect sociopolitical circumstances and remains politically contentious.

According to development historians, the concept of global poverty was invented after World War II when the US and allied nations sought a framework to justify and facilitate intervention in the former colonies (Edelman and Haugerud 2005; Escobar 1995; Rist 2008). Initially, these nations relied largely on modernization theory, which, like colonial ideologies of social evolution, argued that all countries had to pass through particular stages on the single road to development. Modernization theorists contended that promoting economic growth as measured by GDP would propel a variety of desirable changes modeled on US social norms, including the rise of nuclear-family structures, lower fertility rates, capitalist property relations, democratic politics, and liberal legal systems governed by contracts.

In response to criticism that the modernization framework ignored the ways global structural inequalities actively underdeveloped the former colonies, in the 1970s, international aid agencies shifted their focus from development to poverty reduction. In this shift, poverty retained its implicit inverse relation to development even as it was opened to new theoretical, technical, and institutional elaborations. Although global poverty was still often spoken of in terms of the lack of perceived essentials of modernity—asphalt roads, piped water and sewerage systems, electricity, and surplus agriculture products suitable for market—it was measured through biologically informed basic needs approaches that continue to inform the ways many countries define and measure poverty. In Peru, for example, the INEI measures monetary poverty by calculating the price per calorie of all food Peruvians might eat, accounting for variations in diet and pricing in rural and urban areas of coastal, mountain, and jungle regions. The institute then uses the ENAHO to determine how much Peruvians are spending on food each month. If this amount is less than the bare minimum required to adequately nourish household members, the surveyed household is categorized as being in "extreme poverty." The amount of time, energy, and technical expertise devoted to determining the bare minimum an individual requires to survive in different contexts speaks to the political importance of developing poverty metrics conducive to cross-national comparison. It also reveals the infrastructural and epistemological support buoying presumptions that poverty assistance should be limited to preventing starvation despite the rise of more expansive theorizations (Simmel 1965 [1908]; De Waal 2005).

In the 1990s a new development regime emerged that sought to get beyond narrow economic and biological conceptions of poverty and focus more on how the poor are denied the capacity to intervene in society and change their circumstances. In this "capabilities" framework, poverty is conceptualized as a multidimensional deprivation, a state of powerlessness engendered by and made manifest in low levels of education, poor health, malnutrition, and gender inequalities. Proponents of this framework describe it as encouraging a relational and socially embedded understanding of poverty and poverty reduction (Hickey 2010; Roy 2003); critics point out that efforts to measure these aspects of the poverty experience across contexts perpetuate the tendency to reify, exteriorize, and universalize it (Green 2006; Gupta 2011).

A World Bank report entitled *Attacking Poverty* (2000) embraced this multidimensional framework, highlighting the importance of newer measures that could capture diverse dimensions of poverty across countries, such as good governance, gender equality, rule of law, and quality of life. Similarly, in recent years different development institutions have elaborated an array of indicators—among them the Human Development Index, the Multidimensional Poverty Index, the Gender Inequality Index, and the World Bank's Doing Business Rankings—in an effort to embrace the socially embedded and experiential dimensions of poverty while also reducing them to readily comprehensible numerical abstractions that can be easily mapped and compared cross-nationally. In constructing these indices, development agents rely on proxies that can be reliably counted in different contexts, such as calorie consumption per dollar, attendance at reproductive health workshops, and cases of domestic violence reported to the police. They then assign these counts differently weighted values before combining them with other data deemed relevant. The proxies and weights are chosen based on the best judgments of experts and interested parties, but they are judgments nonetheless, and reasonable individuals might make different choices. Although the producers of these numbers are frequently careful to qualify their results and explain what is left out, over time these qualifications fade from view, leaving behind what appear to be objective numerical evaluations.

This brief history of global poverty—from its invention in the 1950s to its current theorization as a multidimensional deprivation with various subjective and experiential but quantifiable dimensions—demonstrates that the idea of a singular "poverty," the objective core of which is the same whether it is measured in Peru, Portugal, or Papua New Guinea, is a product of development thinking. It is an entity "brought into being through the institutions established to describe, quantify, and locate it" (Green 2006, 1111). Even so, tallying poverty in this way has important effects. First, it reproduces particular Western ideas of progress in terms of what is being counted and in the act of counting itself. As Talal Asad (2002, 83) explains, the very idea of progress, so central to the development paradigm, is "in great measure the product of statistical practices" and is inconceivable without the "continuous use of comparative statistics." Relatedly, Asad notes that these statistical practices bolster beliefs in the universality of experience by converting incommensurable cultures into sites of commensurable but nonhomogeneous social arrangements (83).

Second, the consistent reliance on numbers to reveal truth cements beliefs in the supremacy of particular ways of knowing, with important implications for the political legitimacy of governments. Social theorists have argued that the very idea of the state, as an authoritative entity distinct from other institutions, depends on its ability to count, categorize, and administer to the population (Foucault 2007; Li 2005; Scott 1998; Sharma and Gupta 2006). In Peru, as far back as 1930, leading political figures argued that the legitimacy of government depended on its ability to wield statistical knowledge that "rather than invent reality, discovers the space people inhabit and attempts to organize and govern them" (Haya de la Torre 2005 [1931], 254). To this day, the legitimacy of the Peruvian state depends in part on its statistical and technocratic competence, that is, its capacity to render society legible using its chosen categorical schemes and to govern based on that knowledge.

With the rise of global governance practices and democratic ideals, state legitimacy also depends on transparency, which we may understand as a state's capacity to render itself and its actions legible to a host of governments, global development agents, and its national citizens. Sally Merry (2011, S85) argues that the "massive expansion of quantification in recent times comes from a political culture that demands more openness and seeks to drive out corruption, prejudice, and the arbitrary power of elites even at the cost of subtlety and depth." This, Merry argues, is the power, the magic, and the appeal of numbers (S85). For global governance elites, numbers transform an unknowable and anxiety-provoking world into one amenable to governance and manipulation. And in their simplified, commodified, and readily circulating form, numbers make this knowledge accessible to anyone. As statistics and composite indicators become established over time, they become "public numbers," part of the "official language of market and state" (Guyer et al. 2010, 56) and a "discursive currency by means of which government speaks to its subjects, citizens speak among themselves, experts speak to every-persons, everyone speaks back to government—and the media mediate all the incessant talk, adding their own inventions, inflections and inflations" (Comaroff and Comaroff 2006a, 211).

As a democracy where citizens take seriously the assessments of the international community, various numerical indicators of national well-being have an active life in the Peruvian media. They compete for attention in the national imagination and for impact in the policy realm, and they provide a language through which the reality and trajectory of the Peruvian nation can be contested. As a result, the picture of Peru painted by the national media is fraught with contradiction. Any good news about national development is coupled with a troubling story of Peru's current reality. At the time of my fieldwork, national media outlets portrayed Peru as both an economic powerhouse and a nation on the brink of socio-economic crisis. Public service announcements ending with the government slogan "Perú Avanza" (Peru Advances) were immediately followed by rants about government corruption, incompetence, and indifference. The popular newspaper *Perú21* notably placed the *buenas noticias* (good news) and the *actualidad* (current reality) in quick visible succession so that celebrations of economic growth and declining poverty rates were undercut by (re)current national truths.[9]

Good News: Peru Rises in the World Bank's "Doing Business" Rankings
Current Reality: Peru Falls 18 Places in Gender Equality Ranking

Good News: The Peruvian Economy Grows by 8% in March
Current Reality: Disquieting Increase in Statistical Rates of Delinquency

Good News: Government Contains Rising Electricity Costs
Current Reality: UNICEF Study Shows 70% of Ventanilla's Children Suffer Anemia

When not offering contradictory messages about the state of the nation, numbers were splashed across front pages in bold print.

Death Toll from Cold and Pneumonia in the Sierra Rises to **70**
593 Transit Deaths So Far This Year
903 Drunk Drivers Found
217 Social Conflicts So Far This Year

Importantly, these numbers rarely speak for themselves. Instead, their significance is constituted through various expert interpretations, dramatic narratives, graphic images, and attention-grabbing headlines. As numbers and images mingle in people's minds, the messages they transmit are more emotional than technical. Numbers add a veridical gloss to heart-wrenching tales of poverty and infuriating exposés of government corruption and provide metrics by which Peruvians can imagine a nation beyond their own experience of it. Through mediated numbers, Peruvians can connect individual incidents to national statistical incidence (Comaroff and Comaroff 2006a), conceive of their place in a country of thirty million people, and imagine Peru's standing in a global hierarchy of nations.

The gross poverty statistic the Peruvian government releases each year offers one measure of national well-being that Peruvians can contest with myriad other measures produced by different experts and institutions. The credibility of these numbers depends on how they are framed and the extent to which they align with international consensus and a Peruvian common sense that has been produced over time and is reaffirmed through everyday conversations and interactions. In contests between numbers, those generated by institutions described as "global" or "international" are frequently deemed more objective, legitimate, and higher up in the global order of knowledge (Ferguson and Gupta 2002), while national and local government statistics are more readily perceived as partisan and politicized. However, these arguments are also sometimes inverted through discourses that celebrate the apparent proximity of local knowledge to reality on the ground, prompting institutions to use tropes of grassroots participation to bolster their knowledge claims.

Just as Peruvians can argue about reality *with* numbers, they can also argue about the reality *of* numbers. In Peru, questioning statistics is a political tactic used to challenge the competence and moral authority of diverse political parties and administrations. The political importance of accurate counts was on display in 2007 when President Alan García decided to redo the national census conducted just two years earlier under his political predecessor Alejandro Toledo. García pointed to certain statistical "anomalies" that suggested the census had undercounted the population, and he argued that accurate data were critical for optimal governance. A number of critics questioned García's motives, suggesting that new census data could be manipulated to make García's administration appear more effective than it actually was. Yet no one questioned the desirability of more representative data. Accurate statistics were viewed as an unequivocal good, integral to democratic ideals of transparency and accountability as well as to a populist sense that effective policy depended on accurate counts.

García promised that the 2007 census would correct the record and clarify the national reality. Instead, the new census and the political circumstances surrounding it mostly succeeded in muddying the waters; it brought statistical techniques to light in a way that undermined the fetishistic quality of numbers as national truths. For numbers to be accorded special truth-value and have their full communicative effect, their production must be invisible. When the translations, judgments, and manipulations required to convert raw data into usable numerical information are made visible, the resulting numbers are cordoned off from the realm of legitimate and official knowledge (Verran 2010, 177). No matter how impeccable the statistical process, the mere fact of public scrutiny undermines a number's status as truth. In this way, debates about the veracity of

Peru's national statistics challenged the legitimacy of the government and distanced Peru from the ideal of a modern nation, even as the ideal of an objective, countable truth, accessible with the right kind of expertise and ethical commitments, remained unchallenged.

POVERTY ON THE MAP

Although Peruvians readily argue with and about numbers, when statistical assertions are rendered cartographically, they become less contestable. Maps are powerful political and communicative tools. They erase pasts and remake worlds, lay claim to an objective truth "out there," and link the allure of technical expertise to existing structures of feeling about places. And even more so than free-floating statistics, maps' meanings are easy to grasp.

Since the early 2000s, the World Bank has promoted poverty maps as critical tools in their ongoing mission "to fight poverty with passion and professionalism for lasting results,"[10] and today, GIS data specialists feature prominently at World Bank conferences on poverty.[11] The rapid advancement of GIS and satellite technologies in some ways democratizes maps as more people are able to access, make, and deploy them for diverse social and political ends; however, from the perspective of state actors, maps remain exceptionally useful tools in the "centralized management of disorder" (Comaroff and Comaroff 2006a). Maps can extract poverty from political-economic systems and transform it into an attribute of particular places. As a spatially isolable thing, poverty can be attacked through targeted interventions, the results of which can be apprehended at a glance. Socioeconomic levels and various attributes of poverty, as defined by mapmakers, are color-coded, and changing a color means making a difference. Yet by asserting the visuality of poverty and grounding it in specific places, maps also have the potential to undermine statistical assertions of progress, creating new indeterminacies and political possibilities.

As a nation, Peru helped pioneer poverty-mapping techniques in the early 1990s when President Fujimori began using them to target poverty interventions. He created FONCODES, whose function was to identify the poorest of the poor and ensure that funds and projects went directly to alleviating their poverty. FONCODES did this by using censuses and surveys to assign every geopolitical entity a color depending on the number of vital urban amenities it lacked. The amenities that FONCODES chose to measure—piped water and sewerage systems, electrical connections, health clinics, schools, and land titles—meant that maps of poverty were effectively maps of state presence. In this framework, poverty could be fought by increasing the ways the Peruvian state was inscribed in space.[12] The strategic and highly publicized placement of a school or health clinic could change the color on a map, even as it also supported Fujimori's neo-populist agenda, positioning him as a benefactor who provided for Peru's poor while still reducing and rationalizing government.

When Fujimori fell from power, some legislators demanded that FONCODES be dismantled, arguing that the organization was simply an instrument for targeted populism and that its measures were redundant to what everyone already knew. But by that time, the maps had circulated in the realm of World Bank officialdom and returned partially cleansed of their clientelist imperfections, with the added weight of international affirmation. In a personal interview, FONCODES's lead social cartographer suggested that the organization survived the congressional onslaught because "we can target poverty assistance, are more efficient with social expenditures, and because we have a better understanding of extreme poverty and can prioritize." There is no reason to doubt these assertions about efficient poverty targeting. FONCODES found an internationally approved way to define and measure poverty and harnessed powerful visual technologies to show measurable results. Indeed, who would know more about how to change the colors on a map than the mapmakers themselves? Moreover, while some of Fujimori's critics argued that the maps were redundant to Peruvians' commonsense understandings of where poverty was located, this redundancy likely increased their credibility. In Peru, maps add a technocratic gloss to long-standing practices of identifying poverty visually and spatially.

Ever since Spanish colonists established their capital in the coastal city of Lima, physical distance from this center of urbanity and *policia* has served as a proxy for poverty and premodernity. Most Peruvians I spoke with readily identified the mountainous regions of Huancavelica and Cerro de Pasco as containers for the poorest of the poor, with inhabitants of urban peripheries occupying the next rung up on the socioeconomic ladder. The district of Ventanilla, which encompasses Loreto's home of Pachacútec, attracted NGOs and state development programs precisely because of how it fit into this geography of poverty. The regional officer for UNICEF in Ventanilla explained,

> We needed a focal point in Lima because . . . not all of Lima needs assistance. We sought a district [with certain] characteristics. . . .

> Ventanilla, for example, is . . . territorially big, and the indicators of extreme poverty are equal to those of other [rural] regions in which we intervene. . . . Only a third of the population here . . . has access to water and sewerage. [There is] the problem of pollution, access to schools and more importantly quality education, the issue of the basic basket of family foodstuffs, life expectancy at birth, and various themes that add up as requisites [for intervention]. . . . FONCODES and the director of health in Callao identified Ventanilla as the district with by far the most pockets of poverty. And that's for multiple reasons . . . like the issue of migration. You've seen how Pachacútec is.

With this statement, the UNICEF agent demonstrates that even as various indicators are produced to help officials grasp the situated nuances of poverty and facilitate different kinds of interventions, they are parsed only to be bundled back together, combining a number of supposedly distinct characteristics to reproduce a generalized imaginary of poverty as the locus of all social ills. He also links these characteristics to the tenacious idea that Peru's urban poverty and peripheral settlements are a direct result of rural-urban migration despite several generations of scholarship showing otherwise (Collier 1976; Pereyra 2004). Even though most of Pachacútec's inhabitants were born in Lima or lived in Lima for many years before moving to the settlement (Skrabut 2018), the well-meaning UNICEF agent still presumed that most residents were rural indigenous migrants who brought poverty with them, along with their customs and culture, and brought it on through their sudden and collective arrival. Ignoring the Peruvian state and international development organizations' long histories of encouraging homeownership as a route to poverty reduction and national development, the UNICEF agent suggested that it was an inexplicable cultural affinity for homes of their own that led migrants to settle in an unsavory periphery:

> Peruvian culture, not all of it, above all it's the migrants, they want a piece of land to construct their house, and it's cheaper [in Pachacútec] than in an urbanized zone. . . . The idea is, independent of the location, to have a house. . . . "I'll construct my house no matter what," they say. But they don't realize what they've lost. They lose in health, in development. But many people don't care about this. The issue is first the house, and then figure out how to get ahead. . . . It's a cultural issue that isn't just from now, nor has it always been this way in Peru. Since more or less fifty or sixty years ago, the process of migration started. . . . I couldn't justify this [desire for a house of their own], but it's their logic, no?

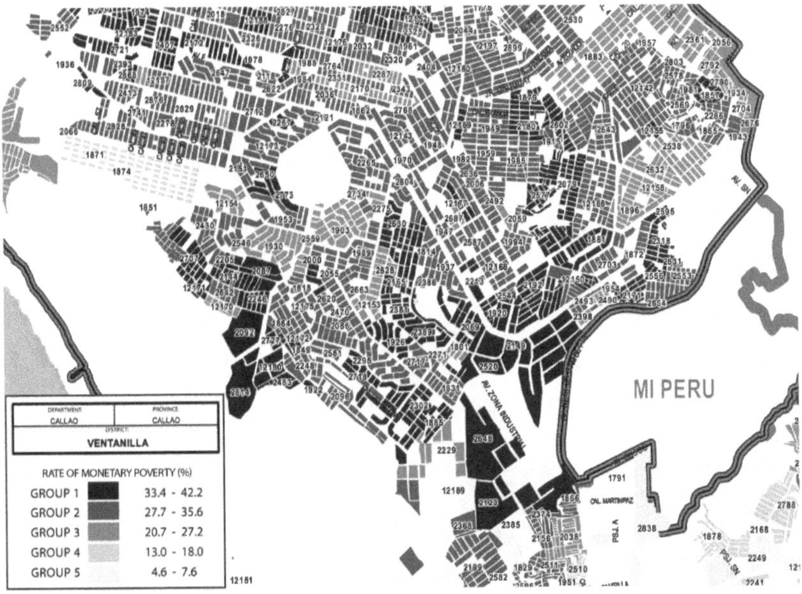

FIGURE 1.1. Poverty map of Ventanilla, 2020. The data are disaggregated to the subdistrict level to show variation in the pervasiveness of monetary poverty by block. *Source*: INEI 2020.

One of the most important ideological effects of spatializing poverty is that the poor appear to be contained in pockets that can be easily segregated from the surroundings using visual determinants alone. A FONCODES field director in Pachacútec explained, "Of course we have extreme poverty here in urban areas. . . . It's like two different realities. On one side of the highway everything is normal, and on the other side you see extreme extreme poverty . . . a poverty of everything; a poverty of health, education, infrastructure. [There is] even domestic and sexual violence!"

Maps that locate poverty in particular places reinforce this sort of grandiose visual analysis as poverty becomes isolated from the rest of the social world and rendered homogeneous within spaces. When poverty is an attribute of place, people are categorized by virtue of where they live and the sorts of urban amenities available to them. This spatial view of poverty is not without merit; piped water, electricity, and other urban amenities make people's everyday lives easier and are almost universally desired by Peruvians as elements of a dignified life. But this spatial perspective also has a number of problematic implications. First, the primary target of poverty interventions becomes the place rather than the individuals within it. This leads to an aesthetic politics and a singular focus on land and housing that encourages the upgrading of spaces but ignores the upgrading of livelihoods, rights, political inclusion, and accountability (Murphy 2015; Peattie 1992; Roy 2003). Second, spatial categorizations tend to generate what Wacquant (2007) describes as "territorial stigmas." These stigmas disparage inhabitants and ignore the degree to which individuals literally move in and out of sites of poverty in their daily lives and as they pursue life projects and suffer setbacks. Although the qualities of places do shape the lives and identities of inhabitants in important ways, people who live and work in extreme poverty zones are often critical of interventions that stop at the district level and do not target the truly needy within these spaces. Without more fine-grained analysis, they argue, politics takes over, and the truly needy individuals within these spaces lose out.

APPROPRIATING EXTREMES

In addition to being assigned colors on official maps, each district in Peru was marked with a letter that indexed the social and economic status of residents. This sociospatial categorization scheme, combined with other official discourses and mediated imaginaries, permeated the ways Peruvians understood real poverty and made sense of their own social positions. Interlocutors of different professions, residences, and class statuses described this social alphabet to me, with slight differences reflecting their past and current social positions. Sicha, for instance, grew up in a middle-class neighborhood that he described as the prettiest district in Lima. Now, though, he described himself as belonging to a lower socioeconomic stratum by virtue of his residence in Pachacútec: "We are classified as sector D. All of Pachacútec, not just me. There's sector A, B, C, D . . . we're almost last. All of Pachacútec is classified as between sector D and E. . . . We're only a little better off than they are in *provincia* [rural areas]. We only beat towns like Huancavelica, Ayacucho, . . . those places that are in extreme extreme poverty."

Dr. Brennan, a wealthy lawyer responsible for distributing land titles to residents of Pachacútec, also articulated a social alphabet to me, but he focused on the ways these sociospatial categorizations reflected and refracted onto the behaviors, tastes, and habituses of different classes of Peruvians:[13] "A person from sector A who takes vacations in [the southern beaches] is going to prefer their 'lite' food—their little salad or their lite yogurt—while a person from sector D, even if he gets money, he's going to prefer his rotisserie chicken [*pollo a la brasa*]. That's how you know them. It's a question of culture and formation."

Charo articulated yet another variant. She and some neighbors had recently invaded a barren patch of land in Pachacútec, a few hundred meters from the homes of friends and relatives who lived farther down the hill. They had been squatting on the land for months, defending their claims from authorities and neighbors who opposed them and seeking a patron in the regional government who could help them gain legal title. When Charo described Peruvian social strata, she used an abridged alphabet. "There are the sectors A, B, and C," she explained. "C is people like us, people of extreme extreme poverty. B are the people who live in the [more settled areas of Pachacútec] down below, people who already have a job and land and all that. Then you have sector A, the people who already have a lot," she said, rubbing her thumb and forefingers together to signal they had money to burn. "Where we are now, this is called extreme poverty because we don't have a dignified house. . . . The people who only have enough money to eat, . . . that's what you call extreme poverty."

Charo had a lot to say about persistent inequalities in Peru: how the big guys made their fortunes on the backs of the poor, how authorities discriminated against them because of their appearance, and how their formal requests were ignored because they didn't know anyone inside the government and didn't have enough money to bribe them. She was an articulate individual who moved fluidly between macro issues of political-economic injustice and poignant personal tales of domestic abuse and police insults. As we stood outside Charo's one-room shack, her older children running circles around us and a diaperless baby in her arms, I wasn't surprised to hear Charo argue that Peru's declining poverty rates were a hoax. But I was surprised by what she said next: "All of that about the decline of poverty in Peru, that is all smoke. If you really want to understand the Peruvian reality, you have to watch that [TV] show *Extreme Lives*. That's where you see it. That's where you see how Peruvians really live."

This was not the first time the show *Extreme Lives* had come up in my conversations. People often directed me to this reality TV show when I inquired about Peruvian poverty. In fact, as evidenced by Charo's proclamation, the poverty portrayed in this TV program was in some ways more real to people than what they saw and experienced in their everyday lives and more representative of the "Peruvian reality." Official categories, numbers, and maps help to make poverty isolable and thinglike, but it is vivid

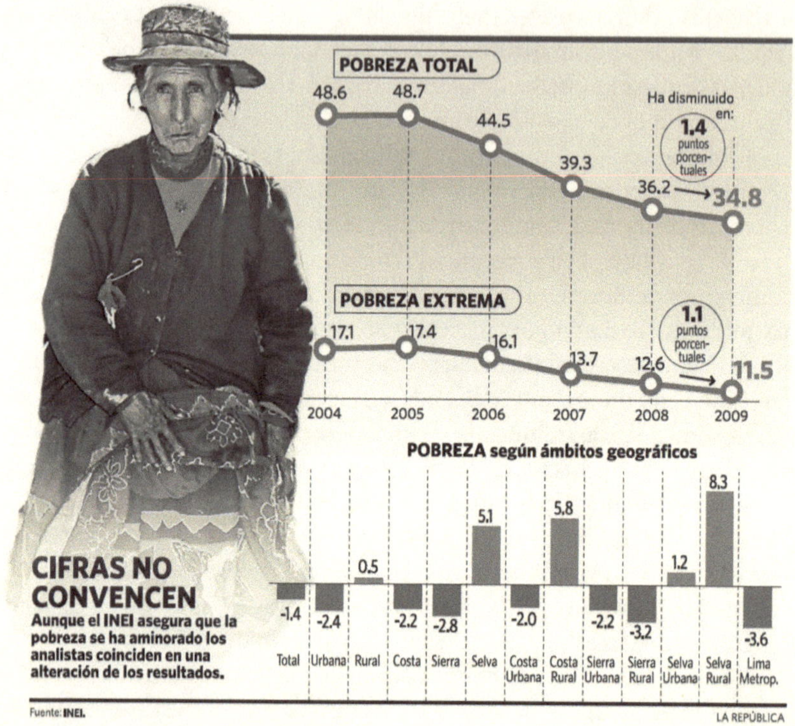

FIGURE 1.2. Newspaper infographic, "Statistics Are Unconvincing," 2010. *La República*'s graphic exemplifies the mingling of images, numbers, and narrative that produces Peru's total poverty fact. Notably, the newspaper used pictures of this same elderly Andean woman in different poverty-related infographics at least four times from 2009 through 2011. *Source*: *La República*, from INEI data, May 19, 2010.

imaginaries and formulaic narratives that give these numbers emotive value and purchase as depictions of the real. They play an important role in contributing to Peru's total poverty fact, a larger-than-life construct of poverty with specific historical and affective connotations and evocations.

Although *Extreme Lives* was the most popular poverty-focused reality show, there were a number of programs that purportedly showcased real poverty and equally real poverty assistance. *Show de los Sueños* (Show of Dreams), a dance competition in which celebrities compete on behalf of different impoverished individuals, had assisted a one-legged man who spent his days standing in the middle of Ventanilla's main market selling newspapers. Similarly, an American socialite, Electra Anderson, collaborated with Peru's Channel 9 to assist a group of *comedores populares* in

Pachacútec until a natural disaster drew her attention elsewhere. In general, my interlocutors were avid consumers of these poverty portrayals, even as they remained skeptical about the deservingness of the individuals who were assisted and suspicious of the intentions of those who assisted them.

Pablo, then a newly appointed political operative for the district government in Pachacútec, raised a number of these issues as he sifted through furniture donations that had come in for the Christmas season. After complaining briefly about all the competing charitable events in Pachacútec and the various politicians and NGOs who used the holiday to bolster their image, he asked something I wasn't expecting: "Kris, in the United States, are the people who beg on the street poor?"

"I assume so," I said, before Pablo quickly launched into his real point.

> Here in Peru, no. Here in Peru, there are people who beg and they are really poor, but there are also people who beg who are millionaires. That's why people have lost that good faith to give the street beggar a few coins. Because they've seen cases where [news reporters] followed beggars and discovered they had cars, houses, good economic standing, but they liked the easy route. They dressed in ratty clothes to give the impression that they were very very poor and people gave them handouts. . . . For instance, you see a beggar sitting with a can on the street. Throw in a coin and walk away. If you turn around and pass the same spot, that can no longer has any money in it. That little can is going to be empty. This gives the impression that he has no money. So what you see isn't always true. They are only appearances.

While scholars and journalists frequently contrast soulless statistics with individuated narratives, in reality these two modes of representation have much in common and work jointly to produce the poverty imaginary. Statistics and graphic portrayals of poverty both help to commodify poverty, transforming it into a thing that can be circulated and exchanged. Similarly, graphic and emotive portrayals of global poverty work like statistics in that they hollow out situated experiences of suffering, transforming them into something that, while arguably universal and amenable to cross-national comparison, is devoid of constitutive contextual substance (Kleinman and Kleinman 1996). These two modes of representation also complement each other in a perverse way. When coupled with numbers, grandiose and dramatic poverty imaginaries take on an air of precision. Statistics help to assure people that individuals who match these imaginaries exist. As such, almost everyone I spoke with believed that social assistance programs had a moral obligation to see through the throngs of unscrupulous scam artists who trafficked in appearances to identify the truly needy individuals who matched the ideal.

THE ANXIETY OF IDENTIFICATION

In 2009 Peru's national government began rolling out SISFOH, a socioeconomic classification system and poverty-targeting database that promised to provide diverse social assistance organizations with access to reliable, fine-grained information about which Peruvians officially counted as "poor" and "extremely poor." The technical definition of "focalization" is to "introduce selective criteria to identify potential beneficiaries for the purpose of attending to them via some social program in a priority matter" (Diaz A. 2006, 4). The term rose to prominence along with Fujimori's neoliberal policies in the 1990s and is used to signal a range of policy initiatives intended to promote efficient social spending and morally upright, targeted, and ostensibly apolitical social assistance.

Using maps to target poverty and social assistance spatially was an important first step in the focalization process, but SISFOH was meant to get beyond spatial indicators and resolve the supposedly ubiquitous problems of urban *filtración*. This term directly translates as "filtration," but in the context of social programs, it refers simultaneously to "leakages" of funds and "infiltration" into the program by inappropriate recipients. Emilio Pacherres, the SISFOH project manager at Peru's Ministry of Economy and Finance, described *filtración* as an urgent problem for social programs in urban areas. Results from the ENAHO indicated that 50 percent of beneficiaries of Peru's national health insurance program, and 70 percent of beneficiaries of Vaso de Leche, a community breakfast program targeting children from low-income families, were officially "not poor." Pacherres described this finding as though the ENAHO had tricked respondents into revealing a carefully guarded secret: "In the ENAHO they ask you lots of things, and while you are entertained by questions like whether you have electricity, phone service, your food expenses, et cetera, one of the questions is if you receive from Vaso de Leche, and the answer is yes. That is how the information comes out."

In response to these revelations, the Ministry of Economy and Finance began establishing SISFOH, which they hoped would one day constitute a comprehensive registry of all the poor people in Peru. By 2009 they had only just started the registration process, which involved a home visit and comprehensive questionnaire to determine a household's socioeconomic status, beginning with known areas of concentrated poverty in Lima-Callao. Pacherres relied on ideas of economic efficiency and on understandings of the wily nature of the urban poor to justify this approach. "You see that red stain there?" he said, pointing to a map of Callao he had opened on his computer screen. "In other areas there are poor and there are nonpoor, but in this 40 percent of households, that's where 80 percent of the poor people live, so it was more efficient to do the registry there. . . . The idea was to hone in on where the poor are located [*ubicar bien a los pobres*]." Pacherres went on to explain that registering rural residents was not a priority, precisely because they were generally poorer and more deserving than urban inhabitants.

> The problem of focalization is principally urban. In a rural zone, the majority of people are poor. . . . The percent of poor in rural zones is 70 percent so the problem of focalization is not serious. . . . Yes, the nonpoor are going to have advantages over the poor. They will benefit and surely before the poor do. But there aren't many. . . . The [focalization] problem is more manageable because the nonpoor are typically the ones who run the program, so in the end you can't exclude them from the benefits.

Urban areas were a different story. Pacherres explained that, in these areas, poverty was more heterogeneous, feigning poverty had more serious consequences, and residents were more likely to lie. "In urban zones, there is greater need for information," he said. "If you make decisions based solely on appearance or personal declaration, you make grave errors. That is what happens now." According to Pacherres, people frequently lied about being poor to obtain benefits from social programs. Moreover, private organizations contracted by the government to provide social services would likely declare all their beneficiaries poor, regardless of their actual socioeconomic status, to ensure they were reimbursed by the state. In both cases the result was the same: the nonpoor unjustly benefitted, and the truly needy were left out.

By 2016 the SISFOH registration process was being rolled out in force. The national government had allocated funds to districts across the country and made local governments responsible for surveying inhabitants and registering them in SISFOH. The national government also made inscription in SISFOH a requirement for accessing national social assistance programs, including national health insurance, student loans, and pension programs. The ultimate goal of the program was to enter every Peruvian into a central government database where their national ID number and biometric information was linked to a socioeconomic classification of "not poor," "poor," or "extreme poor" that would determine their eligibility for all social assistance programs.

Although SISFOH was gaining ground, as of 2016 it was not yet being used by local governments, neighborhood associations, or, to my knowledge, any institution outside the national government. In 2009 Pacherres described this as a political problem. The national government was trying to secure its status as the sole arbiter of real poverty, an initiative Pacherres saw as technocratic rather than political. But local governments, he said, wanted to determine their own program beneficiaries in order to secure political loyalties and create enduring political networks. While there is some truth to Pacherres's claims about politicized social assistance, local political administrations justified their own poverty-targeting efforts using the same skeptical and moral-technocratic language as SISFOH. They described the need for more finely tuned targeting systems that got beyond district poverty maps and made it to the level of the household as well as the need to monitor beneficiaries to ensure they were who they claimed to be.[14]

Local actors' claims to authoritative knowledge about who was truly needy were grounded in proximity and speed. These were two qualities that SISFOH officials also prized and believed their own poverty assessments lacked. Elisabet, a longtime resident of Pachacútec and a municipal employee, explained that NGOs and national government agencies needed people who knew the community to help them distinguish between the *casos normales* (normal cases of poverty) and the *casos sociales* (extraordinary cases requiring immediate social assistance). Additionally, community members could respond to the constant changes in neighbors' poverty circumstances, while SISFOH officials lamented their inability to keep pace with an ever-changing population. In the time between creating Callao's poverty map and sending out SISFOH surveyors, the area of concentrated poverty they were targeting had ballooned. Pacherres pointed to blank areas on his poverty map of Callao that he said were now completely full of makeshift houses bearing all the marks of poverty: "Those people are also poor, probably. . . . The question is, what do we do with these homes?"

As more people are inscribed in the SISFOH registry, concerns about the real-time accuracy of the database persist. Although the registry is supposed to be updated every three years to integrate the newly poor and ensure the no-longer-poor are taken off the rolls, by 2018 Peru's congress had already passed two laws extending the validity of people's SISFOH status, not out of recognition that more sustained support might be appropriate but due to grudging acknowledgment that SISFOH's registrars could not keep pace with these updating requirements.

OFFICIAL IMAGE-WORK

The work of collecting data and producing official imaginaries of poverty and compelling images of poverty assistance depended on the flexible labor of the poor themselves. I ran into my friend Ethel on one of my first days back in Pachacútec following a year in the United States. She lived in Pachacútec's Special Project, and thanks to her friendship with one of the mayor's advisers, she had been employed by the municipality for as long as I had known her. She was wearing a green vest to signal her identity as a district government promoter, while the dark circles under her eyes signaled her physical and emotional exhaustion. When I asked what she was up to these days, she responded with a heavy sigh and a resigned smile, "Igual que siempre, vendiendo imagen." Same as always, selling an image. Like many of the government promoters I knew, she was constantly being switched to different departments and programs. One month she was a cadastral surveyor, the next a registrar for Vaso de Leche, then a vitamin distributor for the child nutrition program Adiós Anemia (Goodbye Anemia), and so on. But for her, selling an image was the common thread in these activities. She was expected to smile and do good works for the community in the name of the municipal government and, specifically, in the name of the mayor, who would be seeking reelection. District government employees understood that it was critical that the mayor look like he was doing good works. Even if the mayor was indeed doing good things, the conspicuous focus on appearances left a bad taste in Ethel's mouth.

While politicians had to produce convincing images of poverty assistance for their constituents, NGO workers were more concerned with producing appropriate poverty and assistance images for donors. For instance, the field manager for an NGO working in Pisco admitted that, although they often came across people who seemed to need assistance, the organization couldn't help them because they didn't look the part: "I know what these donors are looking for. I know the image they have in their heads. They want to help families who are living in straw huts with dirt floors. I'm sure that there are people living in brick houses who are also poor, but I have to respect the image donors have." Although the field manager suggested that he was concerned with matching an image, as he and other NGO workers generated glossy pamphlets and heavily edited videos of their work, they were also complicit in reproducing the specific aesthetic of poverty and poverty assistance that seemed to hold them hostage.

Pictures were only one component of this official image-work. In a policy environment where people are fixated on target populations, tracking monetary flows, and acquiring tangible proof of progress, statelike entities also required numbers, signatures, registries, and formal requests to prove that money was going where it was most needed. As a result, residents in extreme poverty zones became adept at helping institutions comply with this audit culture by documenting both a need for their efforts and the efficacy of their actions.[15] In this regard, Ethel explained, "NGOs are just like the municipality. They have to fill out their registries too. So they go to the *comedores*, mothers clubs, or whatever and say, yeah, we need four hundred kids, so get me information on who they are, how old, et cetera." These events were frequently thrown together with little advance warning. As a result, the people who received donations in these cases were not necessarily the neediest kids in Pachacútec but rather the most readily organized. Ethel explained, "They give to the people who have all of their documents in order, . . . and everyone should be organized already . . . because everyone knows this is how you get stuff."

In my experience, most NGOs operated on the basis of punctuated interventions and documentary overkill. These projects typically began with viable communities that could satisfy NGO desires for local participation. Yet the apolitical, place-based communities that many development programs are based around do not exist a priori; instead they must be cobbled together anew for each assistance project. As Elisabet succinctly observed, "The community doesn't organize itself." For Pachacutanos, creating a documentary image of a poor but virtuous and participatory community out of actually existing neighborhoods, which were composed of individuals with spatially dispersed obligations and shot through with inequalities, jealousies, and cross-cutting political and kin networks, often turned out to be more trouble than it was worth. In one case, when an NGO offered to develop Pachacútec's wetland areas for ecotourism, several weeks of surveys, signatures, and videotapes of community participation resulted in the painting of a single lookout tower that neighbors had installed themselves months earlier. A resident explained, "They painted the lookout tower, took some pictures, and never finished any of the other things they promised. And just imagine how much they charged [donors] for painting that! . . . It must have been a lot, because that's what NGO's do." Though the resident contended that NGOs typically just fed off their poverty, he nonetheless felt obliged to work with them when the opportunity arose on the off chance something substantial might come of it.

EVIDENCE CHAINS IN EVERYDAY LIFE

Spending time with residents of Pachacútec who either distributed or received poverty assistance revealed just how integral the official imagework of poverty was to people's everyday lives, livelihoods, and relationships. Milagros and her mother, Patricia, lived on a corner lot near Pachacútec's civic center. Both women were sociable and energetic, and together they were involved in almost every community organization and social assistance program available in Pachacútec, including the Vaso de Leche program that SISFOH officials critiqued for its systemic filtration issues.

Monday through Friday, they awoke at 4 a.m. to boil a large vat of water, to which they added powdered grains and milk provided by the municipality, as well as sugar and fruit that they purchased themselves. The program recipients, known as *socias*, didn't pick up their milk until 7 a.m., but boiling one hundred servings of it took time. In exchange for their milk, each *socia* paid 2.5 soles a week. Of that, 1.5 soles went to pay for cooking gas and added ingredients, and the remainder was used to fund a Christmas party for neighborhood children and to compensate Milagros and Patricia for their work.

Obtaining the program for their neighborhood had required applying to the municipality with a registry that contained identifying information (names, birthdates, ages, and copies of birth certificates or ID cards) for at least one hundred recipients, including at least sixty-five first-priority recipients (children six months to six years old, pregnant women, and lactating mothers), and no more than thirty-five second-priority recipients (children seven to twelve and a half years old, the elderly, and people suffering from tuberculosis). Once the committee was established, recipients had to be reregistered each year by a representative of the municipality to ensure resources were still being used appropriately.

Milagros had invited me to her house to observe the Vaso de Leche reregistration process. I walked through the yellow plywood door to Milagros's house at 7:30 a.m. to find that registration had already begun. A young woman with dark hair pulled into a tight ponytail was sitting at a large wooden table asking women questions, growing frustrated when they didn't know the answers, and occasionally getting distracted by the telenovela playing on the TV across the room. Around 9 a.m. the young woman's mother arrived to help her with the registration. Apparently, the mother was the real Vaso de Leche promoter, but her daughter was helping her today. "She was my temporary replacement because I was feeling sick this morning," the woman said. "And it's also in part so that my daughter doesn't feel so depressed. She's having some trouble with the father of her child. All men are liars." Milagros and her grandmother, who were also sitting at the table, nodded knowingly. The tension in the room lifted, and the interaction went from an audit to a collaboration.

As the registration continued, we started a countdown of how many more people would be needed to fill out the roster. By 9:30 a.m., we were still far behind the requisite numbers, with only twenty-three first-priority and seventeen second-priority recipients. We began to scramble. The promoter goaded us to find more recipients. "Don't let them take the Vaso de Leche away from you" she warned. "You'll never get it back." Milagros complained that another committee was also doing their registration today and had taken four of her *socias*. "Two of them were pregnant and had other children, which is like getting two for one!" She said other women were reluctant to join because they would only be in Pachacútec for part of the year or only wanted to participate during the summer when rations were distributed raw and they could prepare the milk themselves. "You have to convince them," the promoter explained. "Tell them that they don't have to pick it up. You can give their rations to someone else. The important thing is to keep the Vaso de Leche in the neighborhood so you can manage rations internally."

The promoter seemed to have personal experience acquiring and losing these sorts of programs and was determined to help. She was only supposed to sign people up until noon but promised to stay later to give Milagros as much time as possible to find recipients. The promoter began filling in the new roster with names from the old one so women could stop by and sign without delay. On several occasions, Milagros left to find a *socia* and returned instead with a daughter, aunt, or other family member who said they knew how to sign like the supposed recipient. Meanwhile, I was making runs to Ximena, who ran a small copy center out of her house and charged twenty cents per sheet, to make copies of the copies we had of people's IDs. When I returned, Milagros and the promoters were desperately seeking a woman named Vilma who was on the current roster as a "lactating mother" with two children under six. Within the hour, Patricia came in disguised in a red baseball cap, signed for Vilma, and dashed out. I doubt she was fooling anyone who didn't want to be fooled.

These registration events were as important for promoters as they were for recipients. Someone higher up in the organization would use these registration rates to assess their performance. Generating high registration rates and establishing committees meant they were doing their jobs well, effectively locating the poor, promoting community participation, and creating positive and potentially reciprocal relations between residents and the district government.

The leadership workshops the municipality ran together with a prominent area NGO highlighted the importance of this official image-work for those higher up in the organizational chain as well. Before Pablo worked in the municipality, he had been a block-level *dirigente* in Pachacútec and had participated in the NGO's leadership workshop. He now wanted to make these workshops more widely available. He had five promoters working under him responsible for recruiting participants from different areas of Pachacútec. These promoters knew that Pablo's opinion of them, and therefore their job security, depended on their ability to pull in as many people as possible.

The workshop was offered once a week for six weeks. If participants attended five of the six workshops in the series, they would receive a certificate, which they could use on job applications as tangible proof of their high culture, education, and leadership capacity. These certificates were coveted prizes, and people made certain they signed the attendance sheets even if they arrived hours late or left after only a few minutes. The attendance sheets were important to the NGO representatives, the promoters, and their supervisor, Pablo. The long list of names and ID numbers was among the only evidence they had of the breadth and efficacy of their work. Because I was taking pictures for my research, I contributed the visual documentation of the event. For Pablo, this was another critical piece.

On the final day of the workshop, Pablo stood at the front of the room to arrange a date for the closing ceremony at which participants would receive their certificates. Between child care commitments, jobs, and mandatory community work parties, finding a date that worked for everyone proved challenging. Frustrated, Pablo announced that if participants didn't attend the ceremony, they could not receive their certificates. The audience erupted into angry protests. The situation was made more absurd by the fact that the day's lesson had been on effective communication and problem solving. Julian, the NGO representative, tried to defuse the situation by saying that exceptions could likely be made to Pablo's new rule, but Pablo remained firm in his decision. After about ten minutes, tempers cooled, workshop participants decided on a date, and Pablo impressed upon them the importance of forsaking other commitments to be there.

Walking home after the workshop, I asked Pablo why he had been so adamant about only distributing certificates at the closing ceremony, when Julian would have been happy to accommodate participants and distribute them another way. He explained, "Julian doesn't care about the ceremony because he already has all of his documents. But me, what interests me is the photo, all of those people together receiving certificates from the municipality." Later, when I was helping Pablo put together his monthly report for the mayor, I got a better idea of what he meant. We went through the photos I had taken, and he picked out the ones where the crowds looked densest and there were clear symbols of municipal presence, such as a promoter standing by the crowds with the district government logo on their uniform clearly legible or a speaker lecturing in front of a giant picture of the mayor. We did our best to place these pictures together artfully with a discussion of the event, how many participated, and what people were supposed to have learned. This report was evidence of Pablo's quality work for the mayor.

Despite the conflict surrounding the closing ceremony, in the end everyone seemed to get what they wanted. Participants got their certificates, promoters got enough on-paper participation to please Pablo, Pablo got the numbers and photos he would need to please the mayor, and the mayor could advertise the achievements of these leadership workshops in speeches, political posters, and on the district government website. Yet the focus on producing evidence and images also produced something else, a kind of double consciousness about poverty and poverty reduction. There was the thing, in this case the social program, and the representations of the thing, the attendance registries and event photos that were always partial and polished in ways people both recognized and ignored. Anthropologist William Mazzarella (2004, 356) explains that processes of mediation are simultaneously about self-distancing and self-recognition: "The places of mediation are the places at which we come to be who we are through the detour of something alien to ourselves, the places that are at once constitutive of social reproduction and its most intimate enemy." The individuals who consumed these images remained convinced that this is what poverty assistance looked like, and yet they were also suspicious of the reality behind these images, in part because of their proximity and complicity in their production.

LOOKS CAN BE DECEIVING

Pablo once told me another story. For me, it contained insights about kinship, life course, and ideologies of deservingness. But for him, it was mostly a tale about the potentially misleading aesthetics of poverty and how lucrative poverty could be if you knew how to sell it. The story was about a young man who used to rent Pablo's car to use as an informal taxi.

> The cheapest you can rent a car normally is thirty-five soles a day, but I only charged twenty because he has a wife and a baby boy, and I wanted to help him out. Well, he crashed my car and broke it. I'm a nice guy, but I'm not stupid and I wasn't going to be punished for doing him a favor. Then he found out I planned to sell the car and spoke with his father. His father is a man that holds his pants up with a piece of used rope and dedicates himself to selling candy on buses. . . . He gets up early, puts on his tattered clothing, and boards buses, saying his wife is sick and could you please help him by buying the candy he's selling. . . . Now where am I going with this? The person who bought the car was that young boy with no job. And who lent him the money? His dad, that poor man who you see selling candy on buses saying that he doesn't have any money. But he does have money. . . . He just keeps it in a bank. And you should see him. He's my neighbor. A poor guy with a tiny house. But he went to the bank. "Yeah, how much is it? Here." And he bought the car. He insured it, bought tires, batteries, everything.

Anthropologist Arjun Appadurai (2006, 6) argues that a defining paradox of globalization is that it promises the spread of bureaucratic rationality, precision, transparency, and predictability while provoking suspicion and uncertainty, particularly around categorical identities: "How many of 'them' are among 'us'" and "How might we know whether someone is what they appear to be?" I have endeavored to elucidate how it is that these phenomena travel in tandem, revealing one dimension of poverty's unruly domestication in Peru: the ways efforts to identify, quantify, and thus understand and tame poverty undermine trust in the system. Peruvians' understandings of poverty emerge from assemblages of the nation's most present past, free-floating statistics, truth-asserting maps, and popular media portrayals that affirm both the specificity and grandiosity of what my interlocutors termed "real" poverty. However, stories like Pablo's also contribute to the total poverty fact in Peru, asserting what poverty should look like while also instilling lessons that looks can be deceiving (*aparencias engañan*). Suspicions of appearances are further amplified in this context by my interlocutors' proximity to the official image-work of poverty and poverty reduction. This image-work, which has expanded in importance with the rise of global audit cultures and increased demands for accountability, is essential to the legitimacy of active and aspiring statelike entities, including local governments, politicians, and NGOs. As the stories of ENAHO surveyors, political promoters like Ethel, and aid recipients like Patricia and Milagros demonstrate, this image-work is also integral to the lives and livelihoods of the poor, keeping everyone invested in reproducing poverty imaginaries that they mistrust and maintaining a poverty relief system with which they are profoundly dissatisfied.

Dalia, a resident of a relocation site in Pisco, poetically captured the experience of this disjuncture. When I asked her about the model homes and construction assistance being targeted to residents of her neighborhood, her resentment was palpable.

> They say "Perú Avanza," . . . but what the government doesn't tell you is . . . it's advancing in poverty. . . . Everything looks great on the news, on TV. The internationals come and say, "Oh, what a great president," but those are all just promises. . . . Where do you see that? . . . No water, no electricity, no paved roads, no sewers, no nothing. It's only in the news and it's only for them. . . . Peru advances according to them. *Mentiras, propaganda y dichos, nada mas que dichos.*
>
> Lies, propaganda and slogans, nothing more than slogans.

« TWO »

Ambivalent Developments

THE ENTANGLEMENTS OF POLITICS AND KINSHIP

William and Pablo had been great friends when I first encountered them during Pachacútec's statute-reform processes. On occasion they still were. They would reunite with other *dirigentes*, reminisce about what they had done or tried to do, and talk passionately about transforming Pachacútec from an empty sand dune into an ideal urban community. Over time, though, their friendship had been strained by their divergent views regarding the appropriate relation between politics and development. Like most Peruvians I knew, William considered "development politics" a contradiction in terms. Development was something that benefitted the entire community, bringing everyone closer to ideals of modernity. Politics, meanwhile, was the realm of corrupt subgroups and diametrically opposed to the transparency and integrity implied in terms like "good governance" and "democracy." Pablo had a different view. "Do you really think you can have development without politics?" he asked me one day as we discussed critiques of the district government. As a recently appointed political operative for the municipality, Pablo saw politics as a pragmatic form of constituency and community building; it was about constructing the networks along which state goods and services could travel. Without politics in this sense, there could be no development.

Popular discontent in Peru is as much about the process of development as it is about the products and largely results from the contradictory ways discourses of family and practices of kinship are woven through the politics of development. Like William, most Peruvians I knew depicted developed societies as characterized by clear divisions between public and private spheres, where family, community, and state were nested but discrete realms, each depending for its success on the integrity of the former.

Yet this imaginary exists in marked contrast to the realities of social assistance. Illustrating the double meaning of *política* in Peru as signifying both "policy" and "politics," politicians deploy discourses of family and perform ostensibly neutral but beneficent technocratic tasks, such as installing public works or formalizing community organizations, in order to build an extended kin network that they hope will solidify into a semi-stable political faction. Through these practices, the state materializes as a personalistic problem-solving network that provides goods, services, and information and acts as one of the few paths of socioeconomic mobility in an area where formal employment is scarce (Auyero 2000). The result is that the imagined relation between state and society reproduced in development discourse gives way to real-world divisions between "our people" and "their people."

Although men are often the faces of these political factions, and of Peruvian politics more generally, the everyday labor of politics in Peru's urban settlements is largely women's work. Women's association with the supposedly private and apolitical sphere of the home make them potent political symbols, and their related abilities to quickly activate large, place-based social networks make them valuable political assets and agents. The moral double-binds, psychological burdens, and everyday challenges of development also fall hardest on female community leaders who must negotiate between public and private spheres, expressed in the language of *calle* (street) and *casa* (home), and between two kinds of kinship, one relegated to neatly nucleated households and associated with modernity, and the other flexible, expansive, forged through practice and reciprocity, and associated with premodernity and corrupt governance. As women weave together discourses of family and practices of kinship to build political networks, they also navigate gender expectations that are simultaneously interdependent and divergent. They elaborate different kinds of relational selves and renegotiate their understandings of effective motherhood even as they also embed themselves in other, often exploitative, forms of affective political labor.

These public-private entanglements can be seen in the historical origins and contemporary expressions of ideological divides between political and social work and in the ways these divides are transcended in practice. Producing and traversing social and ideological boundaries—between public and private, social and political, home and street—constitute much of the everyday labor of building communities and political networks in Peru's urban settlements. In my close work with community groups and promoters like Marisa and Anita, I also discovered that this labor was deeply gendered and that women engaged in it ambivalently as a form of personal development.

POLITICS VERSUS DEVELOPMENT

I met William in 2007 when he was leading the charge for a new electoral statute in Pachacútec. Originally from the central Andes, William had arrived in Pachacútec as an anthropology student conducting thesis research when he decided to "go native" (his words) and join the relocation with his wife, children, and extended family. With his university degree, William obtained a good job as a high-level bureaucrat at Techo Propio, a national home-construction assistance program, and spent his evenings and weekends working to help Pachacútec progress. Yet when I visited him at his new office in 2010, he seemed defeated. Six months earlier he told me he feared for his job at Techo Propio. He said he made the newly appointed Aprista officials nervous because he wasn't an APRA party member.[1] I tried to reassure him that he did his job well and they would have no reason to fire him. I wasn't entirely wrong. Instead of firing him, they moved him from the planning offices to a community relations desk. "It's fine," he said softly, his eyes cast to the floor. "Now I have more contact with the people."

I tried to lift his spirits by mentioning that I had seen a new Techo Propio office on Pachacútec's main avenue. He countered,

> Yes, but its empty. . . . It's not operating anymore. Supposedly the government ran out of money to fund the program, so everything is on standby until they can find more money. But it's a lie. It's something political. They have the money, but they're waiting for the [election] campaign so it looks like they're doing more.

William suggested that government funds were now being channeled to FONCODES, the poverty-targeting and development organization that had recently switched its focus from rural to urban initiatives. A cynical reading might suggest that the focus on urban space was merely a political tactic. The concentrated populations in urban areas meant that programs could reach more beneficiaries with less public investment, which would potentially translate into more votes. A more generous interpretation would admit that urban poverty did indeed require urgent attention. William vacillated between the two. He said FONCODES was

President Alan García's new *política* to exaggerate his accomplishments. "That's why the money has been funneled away from Techo Propio. Techo Propio is already known." The president moved resource to FONCODES, William contended, "to give it a famous name so the people are aware of two programs and he can show that he's done more." He then added hopefully, "All this about the *nucleos ejecutores* [a new initiative to create community-based project-execution teams]. . . . It will be interesting to see how far that goes," before reverting back to his disheartened narrative about politics obstructing development and the consolidation of democracy in Peru.

William said that these political games were taking their toll. "The people are getting desperate. They wait and wait but the promises never arrive. The government comes to register or sign people up in whatever program, and people think, 'Why would I give you my information if you never keep your promises?' The people just don't trust the government anymore."

If mistrust was a central problem with the national government, the problem with local government was that relations between administrations and local community representatives were too close for comfort. William suggested that the biggest barrier to development in Pachacútec was the municipality's success in absorbing the *dirigentes*: "The mayor is very clever. He has exploited the necessity of the *dirigentes* by giving them all jobs. . . . With all the *dirigentes* absorbed by the municipality, they can't complain [*reclamar*] because you can't go against your boss."

I asked William if he thought it was possible for this political maneuvering to promote development. Perhaps it didn't matter whether public works were completed quickly during election season or methodically throughout an administration's term or how exactly the government worked with the community to complete them, so long as things got done. Indeed, these products of development were precisely what various poverty surveys and municipal reports captured at punctuated moments of statistical visibility. William responded reticently, "Of course it's possible. But for people like us, people like you and me, Kris, we think differently. We think things should be straightforward and done a certain way."

I let William implicate me in this opinion because it was clear he needed an ally, but I was still thinking the issue through. In referring to things being straightforward and done a certain way, William invoked particular ideals about how a modern state should operate that began to emerge in Peru in the early twentieth century along with the rise of industrial capitalism, modern urbanism, and particularly rigid expectations about proper, gendered relations between public and private spheres. From 1895 to 1940, the city of Lima and the Peruvian state were remade. Narrow colonial streets and Spanish-style adobe homes were demolished to make way for grand avenues, French-style palaces, streetlamps, water mains, and other essentials of modern urban life (Parker 1998, 155). As Lima's governing elite adopted ideals of modern urbanism from the United States and northern Europe, the social, racial, and functional mixtures that had characterized Lima's streets up to that point came to be seen as unsavory, unsanitary, and improper (Aguirre and Walker 2017; Fischer 2014). Distinct neighborhoods were planned for middle and working classes, sites of productive and reproductive labor were clearly demarcated, and homes came to be theorized as exclusive sites of intimacy and affect whose sole function was to produce the personalities of individual Peruvian citizens (Mannarelli 1999).

A new class of public health officials known as *higienistas* oversaw many of these transformations. Prompted by an outbreak of bubonic plague in 1904, these officials initiated citywide public health surveys that, for the first time, brought the state into the homes of working-class urban Peruvians and a particular kind of household poverty to the attention of an increasingly elaborate and reform-minded government apparatus. In a compelling analysis of these survey documents, historian David Parker (1998) details how public health officials commented critically on anything they interpreted as transgressions of idealized boundaries between public and private space. Among these were the presence of animals or productive labor activities in the home; the working-class propensity to keep front doors open and expose private life to public view; bed sharing; and cohabitation with either extended kin or renters.

Public health understandings of poverty qua improper living conditions were further tied to a specifically Latin American form of scientific racism. While Anglo-American racism fixated on Darwinian genetics and natural selection, Latin American elites adopted Lamarckian theories about the inheritance of acquired characteristics. In this framework, biological predispositions were inherited and embodied but also responsive to the corrective power of education and environment, with improvements potentially passed down to subsequent generations.

Interestingly, this Lamarckian understanding resonates with Andean ideologies of kinship and selfhood. As Mary Weismantel finds, in the Andes, "membership in a family—and a race—is indeed rooted in bodily similarities, but this sameness is created through metabolic processes, not genetic codes" (2001, 191). She continues, explaining that as the body "ingests, digests, and expels substances from the world around it, it provides the owner an identity drawn from worldly substances. Body and identity thus originate in the intimate physical relationship between persons and their social milieu" (191).

Marisol de la Cadena (2000) describes how this Lamarckian framework manifested in conversations among Peru's indigenous intellectuals in the 1920s through the concept of "decency." As she explains, "Decency was a flexible norm for the conduct of daily life" that allowed a belief in innate high morality to coexist with liberal ideals of social equality and possibilities for social mobility (47). Political and intellectual elites from this period professed that formal education could "combat and modify inherited tendencies" but also contended that as a primary "conduit of education and morality, the biological family was a central component of decency" (47). De la Cadena (2000, 47) quotes one prominent politician of the time, Humberto Luna (1919), who stated: "The family is the first social element which notably modifies an individual's inherent tendencies, inclining him to good or evil, depending on the parental habits displayed in the home." In Lima, beliefs such as these fueled public policy interest in improving housing conditions as a way of improving the race and civilizing the nation, a move that entangled seemingly progressive housing policies with racist ideologies (Parker 1998).

This fixation on domestic space prompted changes in family structure and household organization that public health officials hoped would reverberate through the whole of society. Historian María Elena Mannarelli (1999) describes how in the early twentieth century, the previously prized "open families" (*familias abiertas*) of upper-class Limeños—composed of extensive networks of consanguineous and fictitious kin that cut across class lines—were suddenly verboten, symbolic of a social structure without limits that impeded the rise of a modern, orderly society. Peruvian public intellectuals of the day asserted that these expansive family structures prompted political corruption, as "the laws of kinship extended themselves over the public realm" and public positions were filled by members of the same family network (Mannarelli 1999, 267). By contrast, the discrete nuclear family governed by a devoted mother was described as the lynchpin of a modern, democratic, and meritocratic society. Household architecture came to reflect these new ideals. Where once the upper classes prioritized creating luxurious salons to entertain outsiders, by the early twentieth century, they focused on enhancing private spaces. Mannarelli (1999, 268) quotes Peruvian sociologist Joaquin Capelo, who, in 1902, instructed that "in a well governed house, order and care begins with the hearth and the kitchen, followed by the bathroom and bedroom."

Although women had long been associated with their reproductive functions in Peru, it wasn't until the early twentieth century that motherhood came to define women's social roles so exclusively and prescriptively. As the field of medicine splintered into distinct specialties (including reproductive health and psychology) and "childhood" came to be theorized as a distinct life stage, maternity morphed from a physiological event into a feminine psychological commitment that required special preparation and education. *Higienistas* saw the mothering project as at once critical to national development and perpetually threatened by women's supposed ignorance, negligence, and proclivities to envy, rage, imprudence, or laziness, which could transform an idyllic nuclear household into a site of moral degradation and an obstacle to national progress. *Higienistas* thus sought to educate women in proper mothering through school curricula, conferences, and household visits (Mannarelli 1999, 127–128). This new conception of motherhood entailed new restrictions for women; it relegated them to the household, limited the individuals who might be included in that household, and demanded the performance of specific maternal virtues. At the same time, it imbued home and motherhood with new political potential. Women's private sphere work of molding children into proper citizens and taming their husbands' worst impulses was deemed critical to civilizing public space. Eventually women's responsibility for the home became a site from which they could make political demands and a carapace they could use to maneuver within the masculine world of the modern state, which, in an interesting parallel to the home, was expected to operate without politics (Mannarelli 1999, 121–126).

At the international level, this dominant understanding of the proper roles, identities, and relations between the private home and the public state was perhaps most clearly crystalized in modernization theory. Despite being discredited by academics for its evolutionist assumptions and obliviousness to colonial legacies and capitalist world systems (Escobar 1995; Wolf 1982), modernization theory continues to shape popular understandings of development in Peru and around the world. According to this theory, as societies progress from traditional to modern, the division between public and private worlds becomes more pronounced. Intimacies are relegated to the private sphere of the home, which is increasingly characterized by small, nuclear families, while the state is managed by a devoted but disinterested bureaucracy that executes plans conceived by democratically elected officials.[2]

Since at least the 1950s, Latin America's designation as "underdeveloped" within the international community has been tied to the perceived shortcomings of its governments. US State Department officials asserted that Latin American politicians were too predisposed to childish individualism and "undiscipline" to faithfully execute holistic programs and obtain the "scientifically ascertained social requirements" for development (Escobar 1995, 26). Within Latin America, this framing has been configured such that politics becomes the enemy of the virtuous family, the functioning state, and the pursuit of social development. In Argentina, Javier Auyero (2000, 72) explains that politics is seen as " 'dirty' and 'corrupt': 'a lucrative business,' 'an opportunity to get ahead,' an activity that is 'deceitful and manipulative.' " Auyero goes on to state, "Almost everyone shares the idea that politics is something 'I don't do'—by implication, something that 'others do.' All agree that politics constitute a universe with its own rules and might serve to improve one's own lot, regardless of the common good" (72).

Gianpaolo Baiocchi (2005) likewise finds that community leaders and activists in Brazil make analytic distinctions between the community, the government, and political parties, such that local government is deemed legitimate and representative of the community only to the extent it is divorced from political parties and the interested actions of politicians. Writing about Bolivia, Sian Lazar (2008, 58) argues that "corruption talk" and critiques of politicians' individualism allow citizens to assert expectations of the state, providing "a foil for the collective ideal" and creating a sense of what "the community" is.

My Peruvian interlocutors echoed these attitudes about politicians and political work, complaining that their country did not progress because politicians were only out for themselves. A Pachacútec police officer argued, "Poverty doesn't go down in Peru because we are not united behind a single goal. The congressmen don't look ahead for development. They just want to see what they can get out of it for themselves." A young business owner in Pisco's outskirts similarly described how politicians hid their unscrupulous activities under the cover of documents and pretensions to transparency.

> The problem is the authorities don't care about poverty and development. They only care about what is in their own pockets, at least until the elections. During election season there's an infinite number of works. Then, the mayor shows you a piece of paper listing all the works he's delivered, all the money he's spent. But it's a lie. This sheet makes it look

like he's working the whole time, but he's not. When this is what our own government does to us, what hope do we have?

In Pachacútec the ideological distinction between development and politics was evident in the moralized distinction between *trabajo social* (social work) and *trabajo político* (political work). A *trabajo social* was understood as something exclusively charitable, often associated with the ostensibly apolitical realms of family and children. For instance, Belén said she enjoyed running a *comedor popular* precisely because it constituted social work that she did in service of poor "social cases" (*casos sociales*) who needed temporary assistance to lift themselves out of poverty. Likewise, many promoters said they liked working for the DEMUNA agency for children and teens because it was social (selfless and charitable) rather than political (self-interested) work. Although promoters still had to drop the mayor's name and hang his photograph at every event, they felt they were doing something good for the community by promoting well-being within the home while also learning to become better parents and people themselves.

People typically spoke proudly and openly about doing social work. Political work, however, was usually discussed through hushed tones and innuendo. Marisa, a district promoter, once explained political work to me this way:

> Political work is something that I do in the name of the administration, in the name of the mayor. For instance, if I need to give a bag of rice to a Vaso de Leche, I talk to the mayor and he says, "Sorry, there's no budget for that. You have to resolve it." So, I go to the market and say to an acquaintance, "Remember when the mayor gave you this or that thing? Well now we need a bag of rice." And he says, "Sure, no problem." But who will sign for it? Not me, Marisa. No. If I'm wearing a municipal vest, I sign it as "the municipality of Ventanilla," that is to say, the mayor. Also, if I'm walking around the neighborhood and my neighbor asks, "What's new Marisa?" I'm not going to say I don't have money for this or that or tell them that I'm fighting with my husband. No. Instead I'm going to say that the mayor has an event or is doing a medical campaign.

For Marisa, political work involved engaging in the quid pro quo of clientelist relations on behalf of the mayor. It was about constructing relationships that would build loyalties to him as a person and an administration, which would lead to his reelection. Other promoters referred to these network-building activities as being "en campaña," in campaign, an acknowledgement that every gift and favor was exchanged with a personal and political end in view. This phrase also highlighted the punctuated temporality of these activities. Like the frequent "medical campaigns," "free ID campaigns," or "tax amnesty campaigns," these exchanges were, in theory, one-time events. The exceptional extension of benefits included individuals in social assistance networks and embedded them in reciprocal relations, but the benefits they implied could not be demanded as formal rights or entitlements.

Despite everyday distinctions between social and political work, the most effective political work masqueraded as or was indistinguishable from social work. *Comedores populares* like the one Belén managed offer paradigmatic examples of the political force that explicitly apolitical social organizations can wield. The first *comedor* was created in 1978 by female residents of Lima's *barriadas* who were tired of their food security being subject to the vagaries of charities and politicized social welfare programs. Drawing on their experiences with community organizing during the initial formation of their neighborhoods, women pooled resources to create communal kitchens. Members contributed to collective food stores and took turns cooking meals on a rotating basis. This allowed members to benefit from economies of scale while also freeing them to pursue other economic activities, knowing that their children would be well fed. As these community-based organizations proliferated, they became primary nodes in the distribution networks of NGOs and government programs that created a class of workers known as "promoters" to facilitate connections between aid institutions and community organizations (Blondet 2004b, 41). Due to their community clout, politicians subsequently sought to coopt and clientelize these organizations, offering modest subsidies in the form of staple foods like rice, beans, and cooking oil. In doing so, they simultaneously institutionalized and factionalized these groups, creating conflicts between autonomous organizations and those that were aligned with this or that politician (Blondet 2004b).

Though often wary of *comedores*' political associations, women continue to participate in these organizations partly out of economic necessity but also because of the array of other benefits they provide. Peruvian historian Cecilia Blondet (2004a, 15) explains,

> Working with this organization is a way to overcome domestic isolation, to socialize, to form part of a network that provides important affective support . . . [and] practical benefits. They [women] learn to

> cook *en masse* and keep records, speak in public, identify objectives, and recognize interests. They learn how to relate to authorities. . . . *Comedores populares* become schools of citizenship. It is in this organization that women of popular classes constitute subjects of rights and obligations. Moreover, women's organizations are networks that permit members access to other, larger networks that they would not otherwise have access to.

Organizations like *comedores*, grounded in discourses of necessity, family, and apolitical assistance, offer women a way to socialize beyond family, a pathway to develop other skills, socially sanctioned opportunities to engage in politics and community development, and expanded horizons and possibilities based on their access to different networks and relations.

Comedores increased steadily in number until 1990 when the economic shock therapy initiated by President Fujimori caused their numbers to skyrocket. Within twenty-three days of the start of structural adjustment, the number of *comedores* in Lima doubled, from 3,500 to 7,000 (Blondet 2004b, 42). The economic challenges of this period were so dire that some scholars suggest women's food-assistance cooperatives were the only reason Peruvians were not dying in the streets (Gandolfo personal communication 2021; Roberts 1995). Despite this chaos, Fujimori remained popular throughout this period, in part due to the effective ways he deployed the politics of antipolitics, with women serving as symbols and agents of his administration.

Fujimori won the 1990 presidential election by positioning himself against what he termed the "partidocracia," rule by political parties. His campaign effectively redefined the popular struggle in Peru: "no longer 'the people' versus 'the oligarchy,' it became instead 'the people'—represented by their elected president—versus the 'political class'" (Kay 1996, 83). At the same time, Fujimori aligned himself with apparently apolitical "social development." He founded FONCODES, an institution designed to locate extreme poverty using objective measures, and then visibly fought poverty through targeted community projects, such as the founding and funding of *comedores*, "that could be directly attributed to presidential initiative" (Roberts 1998, 107).

Fujimori also appointed women to positions of power and aligned himself with women's issues and organizations. Blondet (1999, 18) argues that these associations "cleaned up the image of the President, lending him values that the country demanded but his administration lacked." Women's presumed honesty undercut accusations of corruption, clientelism was reframed as social concern, and arbitrary authoritarian measures were spun as defending family and social order. Then, as now, antipolitical messages that focused on poverty relief, family development, and other so-called women's issues were extraordinarily effective political tools.

During my fieldwork, the political importance of national social programs was evident in how this work was managed and by whom. The FONCODES directors I interviewed were all members of President Alan García's political party, APRA, and were frequently rotated between various programs explicitly designed to fight poverty as Peruvians understood it, moving from the Agua para Todos (Water for All) program to Techo Propio and then to FONCODES, which provided targeted construction assistance. Though these programs all required different kinds of technical expertise, they were managed by political operatives, people who knew how to use purportedly apolitical poverty-fighting initiatives to organize communities and construct constituencies that would support the administration. In fact, organizing politically identifiable communities was the principal goal of FONCODES's efforts to construct *nucleos ejecutores*, community-based project execution teams. After receiving training from a FONCODES representative, community members would elect a small representative body, the *nucleo ejecutor*, to propose one of four pre-approved poverty-reduction projects, oversee the construction of that project with a specific allocated fund, and return the project to the state so it could be publicly administered. If implemented correctly, these *nucleos ejecutores* would result in a small capital project such as a school or a hospital, a sense that the project had been participatory and transparent, and relational ties between members of the *nucleo ejecutor* and FONCODES officials as representatives of García's administration. As one FONCODES official explained clearly enough, "All social work has a political foundation and purpose" (*Todo trabajo social tiene un fondo político*).

THE WORK OF MAKING RELATIONS

Peruvian politicians gain legitimacy by discursively linking the sacred space of the nuclear family to a state that is simultaneously technocratic and beneficent. In this framework, the well-being of the family and the development of the state are united in their distance from politics. In practice, though, family and politics are not mutually exclusive fields but rather exist on the same continuum of informal social relations (Wolf 1966, 2). Javier Auyero (2000, 73) argues that, in neoliberal Latin America, informal networks that appear as kinship or friendship increasingly overlap with political networks and are built by coupling support for everyday survival with a "discursive emphasis on trust, solidarity, reciprocity, caring and hope." The language of apolitical assistance in support of familial well-being is used to construct the very sorts of political networks that these languages oppose.

This ready slippage between kinship and politics in Peru makes more sense if we consider how family is made in practice. Studies of kinship in the Andes have described it as flexible and performative (Leinaweaver 2008; Van Vleet 2008; Weismantel 1995). Relatedness is not a stable biological trait but a product of time, interaction, mutual obligation, and shared residence (Harris 2008). Relatedness thus has a territorial component, but it is not inherent to the territory itself. Catherine Allen's 2002 analysis of the Andean social formation known as the *ayllu* is particularly helpful in understanding this mode of place-based relatedness. She explains, "An ayllu exists through the personal and intimate relationship that bonds the people and the place into a single unit" (84). An *ayllu* is maintained through various kinds of work, including collective labor on local infrastructure projects, participation in communal assemblies, and an elected leader's "informal constitution of consensus and their tricky and difficult representation and defense of the ayllu's interests to governmental agencies and law courts" (18). Although *ayllu* implies a certain connection with the land and cannot exist without it, the word is not a reference to the land itself. Allen states, "Uninhabited places are not ayllus" (84).

In the context of Peru's urban settlements, the flexibility of "community" and its imbrication with kinship results from the ways communities are built up through individual relational ties. Susan Lobo articulates in her 1982 ethnography of Lima's squatter settlements that the concept of "corporate membership" in a formal, place-based community "is not a natural one to the residents of the squatter settlements, who instead visualize social interaction in terms of a network of alliances" (152). She argues that every individual is "already at the center of a kin network" that they can activate in their favor by involving themselves in reciprocal obligations. She further contends that a migrant's success in 1980s Lima depended on their ability to "adapt the kin and alliance systems of their highland villages to life in the city" (176). The clientelist relations between politicians and *barriada* residents are perhaps evidence of this very sort of adaptation.

The power asymmetries of patron-client relations differ from kinship in scope but not necessarily in kind. In the Andes, relatedness is constituted through the circulation and sharing of food and energy (substances) that accumulate in people's bodies during the daily reproduction of the household. By providing these substances to children, parents construct relationships that are simultaneously intimate and hierarchical (Van Vleet 2008). With this in mind, Lazar (2008) argues that clientelism needs to be understood as a particular mode of political engagement that incorporates aspects of Andean kinship practices. Lazar suggests that the asymmetric reciprocities of clientelism in which "politicians exchange gifts for political capital" represent "sound Andean logic" (114). It is a practice frequently embraced by the least privileged elements of society "as a hedge against what is often perceived not as democratization but as bureaucratic indifference and exclusion" (114).

Though political scientists often describe clientelism as a closed-circuit exchange of gifts for votes, an act of "buying consciences," these metaphors do not adequately convey how Pachacutanos experience the clientelism in which they themselves engage. For them, clientelism is not about exchange so much as using favors to construct "personalized ties, an imagined solidaristic community, and a protective and predictable network that buffers the harsh reality" of settlement life (Auyero 2000, 70). Patrons, meanwhile, benefit from "demonstrations of esteem" that create goodwill and contribute to their reputations, fame, and, in electoral democracies, the stability of their positions (Wolf 1966, 17). Clients demonstrate loyalty by attending political rallies, offering various forms of collective support at a moment's notice, and effectively promising to "entertain no other patron"; in the process they become "members of a faction which serves the competitive purposes of a faction leader" (Wolf 1966, 17). Auyero (2000, 73) finds that politicians and their ground-level representatives combine everyday assistance with apolitical discourses of family, cooperation, and solidarity with the ultimate goal of constructing ties that "freeze a particular balance of forces." This is precisely what Pablo was attempting to do in Pachacútec through his efforts to formalize *clubes de madres* (mothers clubs), associations of women connected by coresidence and their affective obligations to children.

With the help of local municipal promoters, Pablo recruited women from different sectors in Pachacútec and met with them weekly to discuss formalizing their organizations: transforming them into juridical bodies based on recognition by the municipality, which would allow them to request assistance from the municipality and other funders for neighborhood parties and projects. Though the weekly meetings also provided regular opportunities to recruit participants for municipal activities, from

Pablo's perspective, their most important function was to build personal relations between club members and the municipal government through Pablo and his cadre of promoters. Although the term "mothers club" is meant to suggest apolitical community organization, Pablo told me that the mothers clubs also had "another purpose, a political purpose." The value of these social organizations for local politics became clearer as the months went by, first as friendships and loyalties were built through reciprocal exchanges of assistance and later as other figures emerged to challenge these social ties.

I ran into Pablo at lunch one day when he was in an incredible hurry. The mayor had given him until 5 p.m. to get one hundred signatures in favor of formalizing what was widely known as Pachacútec's "clandestine cemetery." The cemetery wasn't exactly clandestine; the sandy area where residents had been burying their dead had recently been featured on the reality TV show *Extreme Lives*. Nor was it particularly informal; Pachacutanos were burying their dead in pretty much the same place urban planning maps indicated they should. However, Pablo's goals for formalization went beyond this; they involved renewing documentary recognition of the cemetery and physically marking off the cemetery from the rest of the community, he said, "so that residents can have a dignified, Christian burial . . . a more human burial." For Pablo, it seemed that certain political designations and infrastructural boundaries had a moral status that was constitutive of humanity itself.

Getting the signatures required quick work, so we raced to the headquarters of one of the mothers clubs in search of people to sign the petition. The first signatures came from the mothers who lived next to the headquarters, but soon they too had taken signature sheets and were off to tap their social networks, to get the signatures of friends and relatives and the friends and relatives of these friends and relatives, and so on. People without ID cards were not allowed to sign, since there would be no way to legally verify the existence of these individuals if someone reviewed the petition. However, women were invited to submit the names and ID numbers of husbands and other intimate relations, provided they could convincingly forge their signatures. As we raced back to the *agencia*, the district government field office, to submit the petition to the municipality's official document reception desk, Pablo said he was lucky the women in that sector liked him so much. His ability to activate this social network at a moment's notice and create an on-paper image of political will made it possible for him to meet the mayor's capricious requirements and advance a community project he valued.

Later that week Pablo tried to teach Rebecca, a young DEMUNA lawyer, this technique. Her boss was requiring her to obtain five hundred signatures on a petition for the One Million Friends campaign, which demanded a commitment from Peru's congress to devote a certain percentage of the national budget to protecting the rights of children. When she asked Pablo to sign, he instructed her to give him several sheets so he could get signatures and to do the same with me and any political promoters she had befriended: "You don't do political work [*trabajo político*] one by one. You get as many people as possible to go and tell their friends, and then they tell their friends and their family and the people they run into daily. . . . You see how quickly la política adds up!"

Over the course of several months I saw Pablo draw on these mothers clubs again and again: to participate in leadership workshops, recruit neighbors for government programs, and provide children at a moment's notice when "needy children" were required for charity events and photo ops. Women described some of these events as legitimate development or social assistance activities, while others they described as more superficial. Nonetheless, all of the events served to invoke and reinforce the women's relationships with Pablo and promoters.

Some members of the mayor's administration, however, were concerned that Pablo's tactics were fostering loyalties to him personally rather than to him as an embodiment of the municipality. One week, a new community outreach supervisor showed up to the mothers club meeting with a local councilwoman and the general secretary of the municipal Women's Committee. When the general secretary began her speech, she seemed to be picking up in the middle of a conversation that no one else had heard. "I believe in being honest, upfront, and telling it like it is. The Women's Committee has never marginalized anyone, and we've never obliged anyone to join with us." She went on extolling the benefits of the Women's Committee rather defensively until one woman in the audience spoke up: "Forgive me madam, but I'm confused. Why exactly are you here? What is the difference between the Women's Committee and the mothers clubs? We're here to figure out how to formalize as mothers clubs. What does the Women's Committee have to do with it?" The councilwoman cut in: "The important thing to remember is that all of us here are women with a desire to serve the community and *salir adelante* [move forward]. We have to focus on the positive, not the negative. . . . We are not going to think about who works for what functionary. Rather, we're going to remember that we are all from the mayor."

It soon became clear that the women had a choice, to formalize as mothers clubs or as cells of the Women's Committee. The general secretary explained, "As part of the Women's Committee, you will not deal with promoters. Instead, you deal directly with me as a representative of the mayor's wife." When the issue of member obligations to the Women's Committee came up, the general secretary protested, "We've never obligated anyone to support us with demonstrations or funds or anything like that." Her emphatic protest made me think about the subtle ways obligations between community members and government representatives materialized in practice, the everyday exchanges of gifts and favors that occurred in an effort to maintain relations with the authority figure and to support the representatives and promoters who had, through these frequent exchanges, become friends.

The discussion of the pros and cons of the Women's Committee continued until Gabriela, a president of one of the mothers clubs, said she had to check with the rest of her council before she could make any decision. "As president, it is not my place to decide for the entire group," she said. The councilwoman praised this democratic attitude and adjourned the meeting. When the general secretary and the councilwoman finally left, Gabriela said she worried that if she went with the Women's Committee, all the promoters she had befriended would lose their jobs. In an interesting revelation of who her council really was, she decided to talk things over with Marisa, her local promoter, and with Pablo before she made any decision.

I was watching over her daughter when Gabriela made the call to Pablo, so I only heard pieces of the conversation. It began with her asking when she would get the volleyball equipment he had promised for her neighborhood and ended with her agreeing not to proceed with formalization of any sort until they had spoken in person. Ultimately, it seemed the difference between the Women's Committee and the mothers clubs related to social ties and patronage: who members would go through to get assistance, what that assistance might consist of, and what kinds of support might be requested in return. Joining the Women's Committee meant being part of a larger, established organization that had a president who requested and acquired goods on behalf of members and distributed them based on their own criteria. It was, as the general secretary explained, a "direct line" to the mayor through the secretary and the mayor's wife. The mothers clubs, meanwhile, were supposed to be autonomous. Like residential *dirigentes*, once formally recognized they could request benefits from whomever they wanted. Having spent months forging relations with these women and helping them build their organizations, Pablo and his promoters hoped they would choose to work with them as trusted members of their social network. The promoters who heard about the incident were first angry and then concerned for their jobs. One promoter exclaimed, "So much work we've done with the *mamás* [mothers] only to have the Women's Committee come and rip it up. . . . If the Women's Committee works with them, where does that leave us, the promoters?"

EMPLOYMENT: THE ONLY ASSISTANCE THAT MATTERS

> Without the shield of poverty, the promoters could never get away with all of that political work. . . . Think about how much the muni spends on those promoters. It's more of an employment agency than anything else.
>
> GUILLERMO, RESIDENT OF VENTANILLA

The issue of finding and keeping local government jobs brings up another important way this form of politics is connected to individual and familial efforts to get ahead. While establishing relationships with authority figures could have benefits for the broader community, many women participated in community organizations and municipal programs in the hopes of acquiring jobs, which they viewed as a more sustained form of social assistance that could meaningfully improve their family's economic circumstances. Auyero (2000, 65) argues that in a political clientelist network, "the hope of a job serves as important glue within the inner circle. Although not everyone is employed at the municipality, the fact that someone gets a fixed-term contract or a part-time job has an important demonstration effect. If others in the circle are diligent and 'know how to wait,' . . . sooner or later they will be rewarded with posts."

The more Pablo and other authority figures denied that they had jobs to give, the more obvious it was that local jobs were being used as proverbial carrots to encourage participation. Mothers club meetings would typically begin or end with a motivational speech in which Pablo publicly referenced giving truly committed community servants jobs in the municipality, even if only to deny this possibility.

> I'm going to pay attention to who comes and who does not, who is most consistent in their work. And this work is voluntary. Being a leader

> means you have the capacity to move people. It involves commitment, the hope that you can change things and change things for the better. And your involvement can't be because you think I have a job to give you. You can't do this because you think someone is going to give you something. This commitment to be a leader and serve the community has to be sincere. It has to be born from inside of you.

Pablo also admitted to close colleagues that he was always on the lookout for worthwhile individuals to hire into the administration, typically conscientious, intelligent, and energetic women with large social networks and leadership capacity, a quality he termed "fuerza política," political strength.

Even so, Pablo's work with the mothers clubs revealed how building networks and hooking political administrations into the community, even through something as instrumental as a job, involved combining daily interactions and reciprocities with discourses of affect, service, and solidarity. Women's commitments to these organizations were supposed to be born of selfless desires to serve the community that they themselves helped to produce as they activated social networks to participate in various government-sponsored events and fulfill documentary requirements to formalize their status or request assistance. If women participated consistently and showed themselves to be effective leaders without betraying any individualistic or ulterior motives, they might be invited into the innermost clientelist circle and given a job in the municipality.

These jobs were particularly valuable for women because they allowed them to earn a relatively stable income while remaining close enough to home that they could, in theory, attend to their children when necessary. Although few promoters discussed this openly, it was clear from the way many stole away at lunch or stopped by schools on their routes to attend meetings with teachers that a benefit of doing fieldwork and being out "in the street" was their ability to integrate and flexibly shift between the unremunerated work of care and the paid work of development politics. The capacity to earn stable monthly pay while still fulfilling other gendered expectations and obligations went a long way toward making local jobs stand out as the only form of social assistance powerful enough to ensure political loyalty.

The value of a job as a form of social assistance became apparent one day when I was working with Anita, a sharp, energetic, and delightfully bawdy Pachacutana who was now employed as a municipal promoter. We ran into a friend of hers who was waiting in line to acquire birth certificates for her children through the Right to Identity campaign cosponsored by the municipality and the national identity registry, RENIEC. Because

FIGURE 2.1. A mothers club participates in a civic spirit competition, 2009. Photo by the author.

campaigning was a crucial part of Anita's job, she steered the conversation to what she described as the mayor's "good works" (*buenas obras*). Her friend, however, downplayed these initiatives, saying, "Maybe he does good works, but help doesn't get to the people who truly need it." When Anita countered that everyone in Pachacútec was poor, the woman replied, "Of course, but *you* know that I'm poorer than most."

Anita's friend then quickly steered the conversation to ask how she might get a job in the municipality. Anita gave her advice about whom to speak to in the municipality, what sort of things she should put on her résumé, and the different psychological tests she would have to take to assess her *formación*, her upbringing and education. She also mentioned that, even if the municipality wasn't hiring just then, the woman could rent out the front room of her house to serve as a campaign headquarters since it was located in a politically strategic area of Pachacútec. Doing so would provide her some additional income and give her an opportunity to form relationships with party officials, which could lead to a job or other benefits down the line. The woman was less keen on that prospect than she was on the idea of immediate employment, but she kept the possibility open.

Later in private, Anita offered me more explanation about what this woman's poverty consisted of and how connecting her to the political network of the municipality might be of mutual benefit to the woman and the administration.

> She really is very poor. She lives in a house made of four straw mats with a roof made of cloth. It's not even made of plastic! She has three kids and her husband is very young. He works as a *cobrador* [collecting money on a minibus], but he likes to drink. . . . Her husband is twenty-five and she has to be about forty or so. That's why he drinks, because he's still young and wants to hang out with his friends. . . . Something like that can't last. . . . He's in a different life stage. He's going to get tired [of the relationship] and then it's going to end. . . . But the woman is *muy pilas* [very energetic, hardworking].

If given the opportunity, Anita said, her friend would be able to prove herself the same way Anita and other promoters had. What was striking to me about this whole exchange was that, even as Anita's friend was actively benefitting from a government assistance campaign, it was clear that employment and stable integration into the mayor's personal political network was the only kind of assistance that mattered to her.

Later that same day, Anita explained to me how campaign season was integral to her job and simultaneously impeded her work. Ever since she moved to Pachacútec, Anita had been active in community development initiatives. She had worked with numerous NGOs and had even gone to several women's leadership conferences in different countries around the world. Yet by the time I met her, she had moved away from these activities in favor of a relatively steady paying job in the municipality. She was still deeply concerned with development in Pachacútec and specifically with "la problemática de la mujer Pachacutana," the set of problems faced by women in Pachacútec, but for the time being, her major concern was keeping the mayor in office. Anita and her fellow promoters understood that their livelihoods depended on this, a fact that made it difficult, she said, to focus on community development.

> Before it was good because all the *dirigentes* could sit around a table and work together. . . . Now that we're in campaign season, we can't do anything. Defend. Defend your institution, that's it. Defend your leader, because thanks to the mayor we're working. So we've got to defend against the rivals, against the naysayers. . . . If you look to see if Pachacútec has developed in the last three or four years, it has changed so much! But sometimes people don't want to see it because they say, "I also want to do a campaign because I also want to work." And that's the problem. They form these little opposition groups. That's what the mediocre *dirigentes* do, because they haven't been productive and they

> don't have principles. . . . You'll see *dirigentes*, "Take one hundred soles and support me in the campaign," and that is buying consciences. It's trafficking with the desperation of the neighbor. That is what politics is. Nothing is clean. And now I'm tired. Before I was always up front, but now I just want one day or a week to be in my house.

Anita clearly loved working in the street and the relationships, opportunities, serendipity, and salary that came with it. However, her job required her to connect and collaborate with local leaders to visibly promote development, and she was being thwarted by people who, much like her, would rather have a job that placed them inside the primary political network than work with a promoter to improve their communities from their current positions. Although Anita ultimately tried to discredit opposition leaders, accusing them of giving and taking bribes in exchanges divorced from sincerity and sociality, she understood that what people really sought were more central positions in the political network. The dynamic of distributing jobs to party militants is what might be considered "politics of the belly" (Bayart 1993). Describing similar phenomena in Bolivia, Lazar (2005, 223) contends,

> Politicians are entitled, and expected, to accumulate wealth personally, and use it to benefit their social networks, including above all their family. How acceptable this is in Bolivia varies according to the context, but what is similar is that Bolivian patrons are expected to redistribute their wealth, and the wealth of the state, through the provision of jobs to their clients. . . . Each time a new political party takes over the administration of a municipality, ministry, etc., the previous set of civil servants is fired and the new party's activists take their place. Despite the rhetorical emphasis on obras, the largest part of a municipality's budget goes on wages for its functionaries.

Above all, it is through these clientelist, network-building mechanisms that politicians serve the poor. Yet as evidenced by Anita's complaint, building these networks also produces social and political factions. People who are aligned with the dominant political party become a privileged class with access to state resources and options for social mobility, while others are left outside the state, with limited capacity to improve either their communities or their own economic positions. This disjunctive framing of insiders and outsiders raises important questions about what the state is in this context, how it connects to the community, and the uneasy subject positions of those who mediate these connections.

NEGOTIATING IDENTITY INSIDE THE STATE

Anthropologists have long questioned the nature of this thing we call "the state." A. R. Radcliffe-Brown argued long ago that the state was a fiction of philosophers. What we speak of as "the state," he suggested, is better understood as a "collection of human beings connected by a complex system of relations" (1950, xxiii). Abrams (1988, 81) added to this laic definition the power of the state idea. He contended that " 'the state' is not a fact but a claim, . . . at most a message of domination . . . attributing unity, morality and independence to the disunited, amoral and dependent workings of the practice of government." The state can of course be incredibly real in its effects, martialing law, violence, and expertise to displace, incarcerate, coerce, and otherwise shape populations and landscapes within a given territory in ways that, particularly when combined with discourse, might prompt us to imagine it as superhuman, omnipresent, and omnipotent. Yet the state never arrives at the door of human experience except as mediated by the work of concrete human carriers who belie the fiction of neat divisions between public and private on which the idea of the modern state depends (Poole 2004; Scott 2005).

In Peru, the individuals who mediate state-society relations—and in so doing also help constitute imaginaries of "state" and "society" as discrete social spheres—have historically been morally suspect and often racially ambiguous. Colonial powers, for instance, relied on local indigenous *kurakas* (chiefs) and criollo tax collectors to uphold Spanish rule in the Andes. Though this system allowed distant rulers to profit from colonial populations, their power was always tenuous and dependent upon local leaders whom they could never fully trust or control (Orlove 1985; Thurner 1997; Walker 1999). In the 1900s this intermediary role was filled by *gamonales* (abusive landed elite) and *tinterillos* (notaries, hack lawyers, and paper-pushers). Poole (2004, 45) describes the *gamonal* as embodying the slippage between liberal law and authoritarian rule. The *gamonal* was both a representative of the liberal state and "the spot where state rationality and jurisdiction fade[d] into uncontrollable domains of extrajudicial force," which was visited regularly and capriciously on Andean peasants. *Tinterillos*, meanwhile, mediated state-society relations via the letter of the law and the dizzying materiality of officialdom in ways that promised to promote indigenous access to elite worlds while in practice robbing Indians of their historical land rights (Arguedas 2002 [1941]; de la Cadena 2001). Interestingly, at the time, *gamonales* and *tinterillos* were associated with racial impurity, as though being neither fully indigenous nor fully white explained their ambiguous loyalties and unscrupulous behaviors (de la Cadena 2001).

In the latter half of the twentieth century, the work of mediating between rural communities and an official, typically urban state fell to migrants and university students who had, through force of experience, learned to operate in both contexts and maneuver between them (Ronsbo 2008; Stepputat 2004). However, as hybrid subjects—rural representatives in urban space and urban experts in rural space—these individuals were frequent objects of moral critique. State officials and community members hoped that these intermediaries would advocate on their behalf but remained suspicious that the mediator was really serving the other group, or worse, themselves. Though their identities were rarely tied explicitly to race, the community leaders and municipal promoters I worked with in Pachacútec found themselves in a similar situation, negotiating a layered, hybridized, and conflicted positionality that made them suspicious to those around them.

Transforming oneself into the state begins as a matter of wardrobe, specifically a vest. Regional and district government employees wore green vests, national government employees wore red vests, and RENIEC employees wore blue vests. Over time, many of Pachacútec's most politically active community members had been given vests and jobs by one institution or another. This was true for the mostly male residential *dirigentes* elected to represent their neighborhoods in negotiations with different state organizations, and for the exclusively female *dirigentes* who led *comedores populares* or Vaso de Leche branches. As leaders in their communities, these *dirigentes* had an ability to move people that was useful to organizations seeking community collaboration and participation, and elected officials knew it was better to have these individuals working with them than against them.

In hiring local residents, government organizations effectively divided the population into those who were part of the current administration, and thus inside and constitutive of the state, and those who were outside of it and therefore members of the community. The division between those inside and outside the state was reaffirmed frequently. Promoters wore vests, and the community did not. And while wearing these vests, promoters conducted censuses and took attendance at events while the community was surveyed, they served snacks that the community received, and they orchestrated collaborations on behalf of the mayor in which the community was asked to partake. On some occasions, such as when Pachacutanos rose up to demand land expropriations or water infrastructure from the national government, promoters were instructed to remove their vests and participate alongside protesters as members of the community. This practice reinvigorated promoters' identities as community members and advocates even as a kind of green aura still clung to them, an after-image that, without implicating the mayor directly, would signal his solidarity with the community.

Nonetheless, these orchestrated vest removals generally weren't sufficient to stave off critiques of community leaders who joined the administration. Many residents complained that once people started working in the municipality, they became arrogant or thought themselves better than the rest of the population. We might understand this as a way neighbors experience a municipal employee's apparent remove from the rest of the community. Others complained that community leaders who took municipal jobs had sold out, suggesting that employment in the municipality was at odds with the antagonistic relations required for *dirigentes* to effectively advocate for community interests. A local *dirigente* explained simply, "A peon can't go against his patron." Although having political strength made someone valuable to the municipality, getting a job in the administration put them at risk of losing the very support that made them a political asset in the first place.

This is precisely what happened to Pablo. For a time, he tried to be both a *dirigente* and a political operative for the municipality. However, he soon discovered that maintaining this dual positionality was impossible. "I can't fight with myself," he explained.

> As a *dirigente* you're supposed to work for the population, but as a municipal employee, you have to work for the municipality. So then, when there is a battle between the two, where do you position yourself? . . . There's no clear identification. . . . At first, I tried to be a bridge . . . that could serve both the state and the population, but the other *dirigentes* didn't think of it like that. They thought I was identifying with the municipality and not with the population. . . . I'll give you an example. They [local officials from the municipality] say that out of three roads they're only going to pave one, and people say, "No, you work in the muni, you've got to fix it, so they pave the

> three." . . . They don't see you as a *dirigente* anymore, they see you as a muni worker, and as a muni worker they think that you have all the right and the muni gives you everything you want. But since that's not going to happen it makes the *dirigente* fight with his population. So then the population says, "Oh look, that guy is bad. Because the muni is paying you, you're accepting that they give only one road instead of three because it doesn't matter to you anymore." But it's not that it doesn't matter, it's that you can't. . . . There is always a process. It's not like the muni will say, "Oh, since it's about you, yeah, we'll do it." . . . So the people said I wasn't doing anything, and since there's all that mistrust, I left my position [as a *dirigente*]. . . . That's why I tell you that it's hard to be on both sides.

Pablo's account points not only to the challenges of managing multiple or intermediary identifications but also to conflicts between networked and bureaucratic understandings of the state. The neighborhood critique of Pablo was not simply that he worked in the municipality but that he was not clearly using his position to benefit his community. His neighbors hoped his appointment would give them an ally on the inside, someone who could steer the administration in ways that bettered their neighborhood. Pablo was instead visibly adopting the subject position of a bureaucrat, aligning himself with institutional logics and trying to explain these sympathetically to his community rather than maintaining loyalties to the community and using his insider status to make them an exception to the rules. While Pablo still felt himself pulled in multiple directions, in practice, the municipality had succeeded in quelling any opposition Pablo might provoke, pushing him to understand the bureaucratic predicament rather than looking outside institutional logics to create change.

Anita, who had also been a *dirigente* in her community, agreed that it was difficult to be both inside and outside the state. Still, she said it was possible.

> For the intelligent leader there's another way to manage her group while being inside the municipality. . . . You delegate responsibilities and create a plan. And when you're on the inside, you can channel the project. . . . I, as general secretary [of the neighborhood], delegate commissions in my community. Then, since we [promoters] are on the inside, we know what funds exist, what programs there will be, and when they will be offered. So we say, "Look, on this day the muni is doing this thing," and then you, as a community member, knock on the

door. And there I am in my office as the municipality. As a neighbor, a citizen, a leader you are obligated to ask for things, and my people [in the muni] have to attend to you because it's their job.

Anita's example of how to be both inside and outside the state indicated that working for the community from within the municipality required subterfuge and a subtle form of political labor to ensure that one's bureaucratic performance was simultaneously interpreted on multiple registers. Anita was not in a position to change what the municipality offered; for that, her community, under the official leadership of a different neighbor, would have to rise up in protest. Instead, she used her position to link her informal neighborhood network to the political and social assistance network of the municipality. This maintained and even strengthened her identity as a community advocate despite being on the inside while also promoting development in her community. Her capacity to negotiate these identities and interests was something Anita rightfully took pride in.

Interlocutors often told me that if you didn't have someone on the inside of a political administration, it was impossible to get anything done. For people without connections, or whose connections refused to give them special treatment, these logjams evidenced corruption and Peru's continued moral impoverishment. For those with personally supportive connections, having someone on the inside could create a sense of intimate engagement with the state. In this sense, community and individual development did depend on inclusion in the state, not in a formal, bureaucratic sense, but an inclusion based on real-life contacts, everyday exchanges, and the expansion of social networks. In this context, the relation between state and society gives way to questions of "our people" versus "their people." Local political opponents were frequently explicit about this understanding of the state, having no critique of a politician other than it was time to give someone else a turn.

WOMEN IN DEVELOPMENT

The fact that most promoters were women invites us to consider how gender intercedes in the identity acrobatics required to work inside the state. Like most female promoters I knew, Anita's home life was complicated. She was the mother of three teenagers, one of them with special needs. She had been romantically separated from her husband—the father of her children and a sporadically employed alcoholic—for several years and was actively dating another man, but her husband continued to live in her house due to economic constraints and her sense of marital obligation. Also like most political promoters, Anita was using her job as best she could to navigate the moral double bind in which poor mothers found themselves, while also cultivating a sense of dignity, purpose, and modern selfhood that she could take pride in.

On the one hand, modern women were expected to have aspirations and identities that extended outside the home and to be capable of providing for themselves without depending on anyone else. At the same time, women were expected to be ever-present mothers, devoted entirely to their children, and were frequently reminded that falling short in this obligation put their children as well as the nation at risk. Middle-class women might find some success navigating this double burden by hiring others to fulfill care duties in their homes while they cultivated professional identities outside. These options, however, were not available to lower-class women whose work was typically not esteemed in the way middle-class professions were (Fuller 2005). Nonetheless, employment was perhaps even more important for impoverished women's moral standing. Although single mothers and female household heads were deemed the poorest of the poor and the most deserving of assistance in the abstract, in their encounters with state agents their deservingness hinged on whether they were actively working to ameliorate their circumstances and lift themselves out of poverty (Han 2012). Mothers who did not do so were accused of being *dejada* (lazy, apathetic) and *conformista* (content with the unsatisfactory). At the same time, impoverished women had particularly intense care responsibilities. They were expected to be especially vigilant in protecting their impoverished and thus "at risk" children, and they were readily accused of abandoning their children if they left them in the care of others or were seen as less than fully devoted to raising them properly (Campoamor 2016; Ponce Alegre 2007). For impoverished women, the double burden of care and work manifested as a gendered moral double bind. Working as a political promoter offered women one way to navigate this dilemma.

Women's success as political promoters relied to some degree on their reputations as hardworking and attentive mothers and on their ability to extend a mother-leader identity into the community care work that constituted the politics of development. These jobs also informally afforded women some flexibility to care for their children, even as they cultivated professional and political selves by engaging in different kinds of relationships.

Even so, working as a political promoter constantly threatened to undermine the maternal identities on which the job depended. Female promoters were therefore frequently engaged in complex private-public negotiations. For instance, given the salience of food as a modality of care, Anita and her colleagues made a special point of trying to cook midday meals for their children despite being in the field all day, with some waking up at 4 a.m. daily to cook the large midday meal. Anita explained this practice with profound simplicity: "What nutrition can our children get if we don't cook for them?" Despite these efforts, political promoters' time in the street was critiqued by many as a form of abandonment. Anita explained the problem to me over lunch one day:

> What they're saying is that now the municipal workers shouldn't have small children because what happens is we hit the streets to work and the children end up abandoned. How are we supposed to know what they do all day if we get home at 6, 7, 8 o'clock at night!? . . . Saturday we are working. And the events! Sundays there are anniversaries . . . electoral committees, neighborhood meetings. . . . We're outside all the time. . . . [And] the son or daughter of that promoter is hanging out in the streets . . . or is a *piraña* [child pickpocket] or a *pandillero* [gang member] or is doing bad things in the house. . . . How do you raise [*Cómo formas*] your child if you're not at home? . . . For instance, I recommended this one woman for a job preparing our tortillas, but then I had to ask the age of her child . . . and I had to tell her no, . . . that she's not going to have the time available to do it. Who is going to watch her small children? . . . It is a way to maintain the structure [*formación*] of society, with the mom in the house.

Belén, the head of a *comedor popular*, once commented to me that the problem with promoters and other working mothers was that they were "materialistic," valuing money to buy things for themselves and their children over spending time with them.

Money and semistable employment were indeed important attractions for female promoters, and many construed this paid political work as an extension of their maternal obligations. But what kept most women I knew involved in political work was not the money so much as the freedom it gave them from the household and the extent to which it allowed them to cultivate different relationships and thus different kinds of selves. Despite the difficulties women experienced working in the municipality—which included long and unpredictable hours and inconsistent pay and in many ways echoed the abuses women have experienced in other sites where their paid work is partially figured as an extension of care and filial responsibility—Anita said she persisted in her work as a promoter because she had grown accustomed to it.

> We've been in the administration for two or three years and now . . . we're accustomed to a certain rhythm, . . . to not being in the house. . . . You get used to the people too. At home the majority of us are alone. Jackie is alone [a single mother], Elisabet is mother and father for her kids, and in my case my husband sometimes helps out, sometimes no. And he gets bitter because he says to me, "You work your ass off and on top of it you're feeling bad and they don't pay you, . . . and on top of it you can't even be with your kids on Sunday!"

For all of her ambivalence about working in the municipality, Anita's reference to growing accustomed to rhythms, to the people, and to not being in the house speaks to the power of work to shape subjectivities and to do so not through bodily discipline or rigid economistic scheduling but through forging relations with employers, neighbors, and the community.

The home could and did emerge for Anita as a site of solace in certain circumstances, yet it was also a site of constrained subjectivity and limited relational identities. Mary Weismantel (2001, 58) has argued that, for women who work in female-dominated arenas, "the private home does not appear as the one definitively and unambiguously female domain, where women can feel secure and in control," but can emerge instead as an "ominously patriarchal territory controlled and dominated—often violently—by men." Although municipal politics was not a fully feminized space, street-level promoters were predominantly women. And engaging with community members, attending workshops, and spending time with other promoters in the street provided an important respite from the home, where female promoters related almost exclusively with children and were constantly confronted with the disillusioning absence, or presence, of men and particular forms of economic or familial poverty. Even women who simply attended community workshops or mothers club meetings without aspiring to municipal jobs said they did so primarily to distract themselves from the house, framing the house as a source of their most pressing problems and a site from which they needed reprieve.

Being in the street and having cause to be constantly on the move, encountering new things, and engaging with new people was something that Anita and other women valued immensely. The work energized even as it exhausted them, and in exposing them to new experiences and people, it allowed them to be different kinds of women. Drawing on the relationships she had forged with neighbors, friends, and colleagues through her experiences in the street, Anita was able to construct herself as a *mujer luchadora*, a strong and independent "woman warrior," concerned with her personal and professional development as well as with the progress of her community. She was a savvy leader who understood politics but kept her eye on development.

Yet maternity, which for a century has been framed as integral to the development of a modern Peruvian nation, was always in the background of these identities. Anita told me on several occasions that the major problem in Pachacútec was the "lack of love" in households. She saw devoted mothering as integral to community development and national well-being and understood that working as a promoter could in some ways compete with this mothering project. However, politics also provided avenues for her to care for her children not only by bringing in an income and promoting community improvements but by supporting her children's own entrées into politics and encouraging the personal and professional growth that might come from it.

As municipal elections drew closer, Anita's oldest daughter began working on the campaign of an opposition candidate. Despite critiquing others for opposing the current administration simply because they "also want to work," Anita explained that she had to support her daughter's decision because it was an opportunity for her daughter to grow as a person, to develop a professional-political identity, and to see what life was like on "the inside," indicating that personal development required becoming part of a political network that might solidify into the state.

> It's her decision. She's twenty-one. And these are going to be her first steps. She said to me, "Mamá, I should be thanking [the candidate] for giving me this opportunity to have experience, to get in front of the public, to do something that's different from what I normally do, whether [he] wins or not." This way she can see how you manage everything from the inside. Because as young people we have a different perspective. It's like when we were all passing out flyers for the mayor [years earlier], . . . all of that campaigning to see what it's like from the inside. Because as we said to ourselves, "When you're on the outside, they screw you even worse."

Even as she valued political work for allowing her to develop her own capacities and potentially the capacities of her daughter, Anita often said that she longed for a different sort of job, one that didn't demand a political commitment and the expansion of affect and obligation to her employer, her colleagues, and her broader political network. It was this political-affective commitment that kept her working long hours under harsh conditions, caused her to miss time with her children, and exposed her to critiques from her husband and her neighbors even as it also allowed her to partially escape them. For Anita and women in similar situations, this was the everyday and ambivalent substance of development: a constant negotiation of conflicting commitments and personal relational aspirations and an emotionally taxing struggle to weave the divergent obligations of development into a single moral life.

POLITICAL DEVELOPMENTS

I often returned to Anita's statement "When you're on the outside, they screw you even worse" as I puzzled through the paradoxes of poverty, politics, statecraft, and development in Peru. It seemed to me one of those lines of found poetry that encapsulate a world of truth and contradiction. In this line, the state is an impenetrable monolith, cold, bureaucratic, male, serving the interests of a privileged few and excluding or screwing the rest. And yet this imaginary was being conjured by a woman presently on the inside, a quasi-single mother and woman warrior whose everyday labors and never-ending identity acrobatics helped to produce ideals of an apolitical state—grounded in the gendered, spherical geographies of private/public, home/street, and social/political—as well as the state's disillusioning, gender-exploiting, political, and networked realities. Anita and fellow promoters specialized in traversing the very spheres that their feminine bodies invoked and that they discursively reproduced when they talked about social and political work. Through their persons, the state, mayor, and administration were able to reach into communities and homes, spreading messages, distributing resources, and establishing relations. In the process, female promoters created the community, state capacity, and political networks in one fell swoop. In Pachacútec, this was the political topography that all development and poverty-assistance initiatives traveled along and contributed to and why, for most people I spoke with, development was a farce; it looked too much like politics to be genuine.

« PART TWO »

Materialities of Statecraft

« THREE »

Papering the Margins

formal \ˈfȯr-məl\ *adj*

1 a: belonging to or constituting the form or essence of a thing; b: relating to or involving the outward form, structure, relationships, or arrangement of elements rather than content

4: having the appearance without the substance

MERRIAM-WEBSTER'S COLLEGIATE DICTIONARY, 11TH EDITION

It was early September and the worst of Pachacútec's winter was over. By 8 a.m. the fog had almost dissipated, and there seemed a small chance we might see the sun that day. As I walked the stretch of asphalt from the highway to the district *agencia*, I could make out the figures of promoters spilling off the concrete staircase. With green vests over their shoulders and flyers for formalization programs stuffed in their pockets, they were ready to paper the margins.

By the time I reached the staircase I had already been handed three flyers:

- "And you, what's your name? Campaign for Free Birth Certificates and National ID Cards"
- "Community Marriage: Take advantage of this opportunity and make your Dream a Reality, Sept. 25th Free Inscription"
- "With Us, Your Eternal Peace: Burial Services for 50 cents! Society for Public Beneficence, Callao"

I called up to Pablo, who was standing on the landing. "Pablo, look! Birth, marriage, and death in a single morning. Pretty efficient, no?" He laughed and said all I needed now was a flyer for my land title and I'd have the full set: propaganda for all the programs a person might need to lead a full life on paper. This paper life was one that all Peruvians were expected to lead and maintain. It was a life that could be tucked in a folder and guarded jealously, as inhabitants of Peru's marginal settlements (*barrios marginales*) and anthropologists are wont to do.

Promoting this paper life through formalization programs was integral to most of Peru's antipoverty efforts. In line with the capabilities and good governance frameworks advanced by the World Bank and other international development organizations, the Peruvian state sought to fight poverty by promoting citizenship and social inclusion for people living at "the margins," a term popularly used to index a geographic and social space that ostensibly lies beyond the full ordering capacities of the modern state. The state promotes this inclusion by extending its bureaucratic reach, aligning official records with lived realities to make these areas "legible" to distant actors and "governmentalizing the informal" so that it can more effectively "conduct the conduct" of the population and solidify its reputation as a modern, democratic state.[1] Formalization campaigns are framed as precursors to and enactments of development, where "development" is understood as synonymous with enhancing state capacity. On the one hand, state agents argue that they need to "see" populations in a documented and manageable way in order to properly assist them. Governments cannot allot food assistance to a poor person they do not know exists or grant construction loans to landowners if they cannot determine what land they own. On the other hand, in the age of inclusive liberalism, formalization is also understood as transformative; it helps to produce a more capable state while also creating new subjectivities and sociolegal entities. It turns marginals into empowered citizens, dilapidated shacks into capital assets, and hordes of invaders into organized communities.

Yet what the municipal promoters so freely distributed were flyers encouraging formalization, not the documents that would certify these transformations. Their job was to drum up a desire that could motivate people through arduous formalization procedures that required paying fees, waiting in lines, and filing forms, lists, and contracts to demonstrate broad social recognition of the status they wanted to legalize. Daniel Goldstein (2004, 90) contends that these bureaucratic procedures, known as *trámites*, are best understood as ordeals "undertaken at great personal cost, . . . necessary, unavoidable bureaucratic hassle[s] that you have to face if you want to function as a legal and legitimate member of society, but nonetheless an enormous drain on your time, energy and resources." *Trámites* were painful trials of citizenship, an obligation and an achievement.

Pachacutanos were well aware that they needed documents to prove to the state that someone or something existed, and they described various legal documents as "birth certificates." A land title was a "birth certificate" for a house, a license was a "birth certificate" for a business, and a *reconocimiento* (official recognition) was a "birth certificate" for an *organización social de base* (social base organization) such as a *comedor popular*, mothers club, or Vaso de Leche branch. This one-time status inscription was a necessary step on the road to formality, but it was not sufficient. To become formal, Peruvians had to engage formality as an ongoing project, continuously updating the official image the state had of them to ensure it aligned with their present situation. Anything less, and the person was out of status, informal, illegal, and illicit.

My goal here is to show how these different formalization campaigns, which are integral to Peru's war on poverty and central to the legitimacy and constitution of the state, do much more than render opaque societies legible and governable. They reproduce historical inequalities, generate new subjectivities and forms of marginalization, and bring new and often unruly social entities into being. Accumulating and updating documents aligns with ideals of performative citizenship, and the formal/informal divide provides a guise under which long-standing patterns of racial discrimination persist. Yet this binary distinction between formal and informal is complicated by the diverse sociolegal entities and subjectivities that formalization procedures bring into being and by the moral identities Peruvians associate with document use. In everyday Peruvian parlance, people who do not acquire documents or who fail to update the documents they have are labeled *dejado*, which may be translated as apathetic or careless. The term *vivo*, meanwhile, is used to describe people who are so good at using documents and so adept at navigating the informal cultures required for formal recognition that they become morally suspect. Although the term *vivo* is occasionally used to encourage people to be proactive and attentive to civic happenings, it is more often used as a moral slight. To call someone *vivo* is to suggest that they are too wily to be trusted, that they are exploiting the system to get more than their fair share, likely at others' expense.

Peruvians sometimes associate *vivos* and the quality of *viveza* (guile, wiliness) with documentary specters like ghosts and the mafia. Peruvians use the term *fantasma* (ghost) to depict a document that does social work for an entity that does not exist in practice or in the flesh. Examples include "ghost workers" that allow employers to pull in extra wages for themselves, "ghost committees" that were formalized but have since ceased to function, and "ghost towns" that exist in name and may even take up space but lack human inhabitants to enliven them. Peruvians use the term "mafia" to depict a set of skills and practices that people deeply involved with the state almost inevitably adopt. As several of my interlocutors explained, replacing government bureaucrats does relatively little to eliminate corruption because "la mafia llega muy rápido," the mafia arrives very quickly to anyone who works inside the state. The term "mafia" indexes corruption writ large, acts that allow some people to be included in and benefit from the state while others are left out.

The moral ambivalence of documents partly inheres in their status as mediating objects that purportedly reflect reality when they are necessarily distinct from it. Mazzarella (2006, 476) terms this documentary pretense a "politics of immediation," describing it as "a political practice that, in the name of immediacy and transparency, occludes the potentialities and contingencies embedded in the mediations that comprise and enable social life." The irony of this immediation is that it is precisely a document's capacity for separation from the immediate that makes it so powerful. Moments are fleeting, circumstances change, relationships are reconfigured, and attitudes shift. Documents, however, do none of that. Rather, they persist through time with the promise of capturing what was and bringing it to life again in a new moment and new context,[2] expanding spheres of interaction beyond the face-to-face world and enabling relations with distant actors and institutions (de Soto 2000; Poole 2004).

In everyday life, documents are revered for their role in strengthening the real with the weight of law and ritual. Patricia Ewick and Susan Silbey (1998, xii) observe, "People write letters, save receipts, document events, and sign contracts because they know that 'getting it in writing' makes a difference. It makes what they say more emphatic, more permanent, and more important." Be it birth, marriage, migration, death, divorce, adulthood, inheritance, or property purchase, each of these life events compel individuals to *tramitar*, a grueling, bureaucratic rite of passage that involves being inscribed in a registry and receiving a documentary artifact that evidences this inscription and symbolizes a particular mode of sociolegal personhood. Even after they receive these documents, Peruvians still must deal with the complications created by their strange temporality. Although the purpose of documentation is often to "preserve, represent, or prove the existence of a physical or intellectual phenomenon" (Briet 2006, 10), documents are always created in anticipation of future readings, collapsing past and future in a way that shapes everyday actions and entitlements (Riles 2006). Beyond this, formal documents are also met with the suspicion that they may be form alone, a superficial cover for a different social reality.

RACIALIZED FORMALITY IN A RACIALIZED STATE

In Peru, there is a strong and long-standing association between formality and the white upper classes and, relatedly, between informality and the indigenous lower classes. Contests for recognition and inclusion of historically excluded populations such as indigenous peoples have played out in part in battles over the rights and righteousness of the informals.[3]

Beginning in the 1980s, Peruvian scholars and politicians began to celebrate "informal" Peru as a challenge to exclusionary and anachronistic legal structures established by the colonial and criollo state. In his seminal 1984 book, *Desborde popular y crisis del estado* (Popular overflow and the crisis of the state), Peruvian anthropologist José Matos Mar argues that the historical and hierarchical divide between Spanish *conquistadores* and Andean society was evident in twentieth-century distinctions between "the official Peru of state institutions, parties, banks, businesses, unions, universities, the military and the church, tribunals, bureaucracy and stamped paper" (25) and the informal world of "exocentric associations, community watches, clandestine workshops, street vendors, reciprocity, and mere subsistence" (97).[4] Matos Mar further asserts that Peru's rapid rural-to-urban migration since 1950 had prompted an overflow of the popular classes in Lima that would ultimately produce a "more authentic Peru" as the culture of the informals bled into all sectors of society. For Matos Mar, the rise of the informals was akin to the rise of indigenous peoples and constituted a social movement on their behalf. A similarly influential text, by anthropologists Jürgen Golte and Norma Adams (1990), links urbanization to indigenous revolution in its title, *Los caballos de Troya de los invasores: Estrategias campesinas en la conquista de la gran Lima* (The Trojan horses of the invaders: Peasant strategies in the conquest of the great Lima). This text connects specific migrant survival strategies to ethnic social structures in their places of origin, emphasizing cultural continuity and migrants' capacities to collectively transform lifeways in Lima rather than assimilate to the dominant culture. These anthropological works have been influential within and outside the Peruvian academy. Several of my interlocutors in Pachacútec suggested I begin my research on urban settlements by reading these books. Having been assigned portions of them in high school and university, they considered them important touchstones for understanding Peru's history and present-day political problems. As a result, tacit associations between informals and indigenous migrants are integrated into everyday ideologies and the stories Peruvians tell themselves about themselves (Geertz 1986).

In the hands of economists and policy makers at the height of the Washington Consensus, the slippage between indigeneity and informality was used to link the rights of the informal-indigenous to the rise of capitalism, neoliberalism, and the virtues of market relations for the popular classes. Mario Vargas Llosa, a right-wing author and aspiring Peruvian politician, wrote in his book *Archaic Utopia* (1996, 332), "Thanks to these ex-Indians, cholos, blacks, mulattos, and Asians, . . . for the first time there has developed a popular capitalism and a free market in Peru."[5] Likewise, Peruvian economist Hernando de Soto used his 1986 book *El otro sendero* (published in English in 1989 as *The Other Path*) to popularize the idea that Lima's informal population was creating a new route to development.[6] In contrast to modernist planners and welfare-state developers who viewed shantytowns as spaces of squalor, social breakdown, and potential terrorist uprisings, de Soto and his colleagues saw them as promising sites of economic growth populated by "micro-entrepreneurs" whose poverty had a legal solution in land titles. De Soto argued that official, documented recognition of landholdings would free these assets from the tyranny of the physical world and give them new life in the expanded realm of the market. As de Soto asserts in a treatise on capitalism, "Property is not the house itself but an economic concept about the house, embodied in a legal representation that describes not its physical qualities but rather the economically and socially meaningful qualities we humans have attributed to the house" (2000, 4). Once these landholdings were inscribed in a legal document, they would be transformed into living capital assets that the poor could use to obtain bank credit, start businesses, and lift themselves out of poverty. Reframed as capitalists and micro-entrepreneurs, the indigenous informals were no longer antithetical to formal modernity but an entry point to it. By showing the will to formalize, the informals could overcome the moral and racial connotations of their undocumented state.

The supremacy of the formal and the documented built upon long-standing racial hierarchies that had associated paper documents with white power, privilege, and cultural and moral superiority. During the colonial and early republican eras in Peru, documents facilitated processes of dispossession and all manner of predations upon indigenous populations. Peruvian novelist and anthropologist José María Arguedas describes this process with frightening simplicity: "The judges and the notaries signed papers of every description; that sufficed. . . . The plundering of the ayllus began" (2002 [1941], 6). Colonists demanded written proof of native land claims that only they had the right to distribute, and they defined social institutions through written contracts that made unwritten relations less legitimate by default (Goody 1986). Because documents signified recognition and authorization within the order imposed by the (post)colonial state, written documents had a weight and legitimacy that practice alone did not. As the material of official communication, paper became "the fragile support of the essential" (Kafka 2009, 348).

Indigenous people were not hapless victims in this process. Instead, they learned to use the law, and the legal documents that constituted much of its everyday materiality, to their advantage (Lobo 1982; Seligmann 1995; Thurner 1997). Today, even a superficial inspection of the newspaper stands in Lima reveals the salience of law in everyday life and the popular will to engage it.

Every morning newsstand owners scour the state daily publication, *El Peruano*, for laws that might interest local residents and reprint them for individual resale. Copies of laws governing land titles, small businesses, identity, marriage, and divorce seem to be the most lucrative and are strung up for interested buyers alongside daily newspapers, tabloids, and party propaganda. Although many of my interlocutors said the law could be unjust and served the interests of the wealthy, they also recognized that documentation and the will to legalize made people more righteous and strengthened their positions in disputes with neighbors and authorities.

Popular faith in the value of legal documents that have long been used to oppress the lower classes might be understood as a paradigmatic example of hegemony, in which one class so thoroughly succeeds in putting forth their view of the world that it is accepted as common sense, even by those that this worldview serves to oppress (Gramsci 1971). However, Marisol de la Cadena (2000, 317) argues that hegemony in Peru is not about static domination but rather implies the "endless motion between contestation and acquiescence" as people strategically draw on a network of signs and systems of meaning to advance their own positions. In Peru, law, documents, and the juridical categories they deploy provide the mutually agreed-upon language through which relations of power are negotiated (de la Cadena 2001). Peruvians do not question ideals of documentation or the belief that documents can improve one's rightness and moral standing. Instead, they challenge the legitimacy of one set of documents over another and the extent to which each one accurately reflects social reality.

FIGURE 3.1. A newsstand in central Lima, 2010. The exterior features announcements and reprints of new laws related to property titles, land expropriations, rapid divorce, and recognition of children born out of wedlock. Photo by the author.

FORMALITY IN PRACTICE

Most development programs in Peru begin with formalization, and Pachacútec was rife with formalization campaigns. Land must be formalized before the state can build infrastructure, hospitals, or schools. Organizations must be formalized before they can propose projects or receive assistance from governments and NGOs. Businesses and vendors must be formalized before they can declare that their wares are authentic and avoid police harassment. Individuals are subject to these formalizing processes at each stage in the life course (birth, graduation, adulthood, marriage, death); these are inscribed into a registry, and the individuals are given documents to signal official recognition of their new sociolegal status as wards in need of protection, literate citizens, founding members of new families, or deceased relatives passing on their possessions.

Although formalization is in many ways about legibility and aligning lived reality with official records so that politicians and bureaucrats can govern from afar (Scott 1998), in urban Peru, formalization is also encumbered with a host of social, racial, and moral connotations. The mid-twentieth-century proliferation of squatters, shacks, and shantytowns in Lima's outskirts prompted anxiety among elites for whom the city had long been a stronghold of colonial civility, whiteness, wealth, and order. The presence of indigenous people in Lima upset not only the spatial order but also the dominant ideological order of the day, confounding conventional associations of Indians with rural and whites with urban spaces. Imposing order on these new and illegible urban spaces became a pressing political concern. During my fieldwork I saw these historical dynamics of race, informality, and disorder play out in ways both mundane and spectacular. For clarity's sake, I begin with the spectacular.

I had heard only a few scattered mentions about the land invasion in sector G4 when I was suddenly thrust into the middle of their official recognition proceedings. Right up until the end, the crucial question was recognition as what? Some friends had warned me to stay away from the area because it was still *movido*, unsettled and therefore dangerous since new residents would be wary of outsiders who they suspected might challenge their land claims. Others confided in me about wanting to join the invasion. They were having problems at home or wanted more independence from their families and could think of no other way to escape their circumstances. Across the board, people were curious why G4's legalization was meeting with so much opposition when the regional government had readily supported other area invasions. Although different sides claimed that the G4 settlers were particularly righteous or particularly duplicitous, the dynamic of this debate suggested that G4 was no different from any other invasion. Peru's history of informal urban development and pattern of eventually legalizing illegal land takeovers meant that in real time, land takeovers were simultaneously inside and outside the law. The question of a settlement's legality was determined disjunctively and after the fact (Goodale 2008; Holston 2008). Either the land takeover would be perceived as an assault on the existing order with invaders subject to the full violence of the law, or occupants would successfully demonstrate their dire need for housing and willingness to comply with urban codes, at which point the land grab would be transformed into a state-sanctioned self-help development that discursively aligned with liberal-democratic values of autonomy, entrepreneurship, and grassroots community engagement.

The process of transforming illegal invasions into formal, legal settlements is not simply a common way of accessing low-cost land. As far as many people know, it is the only way. When a man came to Pachacútec's titling office to inquire about obtaining a plot of land legally, functionaries and promoters were at a loss. Officials explained that land titles were only for people who already occupied land without official authorization. Promoters then took the man aside and quietly informed him about which settlements might be amenable to a newcomer like him so he could squat and then subsequently regularize his status. This seemingly irrational system was originally based on a social logic that the government should only provide land to the truly needy. And it was only by living in misery and illegality and risking social and legal criminalization that people could prove they were in need.

I was interviewing Gerald Vega, a lawyer supervising land-title distribution in Pachacútec's Special Project, when he was called to investigate the invasion in G4. When we arrived on site, Vega and a representative from the regional state attorney's office (who described his job by explaining that the state also needs lawyers to defend its rights) climbed up the sand dune toward the far end of the invasion. I hung back in an attempt to distinguish myself from the state representatives who could authorize land claims but was quickly approached by settlers eager to narrate their stories and have me document their living conditions with my camera. They hoped I would relay this visual documentation along with their narratives to the press or a sympathetic government official who would champion their cause. As a community representative guided me from one makeshift structure to the next, he explained,

> The kids are getting sick because of our living conditions, the air quality, the food, the water. All we want is a little bit of help from the state, from the region to get land titles or to be relocated elsewhere. . . . Look at these living conditions. It's unfair! Look at this woman. She just got back from the hospital. Look at all her medicines!

The settlers argued that they were hardworking families who were willing to collaborate with the proper authorities. The problem was that they could not figure out who the proper authorities were. They described numerous violent encounters with land traffickers and police in the battle for this barren patch of land, approximately 50 meters wide by 100 meters long. In subsequent interviews, residents went into more detail, with stories of men beaten until their clothes were stripped, pregnant women struck by police, and men sent on horseback to disperse crowds and trample straw homes. "Like a broken record, those images play in my head over and over again," one woman explained, her voice fading off into a blank stare.

As I was talking with residents, the lawyers had been registering them. They asked squatters to stand outside their makeshift houses so it would be easier to link their names and ID numbers to land in the new settlement. There were seventy individuals on site when we arrived, but the *dirigente* said there were an additional two hundred land claimants and promised to provide their information as well. The settlers seemed pleased with the encounter and chanted Vega's name as we left. Vega subtly shook his head with a mix of remorse and disbelief, as if to the beat of the chorus. "Six months ago, I came here to evict them and they tried to take my head off," he said. "This time, I'm like their savior." When the doors to their black SUV had slammed shut, the state attorney explained that he was also conflicted. He said the information they collected would be used to initiate the "corresponding legal action." Right now, though, it was unclear what that was. It might mean land titles, as the settlers hoped, or it might be used to press charges against them for illegally invading the area. "It makes me sad to be taking all their information," he said. "There were young women there who are eighteen, nineteen years old, and now they're going to have a criminal record. And what's more, the *dirigente* said she'd give me more names later."

State attention and inscription was always double-edged. The illegal invasion could remain on settlers' police records for life, but it could also serve as official evidence that they had maintained continuous possession of the land and might therefore further their claims to it. This ambivalence contributed to Pachacutanos' anxiety about engaging with the state, which they experienced through a disjointed series of nerve-wracking moments, when it was unclear whether the state would guarantee their rights or threaten their gains and potentially their lives (Poole 2004).

In this instance, things worked out in the settlers' favor. When I visited G4 a few weeks later, Charo, one of the more loquacious settlers, told me

FIGURE 3.2. Settlers rally for land rights in Pachacútec, 2010. Following an encounter between settlement leaders and regional government officials, settlers chant Gerald Vega's name in hopes he will help legalize their land claims. Photo by the author.

the good news. Within a few short days, architects, engineers, and cadastral surveyors would arrive to divide the area into legally sanctioned lots. "It won't be long now," Charo said. "Very soon we will have our guarantee of possession." Proud of their accomplishments, Charo and her comrades described the invasion simultaneously in terms of long-standing patterns of discrimination and as a battle between their own righteous community and the various corrupt, mafioso *dirigentes* who used government connections to malign them. Charo recalled, "They had said we were delinquents, thieves, terrorists, miscreants. . . . That's how they described us. . . . So we had to go to the authorities, to the press and say that no sir, we are not delinquents, we are not traffickers. We are respectable people who need a house in which to live."

Having witnessed the precariousness of the legalization process, I asked why she thought things had finally tipped in their favor: "How did you manage to convince them? If they had been saying that you were delinquents and miscreants for months already and had everyone on their side, how did you manage to convince them otherwise?" Charo responded thoughtfully but assertively, "A person demonstrates that with actions, behaving well in the eyes of society, . . . doing the documents and everything by the proper channels."

Doing the documents. It seemed like such a trivial thing, and yet, according to Charo, it was the difference between delinquents and the deserving poor, miscreants and citizens, enemies of order and the righteous impoverished. Doing your documents signaled a commitment to law, modernity, and development, while not doing them implied subversion and clandestine activity, even if the activity was as overt as a land takeover. Charo was adamant that the abuses they had suffered were a "complete violation of their human rights" but admitted that "one also has to recognize one's own errors, because we entered here without documents to take possession of a green area that was set aside to maintain the environment. . . . It was something illicit. We took possession illicitly." In Charo's description, documents had the power to make actions and actors visible and in so doing, give them the moral high ground. Documents were supposed to increase their transparency, solidifying their ability to be known in a modern bureaucratic sense and sacrificing their capacity to negotiate the meaning of their presence down the line (McFarlane and Waibel 2016).

Despite Charo's confession of illicitness, other aspects of her story highlighted the way documentation and the performance of formality helped to constitute settlers' actions as morally legitimate from the beginning. She said they initially made the decision to invade at a monthly neighborhood meeting based on broad agreement about their mutual necessity.

> We touched on the topic of people who were lodged in houses where other people had land titles, lots that are the property of other people. Since the majority of people were like that, the secretaries of G4 decided to expand housing for those who needed homes of their own . . . and solicit land from the regional government.

Charo and her neighbors inscribed this decision in a *libro de actas* (a notarized minutes book), acquired police documents to indicate that the *dirigentes* who opposed the *ampliación* (settlement expansion) were themselves "delinquents,"[7] and then performed this virtuous formality for authorities.

First, they handed these documents to municipal authorities and requested that their land claims be inscribed in official government ledgers. When this failed to initiate more robust legalization proceedings, they protested outside the municipality "to request that the authorities listen to us . . . to make them know the truth . . . that they see our problem, that they see our necessity . . . [and] to make them see what those [other] men are like." Once they had been granted a meeting, however, they had to change their tone. "[When you] go to the office to talk, you're not going to talk arrogantly," Charo said. "You have to speak with delicacy, with *educación* [education and good manners]. If you speak, they understand you. If you yell, they don't understand anything, not even if you yourself went, Kris." In implicating me, Charo indicated that the social capital granted to me by virtue of my white foreignness would not matter if I didn't behave in a stately, cooperative manner. As the settlement was being negotiated, formality was clearly a project related to documents, but getting those documents required the performance of a particular formal disposition. Formality was both a means and an end, a "pretense at obeying rules, following the law," and a resource that could be strategically "woven through certain affectual contexts" to situate oneself in a position of righteousness, for others and for one's own sense of self (McFarlane and Waibel 2016, 6).

FORMALITY AS PHYSICAL-LEGAL ALIGNMENT

The process of formalizing the settlement did not end with that one-time office meeting but instead involved a complex negotiation between the G4 settlers and the original urban plans. Here, formalization required regularizing through a process known as *saneamiento físico legal*, a form of legal purification that brought the physical settlement into alignment with the juridical and bureaucratic imaginary of it. The juridical term *saneamiento* has the same linguistic root as the Spanish verb *sanar*, "to heal," and processes of *saneamiento físico legal* are broadly associated with health, hygiene, cleansing, and their incumbent moral connotations (Echegaray 1887). When Peruvian settlers take over public land with no previous private owners, the process of *saneamiento físico legal* is relatively straightforward. In places with more complex ownership histories, this spatial-legal cleansing involves accounting for all other legal claims, gathering them together in a file and then nullifying what came before by placing a new act on top of it. It is a process of clarification through documentary accumulation and consolidation.

Sometimes, settlement residents and the physical worlds they created prompted changes in urban plans. In these instances, settlers can be understood as "insurgent citizens" who, in demanding the legalization of their settlements, remake law and society in their image (Holston 2008). This is what occurred when the settlers in G4 forced Pachacútec's green areas to be rezoned for housing. More often, though, settlers were forced to acquiesce to official plans and legal prescriptions; the settlers were declared informal and delinquent until they brought themselves back into alignment with the plans and the law.

In places like Pachacútec, where property relations were still in flux, the negotiations of written law and physical reality were particularly visible. The process of *saneamiento físico legal* often involved physically moving homes, deconstructing and reconstructing them as legal ownership was negotiated and neighborhoods were redesigned. In a single settlement negotiation, people might have to move their houses several times; the more established the house, the more violent the relocation procedure. As a result, where property rights were unclear, residents often opted to use cheaper and weaker housing materials that they intended to be temporary. Precarious construction is where the logics of contested legality meet the aesthetics of poverty. Because housing materials were a key means by which state agents assessed poverty levels, poverty and informality were inextricably linked through precariousness and temporariness. Meanwhile, a stable claim to land and corresponding willingness to use sturdier building materials were more likely to signal wealth and civic virtue.

The ideal of formality as a physical-legal alignment permeated other realms of life as well. Even though many street vendors in Pachacútec and Ventanilla were licensed, they were considered informal because of their tendency to stray from their assigned street corners in their efforts to capture more business. In other words, they were informal because they moved beyond the boundaries set forth in their licenses. Likewise, during my fieldwork, the district government was on a mission to formalize brick-and-mortar businesses, promising that a one-time inscription fee of fifty soles would make the business formal for life. That is, of course, unless anything about the business changed. If the business's spatial footprint grew or shifted or it started selling different categories of goods or allowing people inside the premises rather than catering to them on the street, then the business would once again be informal and illegal until owners regularized it, updating its inscription and paying whatever was necessary for that process. Promoters for this business registration effort explained that formalization was not simply a means of extracting revenue but also a governmental good in itself. In their descriptions, the municipality needed to know the reality of Pachacútec if it was to maintain order, promote development, and act as a modern state.

Residents and community leaders in Pachacútec frequently echoed the notion that an administration's political legitimacy depended in large part on its ability to keep administrative pace with local conditions and ensure that what was in the records aligned with what was in the world. A *dirigente* in Pachacútec's Pilot Project, for example, said development delays in Pachacútec were due to the lack of up-to-date information about the area's conditions. Although the INEI had conducted a census in 2005 and again in 2007, by the time the information was fully elaborated and statistics were available at the subdistrict level in 2010, interlocutors suggested it was already out of date. The *dirigente* said, "There are no reliable statistics that reflect our reality. . . . Those statistics came from the 2007 census. That was three years ago, and now things have changed. What we need is another census that can give us updated statistics." For this *dirigente*, the only valid information was immediate information. A development project based on anything less was doomed to fail.

EXPANSIONS OF SOCIOLEGAL PERSONHOOD

State agents and Peruvian citizens alike valued an alignment between official records and lived reality. But formalization did more than capture reality. It brought new beings into existence, creating sociolegal entities such as *propietarios* (property holders), a legal category that combines person and property into a single entity; *asentamientos humanos* (human settlements), a legal category for nonurbanized neighborhoods that makes them eligible for particular forms of state assistance; and *organizaciones sociales de base* (social base organizations), local social assistance cooperatives that register with and are subsidized by state institutions. Although state agencies encouraged these juridical entities because they facilitated the work of governance, the burden of producing them ultimately fell to citizens and demanded the performance of a kind of super citizenship that generated new civic identities, juridical subjectivities, and uncanny political possibilities.

Property Holders

Owning land and becoming a *propietario* is central to ideals of citizenship and propriety in Peru. For this reason, obtaining land titles, state-issued documents that certify and help secure ownership status, was the principal objective of settlers in G4. Charo and her companions explained that they needed land titles and houses of their own in order to live in a dignified manner and have decent places to raise their children. From a governance perspective, distributing land titles transforms land into a standardized, governable commodity while also transforming "lords into landlords, peasants into tenants" (Appadurai 1996, 126). Through land titles, new varieties of legal land-persons are constituted, binding land, paper, and person together in a way that can be split for the purpose of marketing "while retaining some of the metonymic force that binds territories and titles to named persons" (Appadurai 1996, 126).

For many development programs, creating these territory-paper-person hybrids, glossed through the term "land titles," is a necessary precursor for intervention. For instance, FONCODES, Peru's social development fund, measures poverty based on the *lack* of five urban amenities: electricity, water and sewer pipes, health clinics, primary education institutions, and land titles. Although land titles may seem a less pressing concern than something like piped water, areas must be fully titled and *saneados* (cleansed, clarified, updated) before any other construction can take place. A field agent for FONCODES in Lima explained that FONCODES could intervene only after COFOPRI, the agency charged with formalizing titles, had inscribed the land into the public registry: "You can't construct on land unless you know who that land belongs to. . . . Once the land is *saneado*, then you can construct normally." He went on to state that FONCODES considered electrification a basic necessity in part because it prompted squatters to formalize their settlements.

> Electrification is a necessity because without it people are getting their electricity in a clandestine manner. Electrification helps them get it formally. Additionally, this pushes the theme of land formalization because Edelnor [the electric company] needs to see proof of possession. So with the possibility of electrification, people mobilize to formalize themselves. Many don't formalize, but for electrification they have to comply with certain requisites, they have to be *saneados*.

In this framing, formalization is not simply a precursor to development initiatives but part of its defining substance.

Communities

Before people could request individual property titles, they had to be recognized as a geopolitical organization. When I asked FONCODES field agents what happened to poor people who were not organized or whose neighborhoods were not recognized as official *asentamientos humanos*, they dismissed my concern. One field agent said, "Here that simply doesn't happen. . . . The *dirigentes* here are very astute. All of this about formalizing the land is the first thing they do." The field agent went on to explain that the state could never target a place that had not been inscribed in the official registry, not because it was illegal but because unrecognized pueblos simply did not exist. "Impossible. All of the pueblos are registered. . . . They are organized. They are not isolated. They understand that unity makes strength."

I was fascinated by the agents' insistence that organized communities were a natural fact of life because, ethnographically, it seemed that the arduous process of formalization was itself integral to the construction of these collectivities. The community and its representatives first had to be recognized by individual political administrations and legally constituted through bureaucratic paperwork. It would then take a team of surveyors, engineers, architects, and planners to verify and, if necessary, amend its on-paper existence before the territorial organization could be inscribed in the public registries.

Yet before any of this could take place, community members had to agree on what sort of territorial organization they wanted to be. This decision had implications for the sorts of claims the community could make on the state and for the individual land-person entities and juridical subjectivities subsequently created. Within Pachacútec, communities generally had to choose between formalizing as an *asentamiento humano* or a *cooperativa* (cooperative), and battles raged between neighbors over which designation would be more beneficial. Some of Pachacútec's older inhabitants had formalized their individual neighborhoods as cooperatives because that afforded them the most benefits at the time. Later arrivals, who had taken over unoccupied and ostensibly abandoned land, were pushing to reformalize certain areas as *asentamientos humanos*, settlements that were more readily associated with poverty and would therefore have greater access to government assistance. Cooperativists resisted this change. They feared that reclassification would force them to update their land claims, which could subject them to new fees and regulations and put their current land claims at risk. Olivia, a prominent *dirigente* in Pachacútec's Special Project, half-jokingly referred to one of her neighbors as her "institutional enemy" because they were on opposite sides of the cooperative-settlement debate. It was a phrase that suggested the importance of juridical identities in producing interests and subject positions while also acknowledging the existence of circumstances in which these differences might be put aside.

Social Base Organizations

Although property and territory expand legal personhood in important ways, the formalization of social groups was also considered valuable in its own right. By creating new juridical identities, groups of Peruvians could have an existence beyond their immediate worlds that would be recognized and respected by larger organizations and outlast the members who founded it. Lisa, the head of an NGO that tried to curb child labor in Pachacútec, explained it this way:

> We create *redes juveniles* [youth networks]. . . . The goal is to get kids to care about their community and to take part in promoting projects and activities to build community and improve it. Sometimes these groups formalize. . . . Being formal is a good thing because it lets you do more. It lets you participate at the level of the municipality, and you have access to the budget. When you're not formal you can still do things but smaller, at the level of your immediate community. Also, the issue of the name. Let's say Sara, José, and Juan form a youth group. If it's not formal, when they leave, the group disappears. But if they are formal, if they have a name as a group, the group continues regardless of the individuals who are involved in it. They leave their positions and other people take them. They can also ask for things on behalf of the group. For example, Juan and Sara can ask for money from an organization but probably won't get it, whereas the group can send a formal document and make the request in the name of the group.

However, formalization demanded such extraordinary effort that most of Lisa's youth networks never achieved this. "For this," she said, "you need a *directiva*, a certain type of political organization with a president, a secretary, et cetera, and you also have to pay something. As a result, not everyone makes it to this level."

My experiences with the mothers clubs of Pachacútec bore this out. For the twelve weeks they met, the only subject of the meetings was how to formalize the clubs so they could request donations from the municipality and other institutions to finance local children's activities. By the end of the twelve weeks, only one of the fourteen clubs had secured enough signatures, dues, and information from members to formalize their organization. Promoters from the municipality helped the group celebrate this accomplishment with a formal ceremony. Rows of white plastic chairs were placed in front of the neighborhood meeting house, and green and white streamers were hung to designate the celebration area. One functionary described the purpose of the pomp and circumstance.

> They're legalizing. Now they are going to be legal with their recognition from the municipality. The assistant director from Organizaciones

> Vecinales [Neighborhood Organizations, a municipal office that oversees community groups] is going to read them their responsibilities and oaths, explain to them the work they have to complete, and all of that. It's a formality, but it makes things more serious, which is a good thing.

The ceremony, speeches, and certificates all helped to affirm the importance of legal recognition. It was a moment when the quotidian drudgery of proceduralism was transformed into an event, a ritual, and a rite of passage. The ceremony helped reproduce the stately habitus of formality and asserted the value of formalization as generating a weightier legal identity capable of engaging other entities like the state and the municipality on more equal footing. Yet, the emotional significance of this moment had also been enabled by the quotidian drudgery that preceded it. It had built up slowly over time as organizers chased down signatures, shuttled between offices, suffered countless institutional rejections and humiliations, and abandoned other responsibilities in pursuit of this sociolegal identity.

The day after the ceremony, I spoke with Karen about how the mothers club in her settlement was progressing in its formalization efforts. She began matter-of-factly, but by the end she was approaching tears.

> Yes, yes, we're getting close. We just lack a few of the documents of the *mamás*, their ID cards and all of that. . . . But what happens is many of the *mamás* don't want to collaborate. They say yes, yes, but when it comes time to do something, they're not at home. . . . And without the recognition, no one takes you seriously. . . . I've been so disappointed with all the rejections from the institutions I ask to collaborate. For weeks, every Sunday I go to different institutions to ask for help, but nothing. There was even a congressman who said he would help but only after I sent the member registry and everything, but in the end nothing happened. . . . What's more, we're having problems with the *directiva*. I'm only the vice president, but the other president had to work, and another replacement had a baby, so there are problems. But I'm trying. And it's hard. It's hard to make time to be at all the meetings, because I do *trabajos temporales* [temporary, sporadic work], and so any time a job comes up, you have to be available to take advantage of it. Whatever job comes up, you have to go out. Last Wednesday I had to miss a job because of the mothers club meeting. I shouldn't have done that, but I thought, if I don't go, who will?

FIGURE 3.3. Mothers club formalization ceremony, 2009. Photo by the author.

Karen's narrative highlights the sacrifice and singular devotion required to formalize social groups and why formalization is an accomplishment worth celebrating. She illuminates the physically and emotionally draining work of compiling lists, obtaining signatures, and attending meetings and indicates that these efforts are worthwhile because "without the recognition, no one takes you seriously." Once one institution officially recognizes the existence of an organization, other institutions are likely to follow and may even seek out these organizations as part of their community outreach work. Karen's narrative also provides insight into why some Peruvians critique these intense and often frenetic forms of state engagement that may require forgoing other obligations and opportunities such as parenting and paid employment.

DEJADOS, *VIVOS*, AND THE NEVER-DESERVING POOR

Thus far I have described relatively straightforward relations between formality, maintaining documents, performances of active citizenship, and making oneself legible to the state and worthy of assistance. Indeed, the way Peruvians talk about documents and deservingness suggests that documents are integral to how the international development regime of inclusive liberalism plays out in this context. Unlike neoliberal development regimes, which encouraged the state to abandon its social welfare functions and trust the free market to care for its citizens, under inclusive liberalism the state is expected to be responsive to citizens and shield the poor from some of the dangers of market capitalism, provided the poor are "actively engaged in shaping their own futures" (Hickey 2010, 1141). Under inclusive liberalism the poor are to be "empowered via their own agency, whereby they transform themselves into entrepreneurial agents of the market economy whilst also mobilizing themselves as community-based citizens" (1141). Formalizing is a way to perform this agency that, ideally, produces an active, engaged citizen who is legible to the state. Within Peru's dominant cultural logics, this ideal of performative citizenship through documents is almost impossible to attain, particularly as it relates to social assistance programs. The characteristics of *dejadez* and *viveza* are frequently attributed to the poor in relation to their use of documents in ways that frame them as unworthy of social assistance.

Dejado is derived from the verb *dejar*, meaning to leave behind or give up. When applied to Peru's poor, it is often coupled with terms like *flojo* (lazy) and *conformista* (conformist), suggesting that the poor have resigned themselves to their circumstances and don't care enough to lift themselves out of poverty. Instead, they are accused of waiting for handouts in a development era when being a passive recipient of state assistance is morally untenable. The term *dejado* is also frequently used to describe people who are undocumented or whose documents are out of date.

When I asked municipal promoters how the identity-card distribution campaign was progressing, Hernán explained that half of the applications were pending because "people need to finish getting their documents together. . . . Basically the problem is the parents are very *dejados*. They just leave their documents in the muni and don't finish getting the requisites."

Carla had a similar critique.

> The *mamás* don't move by themselves. You have to be on top of them every step of the way. . . . Really, they should be the ones pushing all of this because they are the ones who benefit. But if you don't follow them, *lo dejan por un lado* [they let it fall by the wayside]. . . . They should be the ones going out and determining for themselves what needs to be done. We give them flyers with all the information about where they should go to figure this out, but they never approach [the agencies].

In saying parents should actively pursue formalization, approaching state agencies and identifying requirements for themselves, Carla echoes a central tenet of inclusive liberalism, that the poor had to be transformed from "passive subjects into active citizens" (Hickey 2010, 1142).

Some authorities argued that denying services to people who did not have their documents in order was the only way to overcome this documentary *dejadez*. The head of social services in another peripheral district explained, "Es por flojera y dejadez [It's because of laziness and apathy] that parents don't register their kids. Only when someone demands it of them, it's only then that they begin to worry about this." Given the cost of everyday legality, this logic seems to bear out. Under normal circumstances, legality was a privilege of the wealthy. It had to be purchased in a lump sum from a notary or paid for in dribs and drabs through processing fees, transportation costs, and time off work. Laws and legislators changed often enough that what was legal one day might not be legal the next. For a struggling family, it therefore made good economic sense to avoid formalizing until circumstances demanded it or there was a campaign that made the process easier.

The term *campaña* (campaign) was code for an exceptional moment of state assistance. Campaigns allowed politicians to maintain the norm of prohibitively complex and expensive legality while marking themselves as benevolent individuals, sensitive to the problems of their constituents. The use of the term "campaign" for these temporary initiatives conveniently highlights how exceptions to the rules are deployed in clientelist and electoral politics. It was never entirely clear when these exceptions would be made, but they were frequent enough that one could wait for a moment when a campaign aligned with a need for regularization. Alternatively, if the need for regularization was widespread, constituents could petition for these exceptions.

An NGO operating on Pisco's outskirts had offered to purchase public school uniforms for all students with national ID cards. Given this opportunity, the parents association and school administrators submitted a formal request to RENIEC for a free ID campaign. The local RENIEC branch had limited funds to provide free IDs to Peru's neediest children. It was through these formal requests that officials determined who these needy children were. Constructing need by sending paper through the proper channels is in many ways the opposite of *dejadez*. It is a prime example of ideal social welfare citizenship in which individuals tone down their demands and present requests to benefit from the state's largesse responsibly and politely (Hickey 2010, 1151). Still, this behavior evokes *dejadez* as the supposed precursor to the petition, such as in this assistant school director's assessment:

> The NGO is demanding that all the kids have IDs because everyone has a right to an identity. So we went to RENIEC to request support, that they provide free IDs because there are many poor parents who don't have money to process their child's ID. . . . RENIEC will do [up to three hundred] and that's it. The NGO wants everyone to have their identity. Many parents don't get it out of laziness. They say they don't have money to get the ID. But they sure do have money to go drinking on Saturdays and Sundays!

The assistant director's remark illuminates the easy slippage between documentary *dejadez* and its opposite, *viveza*.

Viveza implies being too familiar with documents and too good at navigating the bureaucracies associated with obtaining state resources for a person to remain above suspicion. The periodic clamor for sweeping government campaigns and the corresponding influx of institutional resources generate predictable opportunities for those with the knowledge and social networks to exploit them. The effect, Peruvians explain, is a society governed by the "ley del más vivo," law of the most cunning. Unlike the "law of the jungle," which references the dog-eat-dog dynamics that dominate in a mythic state of nature, the "law of the most cunning" implies being embedded in social networks and inundated with bureaucratic regulations. Succeeding in this environment requires specialized knowledge of how to navigate in/formal bureaucratic relations and an ability to exploit the space between lived reality and official documentary representation.

"To be *vivo* is not always a bad thing," a Peruvian colleague explained. "You hear it a lot when a person is very passive and doesn't do anything. People tell them 'You have to be *más vivo*.'" That is, you have to be more alert, more proactive, more willing to figure out the system to make your own luck and your own future. More often, though, I heard that the *viveza peruana* was one of the nation's greatest failings. Julio, an amateur philosopher and pirated-DVD salesman in Ventanilla's market, explained it this way: "Peruvians have their reputation. Internationally, they hate Peruvians. Why? Because look, the Peruvian isn't lazy, he's a very hard worker. But he's also clever, and due to necessity, he finds ways to get money illegitimately. . . . That is the *viveza peruana*." Paradoxically, the same practices that connoted ideal participatory citizenship also generated accusations of *viveza*. This dynamic is especially marked in relation to social base organizations.

Gaining formal recognition as a social base organization implied extraordinary work and sacrifice that would ultimately be rewarded with an expanded sociolegal identity that could be used to make claims on statelike entities. Creating this identity was a key motivation for forming organized communities in the first place. In contrast to FONCODES agents' explanations that organized communities were naturally occurring entities, community leaders and municipal employees insisted that the community does not organize itself. The existence of these organizations also made it easier for statelike entities to connect with area residents. Institutions that helicoptered into Pachacútec expecting to locate truly needy individuals often had to rely on mediators from *comedores populares* and Vaso de Leche branches to identify them. Formalization thus often led to multiplying recognitions, both because it is easier for donating institutions to locate formal organizations that are known by government officials and have their information inscribed in municipal ledgers, and because, through the process of formalizing, people learned to navigate bureaucracies and formed reciprocal relations with people inside the state apparatus.

Yet in organizing to be formally recognized as truly needy and thus entitled to various forms of state assistance, people paradoxically positioned themselves outside ideologies of who the truly needy were. In much official and popular discourse, the poor are portrayed as excluded and marginalized. The truly needy are those who have been invisible to authorities and left out of modernity. Once individuals formed an organization that had been recognized and received some form of assistance, they therefore fell outside the colloquial category of the truly needy. Their status as official social assistance recipients even marked them as *vivos*, people who knew how to work the system and access state benefits, perhaps at the expense of not-yet-included and thus needier individuals.

I first noticed this phenomenon when a new NGO in Pachacútec asked for my help locating truly needy individuals who might be worthy of charitable donations. My suggestions that they locate a *comedor popular* or a mothers club were flatly rejected. "Don't you know any *pobrecitos* [poor little people], or communities that haven't been recognized? That no one is helping?" Although social base organizations were founded in part to provide avenues for social assistance, it seemed that in organizing themselves and becoming legal entities, truly needy individuals disappeared. They went from individual social cases to morally problematic political organizations.

Another important factor in the social construction of *viveza* is the disjuncture between the temporality of need and the temporality of poverty assistance. The way my Peruvian interlocutors described poverty assistance suggested that poverty was only moral and worthy of assistance insofar as it was temporary, a product of emergency circumstances requiring only passing, punctuated relief. Yet this ideology is at odds with policies that encourage formalizing grassroots poverty-relief organizations. By the time a social base organization was running efficiently, months or years had passed, and the founding members had official recognition and a form of social capital that placed them inside the networks of the state. This may be one reason government-subsidized assistance programs like Vaso de Leche and *comedores populares* were frequently criticized for not adequately targeting the poor (Málaga 2010).[8] In the course of formalizing their organizations, needy individuals had become established community members, often with well-constructed homes and robust social networks. In gaining official recognition as the deserving poor, peripheral residents went from being members of the excluded masses to gatekeepers of state assistance. Once an organization's status had been formalized, members were reluctant to give it up and could use their knowledge of bureaucratic practice to maintain it, as Milagros did when she borrowed ID cards and forged signatures to keep a Vaso de Leche branch in her neighborhood. It was in moments like these, when documents stood in for individuals and knowledge of the system made it easier to retain benefits, that "ghosts" appeared and "the mafia" was born.

SPECTERS OF DOCUMENTS

specter \'spek-tər\ *n*
1: a visible disembodied spirit
2: something that haunts or perturbs the mind

MERRIAM-WEBSTER'S COLLEGIATE DICTIONARY, 11TH EDITION

Ghosts and mafia are some of the specters of documents in Peru, the shadows or malevolent refractions that emerge as documents generate new social realities while purporting merely to reflect and communicate existing ones (Hetherington 2011; Hull 2012). Ghosts, *fantasmas*, as Peruvians call them, are the more straightforward of these documentary anomalies. They appear when a document exists with no real-world basis to support it. "Ghost workers" were produced when a legal identity was on the books but the pay was going to someone else, typically the purported employer.

"Ghost committees" emerged when a social or political organization existed in name but not in practice. This was the flip side of the perdurance that Lisa of the child-labor NGO described as a primary benefit of formalizing a social group. For several organizations I encountered, formalization was the only thing they managed to accomplish before the groups ceased to function.

Sometimes these ghosts seemed friendly, as when a construction supervisor I knew put ghost employees on the payroll so he could pay workers who did not have up-to-date ID cards. They had deserted Peru's army during the internal violence of the 1980s and did not want to update their identities for fear of government reprisal. More often, though, ghosts seemed to serve nefarious purposes. Pachacutanos complained that ghosts, conjured when land titles were distributed to people who did not need homes as immediate residences, occupied far too many area houses, leading to the creation of virtual *pueblos fantasmas*. Olinda, the president of a *comedor popular*, contended, "It was a mistake to give property titles to those people . . . because once they got them they closed up and left. Here we have many empty lots. . . . Some people have sold them, but a few of them, because they have titles, don't even have *esteras* [straw mats] on them." Housing theorists have argued that land titles, as legal representations of property, promote economic development by giving property a life beyond its physical structure. Residents of Pachacútec, however, have found that in many instances, the resulting ghosts made poor neighbors. They contributed little to community life and development, and the spaces they haunted provided sites where drugs and delinquency thrived.

Manipulating ghosts was a presumed specialty of the "mafia," a more complex specter of documents that resulted from their capacity to simultaneously connect people to and exclude them from the state. To understand the full meaning of this term requires examining the diverse ways it is deployed in everyday conversation. The conventional meaning of "mafia," as a highly organized crime syndicate, was frequently invoked to reference mysterious child-trafficking rings, the fear of which had been used to justify the child ID campaigns that Peru initiated in 2005. An employee of DEMUNA, the municipal child welfare agency, contended,

> They steal children and they put them to work in inhuman conditions. The big, well-organized mafias get identity cards for them. And if the children are not already documented, there is nothing we can do. But if they are documented . . . it will show up that this kid is not [who the mafia says they are], but one who was reported as stolen.

In this instance, it seemed the only defense against the fake, ill-intentioned officialdom of big, well-organized mafias was the legitimate, beneficent officialdom of the state.

In other cases, there was clear slippage between the idea of an organized crime syndicate and the everyday uses and abuses of paper and power. When disgruntled employees approached the *agencia* to denounce their employers' corrupt practices, receptionists couldn't tell if they were describing mafia activity, standard labor practices, or both. The employees stated that they had spent weeks going house to house recruiting paying clients for an association of lawyers and psychologists. An employee said, "We are supposed to get paid 700 soles a month for our recruitment work, but someone told us this is a scam and that the boss is never going to pay us."

One of the plaintiffs showed the receptionist an informational flyer for the organization. After examining it, the receptionist exclaimed, "This is the real mafia! They've got offices in central Lima, email addresses, phone numbers. It's the mafia." Yet after a beat, she remarked that most employers in Pachacútec used these mafia techniques. "It's like that in most jobs. They have a monthlong training or something, and if you do well, that's when they contract you for the work."

Most often, though, the term "mafia" was used to describe the knowledge, practices, and networks of people and paper that allowed some groups to systematically benefit from state institutions while others were excluded. "Mafias" were therefore prevalent in government institutions, universities, and among recurrent recipients of state assistance, such as the poor who had learned to navigate the networks of people and paper that constituted the state. This particular meaning of "mafia" first became clear to me during a lunch meeting with FONCODES employees in 2009. Most of them were Apristas, members of then President Alan García's political party, who had managed various state-run social assistance programs since García's election in 2006. Eventually, César Ramírez, whom FONCODES agents described as one of the president's *hombres de confianza* (right-hand men), joined us, and the conversation turned to problems between the national government and regional administrations in emergency zones like Pisco and Bagua.[9] When I became visibly confused by the slang, acronyms, and nicknames being tossed around, César began to explain. The issue was that people in one regional government were accusing local Apristas of being "mafiosos." I reconstruct his explanation here:

> They say we're favoring our own members and not giving equal treatment to newly elected regional administrations. But in reality not

> everyone knows how to administrate. When you want to do a project, you have to go through certain *trámites* [documentary procedures], and the people who are complaining haven't gone through all the legal requirements, or they don't know them. So they complain when they see other people getting stuff from the government and they don't. The ironic thing is that they accuse us of favoritism, but the regional governments are the most mafioso there is. They don't know how to spend the money they get because they don't have capable personnel. The mayor gets elected and gives jobs to his supporters, and there is no one left who knows the system. They don't know how to legally process things [*tramitar cosas*]. To get money from the government, there are *trámites*, and if you don't know how to do this it takes more time to get your money. Sometimes we also put in our own people. But at least the people we put in can figure out the system and get things done.

Although César was trying to deny the mafia accusations, his explanation seemed to affirm them. There was a sociolegal and bureaucratic system in place, and Apristas' knowledge of the system and willingness to help party members navigate it marked them as a special group. They were also willing to help friends or party members work through or get around the formal rules, while others were simply blocked by them. Much as James Holston has found in his analysis of state-society relations in Brazil (2008, 5), the phrase "For my friends everything; for enemies, the law" aptly describes the potentially exclusionary effects of law in this context, as only those without personal connections have to contend with its most Kafkaesque complexity.

As César pointed out, it was not only Apristas who managed and materialized this sort of mafia. It was also evident in local and regional governments and appeared in Pachacútec as particular individuals developed knowledge of documentary procedures and social relations with bureaucrats that seemed to give them privileged access to state benefits. Vicario was one of these individuals.

Vicario had been a prominent *dirigente* in Pachacútec for as long as I had worked there. Over time he had become well acquainted with the operations of the municipal, provincial, and regional governments and developed friendly relations with functionaries in these administrations. Even during periods when he abdicated his official community leadership position so he could focus on other responsibilities, he remained an important mediator between his community in sector K1 and local government officials. Some people thought of him as a great *dirigente*, adept at following documents and getting things done. Others described him as "mafioso" because of the seeming ease with which he navigated government bureaucracies to formalize organizations and access social programs.

One incident in particular seemed to affirm Vicario's well-connected status, compelling even his friends to describe him as "bien vivo" (very wily) with a mix of disdain and admiration. One weekend he led a group of neighbors in using black plastic tarp to cordon off the empty land adjacent to the K1 settlement. The reason, he said, was to deter invaders and preserve the area as a future ecological park. Several months later the tarp came down to reveal dozens of shacks made of aged plywood so it would seem to outsiders that the shacks were as old as the rest of K1. For Pachacutanos and local authorities who might know better, Vicario produced documents that showed the inhabitants of K1 had agreed to expand the settlement to alleviate crowding, though it is equally likely the new houses would remain empty, potentially populating Pachacútec with even more ghosts until new owners found it convenient to inhabit or sell their land. The land takeover in K1 occurred at the same time as the one in G4 but did not meet with any of the resistance Charo and her comrades described. This was in part because Vicario knew the system, whereas settlers in G4 admittedly did not know who the appropriate authorities were. However, it was also because Vicario had personal relationships with the right officials. When I asked one of the regional governor's advisers why they had permitted the K1 land takeover while opposing the one in G4, he commented simply, "A veces por amigos me hago el loco" (Sometimes for friends I play dumb and look the other way).

BIEN VIVO: ALIVE AND WILY

Documents are woven into Peruvians' everyday lives in complex and morally ambivalent ways. They simultaneously fix facts and bring new and potentially unruly elements into being. Documents play an important role in formalization procedures that involve aligning the social and physical world with the official imaginaries that governments have of it. They are also integral to the performance of formality as an affective disposition, a promise of transparency and integrity, and an assurance that one's identity will remain stable through time and consistent across contexts. Ironically, one proves this transparency through the accumulation of documents that do as much to produce a new reality as they do to represent an existing one. This paradox results in part from the complex temporality embedded in documents. Their ability to fix and represent reality beyond the immediate physical world makes them incredibly powerful but also renders them suspect. As the world changes, documents are transformed from representations of reality to a misleading cover for it.

Things grow even more complex when the temporalities of documents and formality meet the temporality of poverty assistance. In Peru, formalizing plays a vital role in creating active citizens and producing relations with the state that contemporary development theory argues is crucial for eliminating poverty. Yet while formality involves recognizing and fixing poverty in specific places and on particular persons, to be morally acceptable in this context, poverty must be ephemeral and previously unseen. In this framework, sustained assistance for the truly needy presents an ideological contradiction. Having been identified by the state, the truly needy disappear and potentially come to occupy the ranks of the mafia.

These documentary dynamics form the social terrain on which Peru's war on poverty plays out. Here we see that the so-called marginal areas that state antipoverty programs target are not unseen sites outside the state; rather, they are often inundated by state forms and practices that are generated by myriad actors whose intentions, authority, and efficacy are rarely fully understood by those who engage them (Aretxaga 2005; Das 2007; Poole 2004). This reality gives the lie to the visions of the social world articulated in the antipoverty and identity projects of the state.

« FOUR »

State Identities

Every time I saw Luis, a field agent for Peru's Right to Identity campaign in Pachacútec, he was hunched over a pile of papers, jaw clenched as he shuffled through documents and ground out forms with palpable intensity. Across from him there were always at least two people, one peering cautiously across the desk to glean whatever information they could from Luis's various grunts and sighs and another more passive, staring ahead blankly as they waited to be interrogated about basic facts of their existence: full name, sex, place, date and time of birth, current address, and parents' names and places of origin. Often a local promoter for the campaign circled in the background, studying the intricacies of the procedure so they might ensure that this and future efforts to secure national ID cards for Peru's poorest and most vulnerable inhabitants succeeded. If the applicant effectively corroborated the life story communicated by the dossier they had assembled, the inscription process ended with them submitting a fingerprint, a biological trace that promised to connect the natural person to their juridical counterpart. I was always struck by this bureaucratic ritual, a synecdoche for the Peruvian state's broader efforts to produce proper political subjects. Luis would jostle the interviewee's hand, telling them to keep it soft and pliant as he rolled their index finger from left to right to get a full impression of the subject who, now known and duly recognized, was available to be molded by the state.

Applicants and campaign officers alike told me that without a birth certificate, you were invisible to the state; you did not exist. To acquire an official national identity, you needed someone to speak on your behalf, a social connection that could be the starting point for your official sociolegal existence. Though this axiom was not made explicit in any government

FIGURE 4.1. Checking paperwork at the Right to Identity campaign office in Pachacútec, 2010. Photo by the author.

publication, the bureaucratic logics, witnesses, and labyrinthine document requirements made clear to those involved that their existence for the state had to begin with an array of social and institutional connections that painted a clear picture of who the subject was. Medical certificates of live birth, vaccination records, certificates of survival from police, parents' IDs, witness IDs and signed and sworn testimonies, education certificates, marriage certificates, certificates of non-inscription from other municipal civil registries in which the person might have been registered, and proof of residence in the form of utility bills were all potential documentary requirements. A campaign registrar described the requirements for filing birth certificates for unregistered Peruvians this way:

> All of these [supporting documents] have to be filled out correctly. There can't be eraser marks or smudges. . . . The important thing is that everything is coherent and in order. You can't be normal Maria in one document and María with an accent in another because those are two different people. . . . And it's only when you have all of the supporting documents that you can complete the birth certificate.

Cross-checking this dossier and completing the final birth certificate was tedious, precision work and nerve-wracking for everyone involved. Applicants were subject to the whims of bureaucrats and waited anxiously to see if their documents would be approved. Bureaucrats, meanwhile, were subject to the strictures of documents, having to construct everything just so or be condemned to repeat the process. All things considered, I wasn't surprised to hear that Luis had snapped.

"He just exploded," one promoter recounted. "He threw the form in the trash and told the parents to get out." According to promoters who witnessed the event, at the final inscription meeting, the parents of a three-month-old baby could not agree on whether to give their child two names or three. They went back and forth, and Luis began filling in the certificate application form several times before he got fed up and kicked them out of the office. The event was a small hiccup in the grand scheme of Peru's Right to Identity campaign, which aimed to distribute 7,000 IDs in Pachacútec alone. But it was a big deal for the promoters who had spent days identifying this couple, educating them about the importance of documenting their child, and supporting them in compiling their child's identity dossier. It was a big deal for the parents who would have to compile updated and additional supporting documentation of their child's existence as they waited indefinitely for the campaign to return. And it was a big deal for the three-month-old child, who, due to the government's increasingly strict identification requirements, could be denied state medical care or food assistance until she was properly documented.

As promoters for the campaign rehashed the event over lunch, one promoter suggested that perhaps the third name belonged to an ex-lover of one of the spouses. Some in the group seemed intrigued; jealousy, a chink in the couple's romantic commitment to one another, could explain the impasse. Another promoter countered that the reason behind the squabble was irrelevant. What mattered was the couple's inability to keep things in perspective and focus on the larger issue of their child's identity and citizenship. "It was just pure ignorance," she said. "People just don't think about the real consequences of their actions."

Trying to deflect the vitriol being directed toward the parents, I asked if there was anything Luis might have done differently to ensure the child was documented. One promoter replied that he couldn't force the parents to come to an agreement: "Solo puede esperar la buena voluntad de la gente" (All he can do is wait/hope for the goodwill of the people). Citizenship, like community service or formality, was supposed to come from the ground up as a performance born of people's individual desires to comport themselves as proper citizens and to be included and have their children included in the state. Rebecca, a lawyer for DEMUNA who spent most of her time working on couple mediations, disagreed. Identity was too important to leave to parents.

> He can't just wait for people! When are these poor little creatures going to have their birth certificates?! As an authority, you have to put your foot down because . . . for foolishness like arguing over whether the child should have two or three names, you can't let the child go without a name and identity!

Since 2005, RENIEC had been executing iterations of the Right to Identity campaign in the name of the country's broader war on poverty. The link between citizenship and the war on poverty was forcefully established in RENIEC's National Plan for the Restitution of Identity for 2005–2009, which, over the course of 150 pages, mentions "citizens" and "citizenship" forty-nine times, while variants on the word "poverty" appear eighty-nine times. The plan contends that the state cannot assist people that it cannot see. Moreover, the multidimensional exclusions that both led to and resulted from indocumentation were understood by many theorists and policy makers as constitutive of poverty itself (Altamirano et al. 2004). As with various other documents and formalization procedures, state agents interpreted national IDs as instrumental and intrinsic goods.

However, the incident when Luis snapped highlights several important features of the Right to Identity campaign that are obscured by the singular focus on its work to include people in the state. The first is the way the various activities and interactions involved in identifying citizens also work to shape the identity of the state. Contrary to dominant discourses that depict the state as a singular, coherent, and eternal entity, anthropologists have shown that the reality and identity of the state is shaped by everyday encounters with state agents and broader discourses about what the state is and should be (Sharma and Gupta 2006, 18–19). Although propaganda for the Right to Identity campaign represented the state as benevolent and technocratic, through the campaign's enactment the state could emerge as capricious, explosive, and impenetrable. Rights, meanwhile, were not inalienable but rather conferred at the discretion of individual state agents. A second notable feature of the campaign was the way parents, specifically mothers, emerged as critical mediators between the state and individual children-citizens. As a result, creating citizens was not simply a matter of establishing a dyadic relation between a coherent, rational state and a singular individual; creating citizens also required constructing specific kinds of family and gender relations that, as the normative logics went, would produce proper citizen-subjects (Butler 2008).

THE PLAN: CONSTRUCTING CITIZENS AND BUILDING STATES

According to campaign designers and proponents from central Lima, identity cards possessed a quasimagical capacity to transform bearers from faceless members of the marginal masses into empowered, rights-bearing citizens. A RENIEC field officer told me early on in the campaign, "From the moment you're born, we assume everyone wants to be a citizen. As a full citizen, you can vote, you can enter obligatory military service, you can legally marry, you can engage in economic and financial transactions, everything. And what makes this possible? The national identity card." By contrast, Peruvians without this document were at a necessary disadvantage, condemned to poverty as persons excluded from state programs and civic life.

In the report, RENIEC lays out the official logics of the Right to Identity campaign and establishes a provisional plan for its execution. Though few people read reports like this cover to cover, preferring instead to store them like trophies or mine them for key quotes,[1] RENIEC's National Plan for the Restitution of Identity is worth analyzing as a meaningful and world-making text because of the way it crystalizes an elite vision of Peruvian society, illustrating how well-meaning officials understand and seek to act upon the world around them. RENIEC's plan communicates two central messages that filtered down to state agents and the rest of the Peruvian population through trainings and program propaganda: identity cards produce empowered and productive citizens, and documenting citizens is part and parcel of producing a functional and modern state. I place these ideas in conversation with anthropological theories of statecraft and situate them in the context of Peruvians' quotidian encounters with the state, so that we might better understand the distorted and partial visions these messages project into the world, refracting and reproducing Peruvian society as in a funhouse hall of mirrors.

Documents, Citizenship, and Identity

On the relation between documents and substantive experiences of citizenship, anthropologists of statecraft have shown that where colonial and national governments assert control, state-issued documents play an important role in facilitating political inclusion and protecting subjects from state abuse. Gaston Gordillo (2006) shows how historically excluded indigenous populations in Argentina came to fetishize state-issued ID cards as objects that materialized living relations with the state. Those without documents were subject to martial law and the violent whims of state agents, while ID holders were granted safe passage and allowed to conduct their affairs relatively unimpeded. Although identity is certainly subject to special scrutiny at national borders, Pradeep Jeganathan (2004) points out that checkpoints run through the body of the state. ID cards may be required for myriad mundane transactions, from mailing letters to contracting cable service, all of which create opportunities to exclude or abuse undocumented or improperly documented persons.

In urban Peru, these potentially exclusionary checkpoints proliferate beyond official state institutions. To give their actions an air of democratic legitimacy and formality, settlement *dirigentes* mimic the performances of ground-level state agents by doing things like requiring community members to identify themselves with national ID numbers in order to sign petitions or participate in land takeovers (Das 2007; Sharma and Gupta 2006). Additionally, in radio and TV advertisements, people frequently identified themselves with their national ID numbers as they offered testimonials about products or politicians: "My name is Jorge Fulano and my ID number is 1234567 and my new mobile phone has changed my life." Providing the details of one's identity document in everyday speech signified earnestness, integrity, and accountability, as if to say, "I am a real person, and I stand by this message." RENIEC's identity plan affirms the urgency of documenting urban inhabitants because of the outsized role ID cards play in mediating social interactions in urban space.

> In urban marginal zones, the problematic of an undocumented person creates greater obstacles for the development of citizenship. In the city where people live anonymously—in contrast to rural zones where many can accept the identity of the person in good faith—identity documents are fundamental for . . . access to employment, health services, education, property, land, and credits, among other things. (RENIEC 2005, 93)

Beyond the issues of formal inclusion and exclusion, one of the most remarkable aspects of RENIEC's identity restitution plan is the way it positions official state identification at the center of identity production.

Drawing on liberal political thought and psychological theories of selfhood, the plan argues that Peru's Civil Code of 1936 and the guarantees to "life, identity, moral and physical integrity, and the free pursuit of personal development and well-being" named in its 1993 constitution imply that the state has an obligation to maintain an archive that preserves the "particular social aspects" of each individual—specifically their "static" and "inherent" traits such as their name, filiation, and birth date—so they might "recognize and distinguish themselves from others" (RENIEC 2005, 42).[2] RENIEC's identity plan suggests that without the state to maintain a written record of these traits, people cannot fully know themselves. It further indicates that an alignment between the true self and the legal self that is presented in the ID card is critical to psychological well-being, as any disconnect could lead to ruptures in an individual's psyche and an unstable sense of self.

Ideas about inherent characteristics and true selves invoke understandings of the sovereign, self-constituted "I" that dominates liberal political thought and undergirds much of the field of psychology. Interestingly, in its discussion of rural women, RENIEC's identity plan mingles these frames with an understanding of the self that is fluid, relational, and constructed over time with the help of documents. The report states,

> Indocumentation has a negative impact on the construction of identity for rural women in our society, above all because for them identity exists in and is produced through a person's participation in different social relationships and systems of representation, which involve social interconnection and self-recognition, and consolidates as a conjunction of processes of identification. (RENIEC 2005, 102)

By acknowledging this more fluid form of identity construction, the report asserts that documents help create particular types of persons by facilitating the social interactions through which an individual's self-image might be (re)affirmed, actualized, and solidified. When individuals have state-issued ID cards, the state can play an active role in shaping their identities and transforming these subjects into desirable citizens. Without state-issued IDs and corresponding state influence in these processes, a different kind of being might be produced. A civil registrar in Pachacútec described these beings as "shadow persons," frightening not only because the state has not molded them in its image, but because it might not know them at all.

The Place of History

RENIEC's identity plan devotes only three of its 150 pages to Peru's four-hundred-year history of civil registration and identity documentation. Though we can understand this decision as a product of publishing imperatives related to space and readers' attention spans, it nonetheless helps perpetuate the notion that state identification is a novel idea being introduced to a paperwork-naïve population, when documentation and bureaucratic procedure have in fact been helping to shape these contexts for hundreds of years. As the plan acknowledges, during three hundred years of colonial rule, the Catholic Church registered "vital events" and distributed baptismal certificates that certified religious inclusion and gave Peruvians access to other church services and sacraments such as marriage and Christian burials. When Peru declared independence from Spain in 1821, it sought to transfer responsibilities for maintaining civil registries to local political authorities. It took more than one hundred years and the passing of five different if repetitive laws—in 1852, 1856, 1873, 1875, and 1892—before the norm of secular government registration finally took hold and was cemented in Peru's Civil Code of 1936.

This code created a Peru characterized by a decentralized political geography. It affirmed the exclusive right of district governments to maintain civil registries and elaborate vital statistics for their districts, and a subsequent provision explicitly made it illegal for governments to register vital events that occurred outside their jurisdictions. Although central government agencies, like the Ministry of Justice and the INEI, might compile this information for national projects, their knowledge of the population was mediated by district governments. According to the RENIEC report, this situation generated data-coordination problems and introduced "irrationalities" into the system because district bureaucrats were not always qualified for the work of recording vital statistics or, to offer a less condescending interpretation, might make different decisions about the best way to do so.

National identification, meanwhile, had been the purview of Peru's National Elections Committee (Jurado Nacional de Elecciones), which had been responsible for distributing voter registration cards (*libretas electorales*) to eligible citizens since 1931. Over time, the voter registration cards came to double as proof of identity for any transaction that required such proof. RENIEC's identity plan contends that this practice created a juridical condition in which political inclusion and state-sanctioned identity depended on the act of voting rather than being guaranteed as a fundamental right from birth.

In 1993 Alberto Fujimori's administration sought to address the problem of coordinating vital statistics and the dependence of national identity on voting by creating RENIEC.[3] The institution was responsible, first, for centralizing and standardizing the collection of information on vital events. In 2010, RENIEC was still working diligently to integrate district civil registries into a single national system, an administrative reality made evident in Pachacútec, where RENIEC and the municipal civil registry occupied adjacent offices in the *agencia*. The purpose of this work was to modernize and rationalize the Peruvian state by creating a single authoritative vision of the population by which to govern. RENIEC was also made responsible for "accrediting the identity of all Peruvians" and distributing national IDs based on the newly centralized records of every Peruvian's "inherent characteristics" (RENIEC 2005, 38). Thus, rather than depending on civic engagement, under the new regime all Peruvians were entitled, and on some level obligated, to be visible to the state.[4]

Though state agents couch this visibility in terms of citizens' rights to identity and individuation, national ID cards were also an important means of exercising state control. They assert the state's categorization scheme and extend this scheme into the pockets of bearers, where it might shape their interactions with others and their understandings of themselves. At the same time, as a tool of individuation, the ID card provides a necessary counter to state projects of enumeration and aggregation (Appadurai 2006; Jeganathan 2004). Individual IDs help officials reassert the accountability of individuals in the face of mass demonstrations that many Peruvians view ambivalently as both enactments of democracy and opportunities for delinquent behavior under the cover of mob anonymity. When public demonstrations by groups like the Barras Bravas (soccer fan clubs) or Construcción Civil (a construction workers union) degenerated into riots, the Peruvian state's first and only public response was to require the national registration of individual group members, relying on projects of individuation to maintain order and reassure citizens.

The Peruvian government likewise publicized other surveillance efforts to promote good behavior and assure citizens that it was remaining vigilant and in control. SUNAT (Superintendencia Nacional de Aduanas y Administración Tributaria), Peru's national customs and tax collection agency, advertises its activities in daily newspapers with a thin banner featuring a pair of eyes and the message "SUNAT: WE ARE WATCHING YOU" in block print. The roads that lead from Pachacútec into Lima's middle-class neighborhoods are lined with billboards declaring simply that in this town "TE FICHAMOS," meaning "We will write you up" or "We will put this on your permanent record."

RENIEC's identity plan generally downplays these more disciplinary aspects of individuation and, ignoring centuries of government involvement and diverse identification regimes, highlights the power of RENIEC's national ID to transform vulnerable subjects into empowered citizens. The citizenship conferred by the ID is described as a great equalizer, capable of guaranteeing "equality of economic, social, and political opportunities" and combatting "all forms of discrimination" (RENIEC 2005, 17). Ironically, though, "discrimination" is embedded in the activities of the plan, as the state selectively targets "invisible" populations for the campaign.

Known Unknowns: Identifying the Subaltern

To identify and locate the undocumented population, RENIEC officials purportedly relied on population estimates and survey information from numerous government agencies and NGOs. RENIEC's report devotes seven of its 150 pages exclusively to estimating the undocumented adult population in each of Peru's twenty-five political departments before detailing estimates by gender, income, ethnicity, and rural and urban provenance, among other variables. These statistics, however, were largely justificatory, discursive tools used to add weight and precision to predetermined policy agendas. According to RENIEC's most basic projections, approximately 9 percent of the adult Peruvian population did not have a national ID card at the time the plan was published (RENIEC 2005, 51). If readers did not find that statistic compelling, though, the report also asserted that the numbers were likely far greater than official statistics suggested, due to the abject poverty, exclusion, and hard-to-reach nature of the undocumented population (RENIEC 2005, 101). In this way, both statistics and the lack of them evidenced the gravity of the problem. Moreover, most policy officials I spoke with seemed unconcerned with these specific figures and suggested that everyone already knew who and where the marginals were. The "marginals" were women, children, and indigenous people who resided in rural provinces far from Lima or in the sprawling and disorderly shantytowns that surrounded Peruvian cities. A chapter of RENIEC's report entitled "Who Are the Undocumented Citizens?" is effectively a who's who of subaltern populations, with subheadings titled "People in Situations of Poverty," "Indigenous Communities," "Afro-Peruvian Communities," "Women," "Children and Adolescents,"

"The Disabled," "The Elderly," and "Victims of Internal Armed Conflict" (RENIEC 2005, 2). Though distinct, these populations are united by their distance from the normative, white, male, urban, middle-class Peruvian citizen. Indeed, after disaggregating Peru's "vulnerable" populations with chapter subheadings, the report quickly bundles them back together: "The commission would like to highlight the tight relationship between poverty and indocumentation. We affirm that the situation of poverty—and often extreme poverty—its location in rural zones or urban marginal zones, and a lesser level of instruction are general characteristics of the undocumented population" (59).

As if to highlight the intertwined race and class dimensions of citizenship, the report settles on rural Andean women as being at the extreme end of the marginality spectrum. "Women, in particular those who inhabit rural zones, are the most affected by this problem because they confront traditional relations of subordination with respect to men" (53). While the report appears to tread lightly on the cultural ground of "tradition," to avoid overtly favoring western, criollo values, it nonetheless entreats that the state must intervene, educate, and document these women because "the situation of indocumentation of the woman is inherited by her sons and daughters" (59). Thus, far from outside the nation-state, these marginal individuals are preemptively included in the definition of the state as the bodies that mark its limits; they are the vulnerable and dangerous exterior of the state that justifies its existence (Das and Poole 2004).

Based on these imaginaries, one would assume that distributing identity cards would be a relatively straightforward process. You go the distance to locate the marginals who have thus far gone unseen by the state, inscribe their names in the national registry, and provide them identity cards that confer and signal their official membership in the state. The RENIEC plan presents this as a clean and simple transaction between a rational and benevolent modern state and individual would-be citizens. And yet, it is not that simple. While RENIEC agents justify the campaign by invoking imaginaries of isolated, vulnerable individuals, in practice the campaign depends upon a person's social integration and ability to overlay that integration with coherent documentation. In this sense, legal personhood is not simply bequeathed but rather built over time. As a result, the Right to Identity campaign required reconstructing pasts and erasing inconsistencies. Moreover, while the RENIEC plan largely describes citizenship as a dyadic relation between individuals and states, in practice, constructing citizens required (re)constituting families.

THE PRACTICAL PART: IMPLEMENTING THE IDENTITY CAMPAIGN

The job of filling the gap between the ideals of the campaign and the messy realities of everyday life fell to a small army of municipal promoters who had been hand-picked from other areas of the municipal government and specially trained by agents from GRIAS, RENIEC's identity-restoration and social assistance unit, to carry out the important labor of "restoring identity" to the most marginal inhabitants of Pachacútec. "Supposedly they picked us because we're the best," one promoter explained, "but it's a lot of work." Rather than switching areas, promoters were expected to simply take on the additional work required for the Right to Identity campaign without additional compensation. Their wages remained approximately 500 soles a month, which was slightly above Peru's minimum wage at the time and less than half of what their immediate supervisors earned. Adding to this exploitative dynamic, because promoters lived in Pachacútec, the extreme poverty zone targeted by the campaign, they were expected to work odd hours and accommodate impromptu requests for assistance such that the Right to Identity campaign quickly became all-consuming.

Days for promoters might begin with a loudspeaker announcement inviting Pachacutanos who lacked ID cards or birth certificates to come to a table in a marketplace or *comedor popular* so promoters could inform them about the campaign and begin processing their cases. Most of the time, though, the job was about traversing Pachacútec to follow up with people who had already started the ID process. Carla, a promoter for DEMUNA and the Right to Identity campaign, described this facet of her work.

> Once you start someone on the road to documentation, you have to follow them through the process. . . . You end up trying to find them on weekends and after work because, as you do the job, you start to care about people. You become sensitized to the issues and in the end you really want to see that they get their documents. So you work whatever hours you have to . . . just like this, walking.

In 2009, walking in Pachacútec was no small feat. The town was laid out on a large sand dune with few paved roads to ease the trek. Promoters complained of back and kidney problems from spending so many hours on their feet,[5] as well as chronic bronchitis from the winter fog and blistered skin from the blazing summer sun. Carla explained that the medications promoters bought to treat these conditions were expensive, "and there goes your salary!"

Despite these grievances, many of the promoters said the Right to Identity campaign was worth it. It was important work, social work, designed to help the truly needy. RENIEC had explained the value of the campaign, and most promoters accepted the theory behind it, as Carla articulated.

> The problem is you have people who go their whole lives and don't know their real names. They may be written in as one thing, but the entire world calls them something else. So they never learn. What your mom calls you? That is not your identity. It is not an identity unless you have a document that verifies that you are who you say you are.

The idea that a person's real name and identity were the ones recorded and authorized by the state rather than the ones constituted in practice was taken up by promoters and others in Pachacútec who encountered the campaign. Liliana, a caregiver at a local state-subsidized child care center, had seen iterations of the Right to Identity campaign in Pachacútec since 2007; she understood documentation as integral to the constitution not only of identity but of a person's very humanity.

> When a child is born you have to think in the first place of having something [a document] because my child is not an animal, right? To leave a child without a document? Carambas! So, my child is born and grows and grows and grows, but if I don't worry about a birth certificate, my child would be like a little animal, no? My child would be a zero that isn't worth anything because he doesn't have anything [any document].

Anita echoed Liliana's claim about the existential importance of documents while also linking the Right to Identity campaign to the identity of the Peruvian nation and the competence of the Peruvian state.

> Since they weren't registered [by RENIEC] it's as if they didn't exist. . . . They don't have a national identity. Because they're not registered, they don't appear in the photo of Peru. In all of those statistics, where are they? The census says we're 25 million people, but with all of these undocumented people, we are more than that!

Promoters generally embraced the theory and broad messages behind the campaign, messages about the existential importance of state identity documents and the role they played in producing, protecting, and empowering citizens. Still, one asserted, "The practice is different from the theory. RENIEC arrived to teach us all about the theory, . . . but that doesn't always help you with the practical part."

In theory, the national ID card was the document that facilitated all interactions with the Peruvian state. In practice, though, acquiring an "extemporaneous" birth certificate and ID (from the Latin *ex tempore*, "out of the time") required documents that demonstrated a lifetime's worth of institutional engagements. According to the bureaucratic logics of the campaign, every life stage was accompanied by documents. The more life stages a person had gone through at the time of inscription, the more documents they needed to prove their continued existence through time.

Under what RENIEC deemed "ordinary" circumstances, every Peruvian completed a "cycle of documentation." A RENIEC registrar said the cycle began the day one was given a certificate of live birth written "correctly by the delivering doctor without any stains or erasures." Parents then had thirty days to take this certificate and register the baby with the Peruvian state, obtaining a birth certificate that would serve as proof of identity until the child came of age and received their national ID card and number. When I began working in Pachacútec, laws about precisely when a person could exchange their birth certificate for a national ID card were changing quickly until finally, in 2010, RENIEC began distributing IDs to newborn babies. RENIEC agents photographed each infant's squished purple face and took prints of their tiny fingers to create a yellow ID card that featured the newborn's photo, full name, ID number, date of birth, city of origin, parents' names, and one guardian's ID number. A RENIEC agent said the point of the child ID was to "close the cycle of documentation as quickly as possible. When you have an ID number, that number is yours until you die. So, we are trying to give IDs to newborns in the hospital, so you go directly from the birth certificate to the ID and fewer people fall through the cracks." The agent went on to explain that closing the cycle of documentation early on allowed children to have access to state insurance while also preventing fraud by shoring up the boundaries of families.

> Nowadays, the SIS [state health insurance] won't attend to children who don't have IDs. . . . Before, many insured people tried to get children medical attention at the state hospital when they weren't their kids but rather a nephew or some other kid that isn't their child. . . . So now they [SIS employees] require an ID to ensure that this is your child and not a family member that doesn't really have anything to do with the insurance.

When the cycle of documentation was not completed according to the official timeline, the process of obtaining an ID was transformed from a civic right to a request for exceptional treatment that demanded careful scrutiny. Although the report describes the work of itinerant RENIEC agents as identifying the invisible, it seemed that somewhere along the way RENIEC agents became primarily concerned with preventing "double inscriptions," which criminals might use to disappear and escape the law. An agent explained,

> Now we take fingerprints of all people who get identity cards. That way we don't create a double identity. . . . We want to avoid the issue of usurpation of identity because people who commit crimes would like to have another identity, so it's only when I have all the proof possible that I proceed. . . . The functionaries of RENIEC can prioritize which documents are more important than others, so we work with citizens to verify who they were before now. So, bring me certificates, registries, whatever documents can help us. The more documents you have, the greater your identification.

The number and kinds of documents RENIEC agents required to ensure a person's identity depended on the age of the applicant, that is, the time span over which their identity had to be accounted for, and the particular disposition of the RENIEC agent. For children under six, whose official lives were imagined to be relatively limited, agents only required a certificate of live birth from a medical professional or a certificate of survival/existence from local police; the ID cards of the parents; IDs, signatures, and fingerprints of two witnesses; and a certificate of non-inscription from the district in which the child was born. In short, agents required a documented consensus that the child existed, was who the parents claimed the child was, and was not already registered with another branch of the state. As children grew older, though, even more documents were required. A RENIEC agent explained,

> When the kids are six or seven, an age when the state presumes the child should be in school, the certificate of live birth isn't sufficient any more. . . . They need a certificate of studies, . . . a document that demonstrates the grades the person has completed until they are seventeen. . . . And when the person is an adult, it's completely different. You still need a certificate of non-inscription from the district where you were born, . . . but in addition to identity, RENIEC is also the registry of vital events. If you got married, you have to prove that

with other documentation. You could have kids, so again we need a document.

Because individual RENIEC agents had discretion in determining which documents constituted sufficient proof of identity, an important practical component of promoters' training was helping applicants construct dossiers that would satisfy particular RENIEC agents. In this way, promoters served an intermediary role with the potential to change the nature of the state that Pachacutanos encountered as they sought to acquire national identities. Without the help of promoters who knew the campaign and the personalities behind it, the state emerged as inscrutable and impenetrable, an all-powerful gatekeeper that exercised control over "space, time, and access to resources" (Ferme 2004, 89).

This inscrutable and impenetrable gatekeeper was precisely the kind of state that Yana, a savvy and energetic female *dirigente*, was encountering. A few months prior, she had given up her community leadership role in order to care for her aging parents and specifically to help her eighty-seven-year-old mother obtain a national ID card. Rather than go through the free Right to Identity campaign and be subjected to its institutional vagaries, Yana decided to pay for the document on her own in the hopes of speeding up the process. The municipal registrar she was working with explained that since Yana's mother was quite old, she didn't have time to waste. "If you die without a birth certificate," he said, "you can't be buried in a registered cemetery." It seemed a state-authorized identity played a crucial role in constructing one's humanity, even in death.

Despite devoting herself entirely to the task, it had taken Yana more than a month to acquire all the necessary documents. They had used Yana's birth certificate as a master document and then gathered materials to construct a documentary life consistent with who Yana's mother was at the moment of giving birth to her. The final dossier was over an inch thick and contained the following: copies of witness IDs together with their fingerprints; certificates of non-inscription from the municipality in Trujillo, where her mother was born, as well as from the municipality in Lima; a certificate of survival from Pachacútec's police station to prove to anyone who might review the file that the documents referred to a living person; a certificate from the police that Yana's mother did not have a criminal record (*certificado de no antecedentes penales*); and an authenticated print (*copia original*) of Yana's birth certificate. To acquire these documents, Yana made the ten-hour bus trip to Trujillo twice, once to get her mother's certificate of non-inscription and again to get an authenticated print of her own birth certificate. Unlike others who grew frustrated by this kind of back and forth, Yana seemed to take these challenges in stride, accepting that these dynamics were intrinsic to any dealing with the state: "That's just how they manage the information. They don't give you everything at once. They give it to you piece by piece."

I watched as Yana escorted her parents up to the RENIEC counter. The agent jostled Yana's mother's hand before pressing her finger into the ink pad and then onto the official extemporaneous birth certificate application. When Yana asked if the document would show that her mother and father were married, the agent handed Yana another form to fill out with requests for additional supporting documentation, and the three sat back down to discuss what to do next.

It was the job of campaign promoters to help applicants avoid these frustrations. In the process, they became allies to impoverished applicants and also acted as low-level gatekeepers who presented bureaucratic barriers to the people before they wasted their time at documenting agencies. Promoters themselves described their role as "orienting" the public. In the beginning, this orientation took the form of kindly but efficient rejection. Promoters sat on one side of a wooden table set up at a market or community meeting hall where they gossiped and exchanged bawdy jokes in between responding to inquiries.

- "This isn't the land title campaign. This is for identity. To process your title, you have to talk to Dr. Brennan in the *agencia*."
- "Sorry. This campaign is only for the people who have never been identified. We don't work with changes of address or expired IDs."
- "Since your baby is already eighteen, he is going to have to come in himself."
- "Unfortunately, you can't pick up your nephew's ID without a juridical declaration from him. Of course, in Lima it wouldn't be that way. There they would just give it to you. But because the government assumes that the people here are more wily [*son más vivos*] and that they might use it for some other purpose, at this agency they require a juridical declaration."
- "This campaign only corresponds to people living in Pachacútec, so you should bring your niece to live with you at your address. Maybe talk to the *dirigente* of your zone so you can process things from here."

Once they had taken on a case, the orientation became more involved. A promoter said, "We're helping them make sure everything is in order so that when RENIEC comes . . . they're not told the documents aren't valid and sent away." Sometimes this simply involved telling applicants what they needed all at once, to reduce the number of trips to RENIEC offices. Other times it meant helping people acquire the documents themselves.

At eighteen years old, Elvis was about to graduate high school but still didn't have a birth certificate. When his mother went to the school to get his certificate of studies so he could process his birth certificate, they only provided the certificate for the most recent year he had completed. "That will never work," the promoter said. "If you bring only that, the [RENIEC agents] will ask you where the person was for all of their primary school and every year in between." The mother explained, "The school won't give me any of his previous records because we still owe tuition money. . . . Right now we're strapped and don't have it to give to them." The promoter understood and knew firsthand what it was like to have to explain yourself to creditors. The municipality was already three weeks behind on her pay. "They pay us when it suits them, but we're expected to pay our bills exactly on time!" she told me. The promoter promised to call the woman when she had resolved her problem, either by reasoning with the school director or finding a viable loan option for her. When the promoter asked the woman how she spelled her name, the woman handed over her ID card and said, "That's how you spell it. Exactly as it says in my ID." In doing so she provided a subtle indication of her personal integrity as someone who understood the importance of consistent, accurate, and up-to-date documentation.

In another case, a young mother wanted to acquire birth certificates for her children, but because she had lost her own ID, the civil registrar wouldn't let her. As a single mother with no stable job, the woman explained that she simply didn't have the thirty soles required for a duplicate. A promoter pondered the issue and replied thoughtfully, "Well then, go to DEMUNA, very humbly, and explain your situation. Present yourself as a very poor social case that needs some support. Then they will help you." In this instance, the practical part of documenting and creating citizens involved not simply telling people where to go, but explaining how they had to comport themselves and who they had to be to get the assistance they were after.

In theory, undocumented women were a principal target of the campaign because, according to the RENIEC plan, they had the potential to pass their undocumented status on to their children. However, because adults were challenging to document, children quickly became the focus of promoters, who had quotas to meet, as well as of the larger Right to

Identity campaign, which had an interest in inflating its success. The director of operations for the Right to Identity campaign told me, "It's a question of numbers. Since everyone wants to see results, if we do children we can say, 'Oh yes, we've distributed ten thousand IDs,' while at the same cost we can only do maybe one thousand adults. So, with the children it looks better." In this way, the official image-work of the campaign had an important impact on its substance.

TWO LAST NAMES: IDENTITY AND FILIATION

Despite the consensus that children were easier to document than adults, time and again promoters confronted the fact that the couple, and the legal appearance of a two-parent family, was the starting point for the child. Norms that define children in terms of parentage are inscribed both in international and in Peruvian national law. The International Convention on the Rights of the Child stipulates that every child has the right to "know their parents" and that states have a responsibility to "preserve the child's identity . . . including the name and family relations" (in RENIEC 2005, 24-25). The Latin American Convention on Human Rights places a child's last name at the center of the right to both filial and self-knowledge and directs signatory states to guarantee that every child carries the last names of at least one and preferably two parents (RENIEC 2005, 25). Peru's civil code further specifies that every Peruvian has a right and responsibility to carry a name and *apellidos* (last names) in the plural, with special discussion devoted to which last names a child should carry depending on the marital status of their parents (RENIEC 2005, 29).

The requirement that each child be identified through two last names to index a biological and legal relation with a mother and a father marks the point at which legal citizenship intersects with normative ideologies of family. Andeanist anthropologist Jessaca Leinaweaver (2008, 145) describes Peruvian naming customs as part of "a bilateral [kinship] system with patrilineal skewing." Connections with relatives on both the mother's and father's sides are identified through the same terminology, but because mother and father pass down only their paternal last names, the system is skewed patrilineally. This naming pattern does extraordinary social work, locating every individual in a broad network of kin relations and in a social hierarchy grounded in geography and race (Leinaweaver 2008, 145). Having an expansive kin network is useful in rural agricultural communities and in urban settlements where periods of intensive work—such as farming, installing infrastructure, fundraising, and lobbying politicians—require calling on as many kin as possible (Leinaweaver 2008; Lobo 1982). Last names also index geographic and ethnic origins. Peruvians readily distinguish common Quechua last names such as Quispe and Yapanqui from Spanish last names such as Morales and Perez. Additionally, certain last names have strong regional associations that help to connect second- and third-generation Limeños to specific provinces and their attendant customs and communities.

The bilateral naming system also indicates that connections to both biological parents and their families are integral to a child's identity. Historically, deviating from this two-name norm in Latin America stigmatized children as illegitimate. Illegitimacy functioned in concert with other characteristics such as race, class, and ethnicity to shape social status. Historian Nara Milanich (2002, 75) observes that in colonial South America, an out-of-wedlock birth was considered a stain that dishonored a woman's entire family and made it impossible to assure *limpieza de sangre*, a pure bloodline free of "contaminating influences" from Africans or Indians. Colonial law reflected these discriminatory attitudes and prohibited "illegitimates" from entering certain professions, inheriting property, or bearing the presumptive father's last name.

Even if "the discriminatory spirit of colonial law was patently clear," the law revealed filiation to be a "flexible concept" subject to legal and economic intervention (Milanich 2002, 75). To begin, there were gradations of illegitimacy. Distinctions were made between the offspring of single parents who could technically marry (*hijos naturales*), the offspring of adulterous unions (*adulterinos*), and the children who were products of priests, prostitutes, or incest. Colonial law also allowed people to legitimize their status by purchasing a legal dispensation known as *gracias a sacar*. The price of legitimacy was based on a sliding scale. *Hijos naturales* paid less than *adulterinos*, who paid less than the products of "other punishable and damaged unions" (Milanich 2002, 76).

As the power to define and supervise family formation shifted from church to state in the mid-nineteenth century, questions of legitimacy "based on the identity of the child's progenitors and the nature of their relationship" were replaced by distinctions "between recognized and unrecognized children" (Milanich 2002, 77). Still, the custom of asserting bilateral relations through the ascription of two last names remained. As part of an effort to prevent discrimination against unrecognized children, Peru's Civil Code of 1936 contained provisions to ensure that each child would be equipped with two last names regardless of the circumstances of their birth.[6] Children born in wedlock were automatically given the paternal last names of the mother and her husband regardless of whether the husband was the biological father. Children born out of wedlock were to be given the maternal and paternal "last names of the progenitor who had recognized them," which in most cases was the mother. Only if the child was legally recognized by both progenitors would it carry the paternal last names of both parents. Moreover, if the mother and father officially recognized the child on separate occasions, they were legally prohibited from revealing the name of the other progenitor, and no indication of the absent progenitor's identity was to be registered. The most frequent implication of this was that a mother could not legally register her child with the presumptive father's last name.[7] Instead, children were given the same last names as their mothers.

These various laws and stipulations were originally intended to reduce discrimination against children born out of wedlock. In a context in which everyone is supposed to have two last names, one to link them to each parent, being absent a last name signals a legal incompletion and a conspicuous gap in a person's origins and personal identity. More recently, the issue of last names has been framed less in terms of legitimacy and more in terms of a child's right to biological self-knowledge. The 2005 RENIEC report contends that laws that automatically assign the child the last name of the mother's husband "threaten the identity of the child and impede their ability to know their true and corresponding last name" (29). By extension, women who registered their children using only their own last names were likewise denying their children critical self-knowledge. The moral imperative to properly identify a child with two last names that indexed their bilateral biological origins was one of the more challenging components of the Right to Identity campaign and was overlain with moral judgments about women's sexual behavior.

When I accompanied Carla on her rounds for the Right to Identity campaign, she felt it necessary to warn me about the distressing cases I would see of young women who already had three or four children without birth certificates. She indicated that these cases were distressing not only because of the women's lack of modern moral sensibilities but also because of all the work it implied, particularly when women had children with various men. María, for instance, was nineteen years old and had four children. But, Carla explained, "since she has a husband who works, it's not that bad." Although María was young, her stable partnership made her situation more morally proper and bureaucratically simpler, a coincidence that suggests how normative, morally inflected ideals are refracted onto and reinforced via documents. Teresa was more problematic for Carla: "She is twenty-one years old and has three children all from different men. . . . So none of them have the same name!" Tracking down these men to get them to officially recognize their children was time-consuming, and Teresa alone had to shoulder the financial burdens of locating the fathers and acquiring the documents necessary to take advantage of the free campaign. As a general rule, the more united the couple, the easier it was to get them to collaborate on onerous documentary procedures that both invoked and produced social ties.

Although many women were aware of long-standing laws allowing them to register children with their own two last names, most did not consider this a viable option. Ethel, herself a promoter for the Right to Identity campaign, had never obtained a birth certificate for her daughter, who was nine years old at the time of the campaign. She explained that her daughter's father wanted to recognize her, but he himself lacked a national ID. His birth certificate had been destroyed when the insurgent group Sendero Luminoso burned the civil registry in his hometown. Burning civil registries was a standard Sendero Luminoso tactic, part of their efforts to produce a new society by destroying the institutions that supported the existing one. Without a birth certificate of his own, the father of Ethel's child was not legally permitted to recognize the child as his. When I asked why she had not registered the baby herself, her reasons were twofold. First, a formal name change was bureaucratically complex and expensive, so she and the father decided to delay registration until he was able to sign for his daughter. Neither of them had expected processing his ID to take so long. Second, Ethel's mother had been against it: "My mother said, 'How are you going to let your daughter be like your sibling,' because if we have the same last names, we seem like siblings rather than mother and daughter."[8] Although Ethel's daughter could be said to have technically inherited her undocumented status from her father, this inheritance was mediated by Ethel's assertion that having a name that correctly signaled her daughter's biological origins was more important than an immediate legal identity, which she was empowered to bestow.

Similarly, for Kathy's parents, ensuring she had the last names that biologically corresponded to her was important enough to sacrifice properly documenting some of the other ostensibly inherent characteristics reported on ID cards, such as her date of birth and place of origin. Kathy was in her mid-twenties when she told me this story; her father had died when she was very young, so some of the details were unclear to her. What she did know was that her mother told her she had been born on September

18 in the Maternity Hospital of Lima. "But," she said, "on my ID it says the 27th of September, . . . and my father registered me as Huarochirino," that is, from the rural mining district of Huarochirí. "One would assume that they register you in your place of origin, in the place you were born, . . . but no, they register you in the place where they can sign for you."

Based on what she had learned from her mother and grandmother, Kathy said,

> When I was born, my father . . . was in Matucana in Huarochirí. And so, when my grandmother found out that I had been born, she called and told him, "Go sign for the baby." And I guess they wouldn't give him enough time off work to go to Lima, so my father said, "No, it's really far. Why should I go all the way to Lima? I'll just sign for her here." So that's why I'm registered in Matucana. . . . But he signed on the 27th of September . . . so I'm registered like that.

When I asked if her mother had to bring her to Huarochirí for the inscription, Kathy responded, "No, no. Before it was only the man, only the man signed. . . . And at the municipality, he probably gave a little something to those people who register you. . . . Here everything is corruption."

In her ethnography of child circulation in Andean Peru, Jessaca Leinaweaver (2008, 148–150) describes a similar story in which, rather than travel to a far-off municipality to obtain a copy of her adolescent stepdaughter's birth certificate, the stepmother, Margarita, asked a priest to baptize her stepdaughter using Margarita's last name and to provide a baptismal certificate that declared her town of residence as her birthplace. With this certificate and two witnesses, Margarita inscribed her stepdaughter in the civil registry and used proof of this registration to acquire the child's ID. Since the civil registrars knew Margarita and her stepdaughter socially and were reasonably sure no one would ever complain about this reconstructed identity, they were willing to fudge the facts to help Margarita's stepdaughter obtain a legal identity that more closely reflected her social reality. This technically illegal identity change was an affirmation of relations that existed in practice between Margarita and her stepdaughter and between Margarita and the various officials who helped her. It was also an affirmation of the popular importance of legal identity and citizenship. In this case, people were willing to rewrite the past and circumvent the letter of the law in the name of aligning the stepdaughter's legal existence with her lived reality.

Kathy, however, interpreted her own story not in terms of the fight for citizenship but in terms of government corruption and ineptitude. "Here, there is no control. There is no support," she asserted. She feared that her inconsistent documentation would lead to problems if she ever had to present all of her documents at once, as people did in the Right to Identity campaign or as might be required if she applied for a passport. "I could never get a certificate from the hospital, because to get that they look at the birthdate on your ID and find your file. But my ID says the 27th and my file is under the 18th." The issue was neither the state's absence nor its totalizing control but rather its unpredictable fluctuations between these extremes (Das and Poole 2004). Life was fine with inconsistent documentation until some state agent decided to assert the state's prerogative that everything be "coherent and in order." In those moments, the inconsistently documented population found themselves in the precarious position of asking to be an exception to the official rules.

Kathy went on to suggest, somewhat cynically, that while some things were changing in Peru, others were staying the same: "Now the woman can sign for the child, and they let whatever man sign for it. . . . The important thing, the custom is that the child has two last names." Kathy was largely correct on both points. Peru's Right to Identity campaign was accompanied by an information-diffusion campaign that municipalities termed "Now, I Have My Two Last Names." Its purpose was to raise awareness of Law 28720, which went into effect in 2006 and modified articles 20 and 21 of Peru's civil code to allow women to register their children with the names of the presumptive father, even in his absence. The registering party had thirty days to notify the progenitor of the child's inscription, giving them an opportunity to contest the inscription and file suit denouncing the registrant for "name usurpation." If the inscription proceeded uncontested, the birth certificate could later be used by the mother to sue the presumptive father for child support.[9]

Given the timing, it seems likely that Law 28720 was a response to a high-profile paternity scandal in 2002 involving former Peruvian President Alejandro Toledo. Despite laws prohibiting it, in 1987 Lucrecia Orozco registered her daughter Zarai with the last name of her presumptive father, officially naming her Zarai Toledo Orozco and later suing Toledo for child support. Toledo denied his paternity publicly, criticizing Lucrecia Orozco and Zarai for what he suggested was a naked grab for money and fame (Arriola 2001). Confronted with genetic evidence of his paternity and increasing political criticism, Toledo reversed his position in 2002 and recognized Zarai as his own.[10] Newspaper articles portrayed the outcome as a victory for Zarai, whose father had so long denied her affirmation of her origins (Forero 2002).

It took a while for people in Pachacútec to put new inscription norms into practice. Pachacútec's civil registrar stated, "Since they change the laws all the time, it's hard to keep up." Even so, by 2009 the new law had begun making a difference. It was somewhat easier for children to be citizens of the Peruvian state, identified with the last names that their mothers said properly corresponded to them. As Ethel was discovering, though, the process was still arduous.

> Now that there's this law, her father can just sign for her whenever he gets his ID, . . . but it's still not that easy. I'm processing the whole thing in Callao, but I've been back to that agency three times with documents that they keep rejecting. First it was because the school wrote her name with an accent and her certificate of live birth doesn't have an accent. Then it was because of a misplaced stamp. The third time it was something else, and who has the time to go back and forth to Callao just for the hell of it! Why can't they tell you all of the things that are wrong with the document at once rather than making you go back and forth for each one?

Even as the issue of legal identity and its relation to biological kinship was being resolved, the identity of the state was still in the making. And in Ethel's case, the process of securing her daughter's identity was producing the state as a capricious, irrational, and impenetrable entity.

Nonetheless, many successful inscriptions were occurring, and I was asked to take pictures of people processing their birth certificates to help the district government publicize this success. RENIEC agents interrogated applicants who, with some coaching from promoters, could recite the correct answers to questions about their cities of origin and current residences and could compose juridical declarations to fill in any documentary gaps that remained. Mothers tugged at their children's arms as they waited in line, imploring them to be patient and occasionally barking orders like "Calm down. You have to legalize!" Other children, who had already had their prints taken, chased each other around the courtyard trying to ink each other's faces, unaware that they had just been brought into legal existence. They wouldn't get any other evidence of their inscription, such as the identity card, until several months later, when they would retrieve it unceremoniously from a lockbox at the DEMUNA office in central Ventanilla. Progress was slow, but it was progress nonetheless. The undocumented, or more accurately, the insufficiently documented, were getting national identity cards.

As the campaign progressed, it was also having other effects. It affirmed the correctness of particular kinds of states and particular ideals of state-society relations while also subjecting Peruvians to the caprice of bureaucrats and the idea that insider knowledge was necessary to access the state. It was also putting families, and specifically single mothers, at the center of the war on poverty. The law that allowed a woman to register her child with the presumptive father's last name was effectively honoring the norm of the two-parent family in the breach. It affirmed the correctness of the two-parent family and the importance of this family structure for the well-being of the child while also making women singularly responsible for the maintenance of this family. Mothers, in this sense, were a route to documentation, modernity, and development, but also a central impediment to them. Liliana was incensed as she watched the long line of women and undocumented children creep forward: "It makes me furious, all of this about ID cards. How are we so irresponsible as mothers that we let our children be without an identity?" She continued, "Now there's a law that lets the woman give the child both the last names by herself. . . . And what's more, in the end, men are just men. As mothers, we are really the ones responsible."

MOTHERS OF THE STATE

Peru's Right to Identity campaign, which was depicted as integral to Peru's broader war on poverty, frames identity cards as establishing a dyadic relation between a technocratic state and previously unseen individual citizens. In practice, however, the campaign depends on an array of mediators who inform how the state is encountered and experienced and ultimately what the state is in this context. If we begin from an anthropological view of the state as produced through other institutions and relations rather than an exterior entity that overlays and manages them (Sharma and Gupta 2006), it is easier to see how the documents, bureaucrats, and promoters involved in the Right to Identity campaign simultaneously produce normative visions of what the state should be as well as the often disillusioning reality of the state as illegible, impenetrable, and capricious.

Peru's Right to Identity campaign also reveals how documenting identities depends on producing particular kinds of kin relations and illustrates how holding mothers responsible for Peruvian poverty and development is at the heart of Peru's state-making project. Laws intended to empower women by allowing them to identify their children with last names corresponding to two biological progenitors have other paradoxical effects; they reproduce ideals of heteronormative nuclear families that marginalize single mothers even as they place the burden of developing citizens and the nation squarely on women's shoulders. In the process, poverty morphs from a problem of political inclusion to one of domestic relational failure. This domestic framing informs Peruvians' individuated experiences of poverty and the development patterns that characterize Peru's urban periphery.

« PART THREE »

Intimate Expanses

« FIVE »

Domestic Ideals, Single Moms, and Elastic Relations

I initially didn't take much interest in Peruvians' romantic lives. Although I still played along with three-year-old Sylvia's family when they teased her about her preschool "boyfriend" and took note of the ten-year-old girl who warned me to watch out for Peruvian men—"Ellos te sacan la vuelta!" (They cheat on you!)—as a general rule, romantic melodramas, gendered stereotypes, and directives about how men and women should behave in relationships were topics I politely endured rather than actively pursued. Yet somewhere between my interlocutors' recurrent narratives of heartbreak and loneliness and their explicit advice that I investigate why there are so many single mothers in Peru, I realized that the figure of the single mother and experiences of relational loss and failed domestic projects were integral to how poverty materialized in their lives. Moreover, it became clear that women's relational identities as mothers, as single, and as household heads were important to their official and everyday designations as members of the deserving poor.

Peruvian understandings of poverty are knotted together with ideals of family and realities of intimacy in complex ways. Women's empowerment workshops, educational materials, and social assistance programs support the association of nuclear families and companionate relationships with developed societies, and help to domesticate poverty by locating its source and tenacity within the home and making mothers singularly responsible for it. In this context, single mothers are potent and problematic figures. Women negotiate this ambivalent social identity by tacking between self-presentations as larger-than-life icons of virtuous maternal struggle and as separated beings whose loss of a companionate relation has rendered them permanently incomplete. By identifying the dominant discourses in and through which women negotiate their identities and attending to women's speech and silences around their romantic relationships, we are able to get closer to women's lived experiences of these intimate relations; however, we never fully capture them (Van Vleet 2008). In part, this is because relationships and the ways women understand and narrate them shift over time and across contexts. Relationships may be strengthened and attenuated in different moments and change as they are (re)constituted through different materialities and channels of connection. Critically, the ambiguous and elastic quality of relationships is at odds with bureaucratic practices that seek clear-cut categories and with hegemonic discourses that associate decisiveness and officialdom with modernity. The juxtaposition of real-world relationships with rigid legal categories exacerbates the marginalization of single mothers and foments accusations by community members and state agents that these women are not truly needy. Together, these findings point to how official ideologies of family inform women's intimate experiences of poverty as well as how the vagaries of private life make deserving poverty an impossible category to inhabit.

MOTHER-LEADERS IN DEVELOPMENT

The thud of my boots on the tile floor bounced off the bare plaster walls as I entered the empty clinic auditorium. I checked my watch: 3:45 p.m. The leadership workshop for Pachacútec's nascent mothers clubs was scheduled to begin at 3 p.m. But if previous weeks were any indication, the workshop would start at least ninety minutes late. By 4 p.m., workshop organizers from the municipality and the Good Governance NGO who weekly chastised women for their tardiness had finally arrived to set up. I helped Marisa and Anita, the two political promoters working the event, paste a large attendance sheet to the wall and prepare a snack of buttered saltines and sugared coffee for participants. As women trickled in for the workshop, they helped us pack plastic chairs into tight rows facing the front of the room, easily identified by the green paint on the wall. Green, the signature color of the current governing party, formed the backdrop for every public event. To pass the time, participants complained about Peru's "culture of tardiness" and how time spent waiting for meetings was time spent neglecting their children and households. I found myself preemptively irritated at the thought of the male workshop organizers lecturing us, yet again, about the importance of punctuality for the construction of a modern and orderly society while in practice teaching us that punctuality was a waste of time.

But today's workshop was different. Today, Natalia, the regional supervisor for the Good Governance NGO had planned a workshop on "logical frameworks" to help Pachacutanas identify problems and propose well-reasoned solutions to potential project funders. "NGOs and also the state use this strategy, the logical framework, for projects because finance organizations don't want to read a four-hundred-page report!" Natalia said. "They need a simple rubric to understand the issue and know what to do about it."

The workshop began with participants writing down Pachacútec's biggest problems on index cards and handing them to the front of the room for Natalia to read aloud: "Lack of water and sewage systems. Domestic violence. Leadership conflicts. Lack of communication within families. Unemployment. Domestic violence. Adolescent pregnancies. Trash. Gangs. Domestic violence. Unemployment. Lack of workshops." Natalia stopped. "Wait, is this a problem?" A few hesitant voices answered "No." Natalia continued.

> We have to clarify what we're talking about. . . . [A lack of workshops] is not a problem. That is a solution written as a problem. . . . The logical framework, which you are going to produce today, is a matrix in which you organize the problems and then identify the corresponding actions to resolve them.

Natalia modeled this style of thinking by evaluating one issue that attendees identified: the problem of gangs.

> The problem of gangs has many associated problems. You have delinquency, murder, domestic violence, abusive parents, all of these things are related. But when we're talking about gangs, what is the CENTRAL problem? The CENTRAL problem is domestic violence! Gangs are a consequence of abusive parents. For example, the woman accepts it when the man is only in the house three days a week, but she gets sad and as a result she loses patience with her kids. Of course, we're talking about gangs, but we have to first talk about domestic violence because that's where the problem comes from. . . . The child feels rejected by his mother who spoke harshly with him, so he joins up with other children who feel rejected. . . . He has low self-esteem and he

wants to integrate himself with a group. He is looking for protection, for people who will defend him.

Natalia diagrammed this dynamic, her red marker squeaking as she dragged it across chart paper to form large arrows. "Domestic violence, which leads to children with low self-esteem, which leads to gangs." The all-female audience seemed transfixed by the clarity of her argument. "Remember, the family can be a space where the child develops fully or where he is driven to gangs. . . . So what is the central problem?" Natalia contended that any successful anti-gang program would have to stop the problem at the source, that is, in the space of the home.

Step 2 was to identify actors who might be involved in solving this problem. Workshop participants called out responses: "The family." "Kids and adolescents." "Parents." "Schools." "Local governments." "Society. . . . Society must also be involved because of the issues of employment." Here, Natalia intervened again. "Society is getting really big. That has to do with corporations. But for a person who is a delinquent or in a gang, [corporations] will never give him a job to enter society. So, where does the problem start?"

Natalia redrew the problem in the form of a tree. As with all trees, she said, one had to start at the roots. "What is the root of the problem? What is the central problem?" Audience members called out responses that, with some coaching from Natalia, grew increasingly precise: "The child at risk." "A lack of love." "A lack of communication." "Maybe it's just a child with lack." "The problem is a child that lacks family protection." Eventually they group settled on "the child who lacks family protection due to mistreatment in the home."

"And why is the child being mistreated?" Natalia asked, before quickly answering her own question: "Because of conjugal problems and conflicts. . . . This generates physical and psychological violence. . . . So you see, in a project, you have to look at everything. . . . We have to look at the causes and consequences of our problem. We see that poverty generates delinquency, which generates more poverty. And now it's time for a break!"

As we sipped cloyingly sweet coffee and chewed buttered saltines, Anita complained to me about things women remained silent about, like their everyday experiences with jealous and abusive husbands or the child prostitution that she blamed on parents who were too lazy to work themselves. Pablo interrupted our conversation to remind me that if we broke into groups, I needed to step back and let women from the mothers clubs take charge. He was interested in seeing who emerged as leaders in these groups, so he knew who to tap for jobs as political promoters. As soon as the break was over, we returned to our problem tree.

To address the clearly identified problem of "a child without family protection," Natalia explained that we had to identify a positive corresponding objective, in this case, "protected children." She said, "We always have to keep our ideal in mind, but we also have to think about the reality, . . . about the context." Natalia went on to describe feminist movements that had failed in Peru's provinces because "out there, the culture is different. Here [in cities] women can realize their goals on their own, but in rural areas, it is not like that."

Natalia quickly shifted from describing how urban environments empowered women to be independent to explaining the importance of conjugal stability for the development of children.

> If we know that conjugal instability is a problem that generates physical and psychological abuse of the child, we need to imagine the corresponding positive framing, which would be constituted marriages, . . . that the family is well. . . . Being well has to do with communication between partners. Remember, conjugal stability has to do with the man and woman as a couple and not as parents. . . . We make a mistake in thinking that, when families stay together because they want to be good parents. If the problem doesn't come from being bad parents but instead from conjugal instability, staying together to be good parents isn't going to resolve the situation.

Marisa whispered to me, "What she says is true. A lot of times the woman hits the child because she knows the father is going to suffer."

Natalia continued, "The positive objective that corresponds to conjugal problems is stable couples and relationships. So, you see, if you don't clearly identify the problem and offer a solution to something else, the project is going to fail."

Having determined that gangs were a symptom of more fundamental problems of conjugal instability, workshop participants now had to find a solution. One of the first solutions women proposed was that they find a way to improve mothers' self-esteem. If mothers had high self-esteem, the logic went, they would demand good treatment from their partners and be willing to leave if they were being abused or were otherwise unhappy in the relationship. By working on themselves, mothers could ensure they either had a healthy marriage or were capable of being independent, empowered, complete social beings on their own.

"And what action might improve the mother's self-esteem?" Natalia asked rhetorically. "Remember at the beginning you said the problem in Pachacútec was the lack of workshops? Well, now we see that's not the problem. That's the strategy to resolve it. That comes at the end."

As Natalia finished her exposition, the audience erupted in applause. Although they had come full circle and were back to requesting workshops delivered through collaborations between local municipalities, professional experts, and NGOs, the journey they took to get there was crucial. Before learning the logical framework, the proposed problem of a lack of workshops was a knee-jerk reaction based on Pachacutanas' frequent encounters with development and state agents who consistently offered workshops to resolve Pachacútec's "social problems," those problems that were prefigured in Peru as separate from but foundational to the more official spheres of politics and economics and that, as Natalia suggested, kept people from entering society (Biehl and Eskerod 2007; Escobar 1995). Because workshops were so often offered as solutions, many Pachacutanas tacitly assumed that social problems remained because they and their neighbors had not been trained thoroughly enough. Means and ends are frequently conflated in development work (Ferguson 1994; Sen 1999), and Natalia wanted better from these emerging mother-leaders. She wanted to make sure they were capable of clearly parsing cause and effect, problems and solutions. It was not enough for women to ask for workshops. They had to understand why workshops would be effective. They had to internalize the idea that the problems they confronted living in Pachacútec and in Peru were products of their own behavior and specifically their failure to create healthy family environments by maintaining good relationships with their spouses.

Workshops like this epitomize the domestication of poverty in Peru as a multivalent and ongoing process. In parsing the issue of gangs, women examined a complex array of interconnected problems and actors, only to filter them out and determine that the central problem could be traced to their own behavior as mothers and partners. Anything that might challenge this received wisdom—such as acknowledging the lack of local employment opportunities, the behavior of abusive husbands, the profound social inequalities evidenced in officials' disregard for women's time, the way party politics permeated women's everyday efforts to improve their lives, and other contextual challenges to women's empowerment—was systematically placed out of view with Natalia's gentle exhortations: "What is the central problem?" "Where does the problem really start?" By the end of the workshop, most women understood the responsible answer to be that violence began in the home, and more specifically with their own self-esteem, behavior, and identities as women, and that the solution was to collaborate with authorities and professional experts so that they might address their personal deficiencies.

If Natalia's explanation made sense to women, it was because they had encountered these self-immolating logics before, through institutions and discursive arenas that collectively operate as "forces of governmentality," linking the management of the population to the regulation of "sexual behaviors, and intimate relations within the private and domestic realms of heteronormative families" (Gupta 2012, 238). School curricula and NGO workshops teach women about the kinds of families they should aspire to, encouraging them to construct life projects that emphasize sharing their lives, establishing deep emotional connections, and building democratic families with open lines of communication.

Meanwhile, popular media and everyday gossip illustrate the stakes of domestic failure and women's singular responsibility for it, too often in grisly ways. When police found the body of a young woman, one of Vicky's neighbors, dismembered and stuffed in a suitcase, speculation about what happened spread quickly. In one group conversation, a neighbor offered, "It seems the girls [the victim and her sister] were *media ruca* [kind of slutty], and they liked to go out a lot. . . . The sister went off with one guy and left the other sister with some Arab. . . . She was raped and then he killed her. The worst of it is that it seems the girl was two or three months pregnant." A second neighbor expressed surprise that "the girl would be like that because her mom is a police officer." A third clarified that the mother's job was likely the problem: "Since the mom is out working all the time, she is not there to control and guide them. What's more, it's not like police are the most upstanding of characters either." In short, female immorality and motherly failure were responsible for the girl's fate.

In this context, what made Natalia's workshop remarkable was how elegantly it synthesized diffuse poverty-domestication messages and combined multiple poverty-domestication projects in a single event. The household was ideologically positioned as a container, index, and site for the reproduction of poverty, and political solutions were limited to constructing formal and legible requests for training. Additionally, in Natalia's example, the most troubling effects of this household-level failure were the unprotected children who ultimately formed gangs, groups whose problematic nature was defined by their appearance in the street, disconnected from home and proper family structures. At the same time, in the workshop full of mothers, many of whom self-identified in

FIGURE 5.1. A poster listing "Norms of Cohabitation," 2010. The handmade illustrated list is posted on the wall of a *comedor popular* that hosts a Healthy Home workshop. Photo by the author.

different circumstances as single or separated, we see a central problematic emerging as women are taught that constructing a proper home and being an effective mother depend on establishing stable, heteronormative, companionate relationships. The emphasis on pursuing particular types of conjugal relations is somewhat at odds with other dominant framings of motherhood in Lima as an asexual and all-consuming relational identity (Gandolfo 2009). Nonetheless, these different relational ideals have important implications for the kinds of relationships women pursue throughout their lives and for how they evaluate the success or failure of their intimate life projects.

RATIONAL LOVE AND NATIONAL PASSIONS

A dusty Ministry of Health pamphlet from the 1980s offers a useful caricature of what modern companionate marriages are supposed to be from the perspective of the Peruvian government.[1] The pamphlet, entitled *Mi derecho a decidir* (My right to decide), offers the pink-complexioned Marcela as an example of how women should rationally choose their intimate partners. According to the text, at twenty-three years old, Marcela has finally found the man of her dreams in Alberto. Because she is in love, she has decided to get married. The caption explains that she has considered this decision thoroughly, "knows why people get married and what its purpose is," and only takes this step having already worked hard to become a nurse. She and her fiancé, Alberto, are then pictured on a couch discussing how wonderful it is that they both know what they want and are ready to take a premarital orientation course. Thought bubbles percolate from their heads.

> Alberto: "I feel so happy that I can marry Marcela! She is everything a woman should be and is happy to be so!"
> Marcela: "I feel so sure of what I am going to do. I am sufficiently mature and Alberto is as well."

In the next frame, Marcela speaks to her mother at the dinner table. "My last month as a bachelorette! I am happy because now I can put into practice my right to decide about my sex life. I owe you so much, Mom." The blurb below them introduces a narrative twist: "Marcela is talking with her adoptive mother."

The story then moves directly from Marcela and Alberto's mutual decision to get their prenuptial health exam to a picture of them embracing in bed a few years later. "Several years have passed. Marcela and Alberto form a happy couple. They converse and have mutual admiration for each other. She is pregnant." We witness the couple whispering sweet gender affirmations to each other. Marcela: "Our child will be a good man like you!" Alberto: "Or perhaps a good woman, like you!"

The next frame shows close-ups of Marcela and Alberto individually, their large floating heads presented as far away from each other as the page allows. Marcela thinks, "How wonderful it is to feel like a mother. Where must my real mother be? She surely had me by accident." Alberto guesses at her thoughts. "I can guess your thoughts! I think that in our neighborhood there are many women who are not as prepared as you to decide about their maternity." He comes close but misses the most intimate and most governmental aspects of what she was thinking: her personal sense of loss and incompletion and the ways supposedly irresponsible parenthood infringes on the rights of children to know their origins and by extension themselves. His misreading affirms a sentiment I had heard from several Peruvians regarding the limits of interpersonal knowledge in couples. As one elderly woman counseled me, "You have to know your partner well before you marry. But you never know them completely. They can always surprise you." Rather than correct Alberto, Marcela responds, "Nor are they prepared to decide about their right to the love of a man."

The rest of the pamphlet consists of scenes of Marcela and Alberto holding hands and staring into each other's eyes as they discuss how much they love each other and how well they understand what real love is compared to others in their neighborhood whose backward and antagonistic gender identities impede the formation of loving companionate unions. They applaud themselves for being responsible gendered beings who respect each other's rights to a "tender and pleasurable intimate union" and decry men who "impose their sex on women in every aspect of life" and women who "use sex to dominate men . . . or simply to secure a stable future and obtain physical pleasure." The pamphlet concludes by summarizing what is portrayed in the preceding narrative—"a happy couple . . . two people who love and respect each other as spouses, lovers, and as responsible parents and providers"—and the stakes of emulating Marcela and Alberto's example: "Responsible partnership is the basis of responsible paternity. Responsible paternity is the basis for responsible families. Responsible families will construct a better future for their neighborhood and country."

The pamphlet is clearly targeted toward women. The front cover features the faces of several dark-haired, pink-faced women with a caption that reads, "Women in the Community: Girls, Youth, Adults. Half of the population of the community is women." The substance and implications of this targeting become more apparent when compared to a contemporaneous pamphlet apparently targeted toward men.

The pamphlet entitled "Project of Holistic Attention for Children

FIGURE 5.2. Pages from "My Right to Decide," 1980. The booklet published by Peru's Ministry of Health takes readers on a woman's journey as she pursues a modern romantic relationship and responsible parenthood for the good of the nation. *Source*: MINSA 1980.

FIGURE 5.3. The Ministry of Health pamphlet "Holistic Attention Project for Children and Their Families," 1980. The booklet features a male narrator describing the challenges of serving a rapidly growing urban population. *Source*: MINSA 1980.

and Families in Lima's Southern Cone" features a cover image of a man looking down concertedly at his wife and child. This father figure introduces himself as "a resident of a Young Town, like you," who wants to talk about the crisis of rapid population growth, the lack of infrastructure and economic resources, and what community members can do about it. In this way, men are encouraged to participate in development and enact their citizenship by thinking like a state in terms of "the population," "infrastructure," and "economic resources." Women, meanwhile, participate in development and enact citizenship through the home, their gendered relationships with men, and the control they exercise over their own bodies.

While these pamphlets are antiquated and imbued with the surreal platitudinous aura of public service announcements, they nonetheless reveal how Peruvian women's pursuits of companionate relationships that are "*chosen* according to and based upon a relationship of *mutual affection and intimacy* between two partners" are deemed integral to both personal and national projects of modernity (Patico 2010, 373, my emphasis). Contrary to discourses that naturalize current manifestations of romantic love around the world, anthropologists have shown that this form of love has risen to global prominence in connection with broader processes of urbanization, capitalist modernity, consumerism, individualism, global media circulation, and, critically, through men's and women's situated efforts to identify themselves as modern individuals in a context where this identity may otherwise elude them (Hirsch and Wardlow 2006; Pribilsky 2007). Elizabeth Povinelli (2002, 217) has further connected companionate love to the rise of the democratic nation-state, in which "stranger sociability . . . and membership in an abstract human order, rather than in a family (aristocratic) grid, increasingly defined civil, social and political rights and obligations." Povinelli finds that "intimate love" became the "tender of the democratic marriage contract, the true grounds for the union between persons, and a necessary basis for a community of people" (233). She goes on to contend, "So tightly has the narrative *I* of intimacy become associated with the human and humanity that to be without it is to risk being dehumanized and subject to all the harms of the dehumanizing practices of modernity" (234).

This form of love, though, harbors an internal contradiction. While the Peruvian state emphasizes the role of rational choice in intimate relations, the "blurring of choice and compulsion" is a defining feature of modern intimacy (Povinelli 2002, 229), and one that Peruvians are regularly exposed to through telenovelas, nightly news, social media, and everyday gossip.

The articulation and blurring of choice and compulsion as defining dimensions of modern love became evident in conversations Peruvians struck up with me about national characters and cultural attitudes around love and family. As an unmarried, white, American woman in my twenties at the time of this fieldwork, I was frequently asked by Peruvians about differences between Peruvian and American men and about national differences in relationship styles more generally.[2] I quickly learned it was best to respond to these questions vaguely and impersonally, at least at first. This helped ensure I didn't say anything that would alienate my interlocutor and gave them an opportunity to articulate their own theories of national romantic character.[3]

The most frequent theory I encountered was that North Americans were *más frío*, colder, meaning that they were less emotional, more pragmatic, and more self-centered than Peruvians. Peruvians further used characterizations of Americans as *más frío* in culturalist explanations of US economic development: the United States progressed economically because its rational, self-interested citizens sought fulfillment through their careers rather than through family. Sexually, being *frío* could mean someone was conservative, unemotional, and dispassionate, but being *frío* could also make someone more liberal or sexually promiscuous. Diana, the coordinator for a local INABIF after-school program, told me matter-of-factly, "According to the statistics, in the US and Europe people are more liberal. . . . That means they don't love their own bodies because they let anybody use it." I recalled this conversation on a bus a few weeks later as I found myself seated below a sticker bearing the slogan "Mejor una chola conocida que una gringa con SIDA" (It's better to be with a local/Andean girl that you know than with a foreign/white girl with AIDS).

Peruvians described themselves, by comparison, as *más caliente*, hotter, and *más cariñoso*, more affectionate. This imaginary permeated serious discussions about culture and intimacy, bawdy exchanges of sex jokes, and the many conversations that lay somewhere in between. In a long conversation I had with three Peruvian men about marriage and fidelity, one man tried to offer scientific support for his assertion that Peruvians were more passionate than American men. "They've proven it genetically that Latinos are hotter. That is what a Puerto Rican sexologist said, that Latinos are hotter due to their nature." His companion echoed this sentiment: "It's true. If a Latino man meets a woman, he wants THAT woman and he pursues and pursues her until he conquers her. He anguishes over her. He falls completely in love." Women I spoke with tended to affirm this characterization but suggested that this passion came at a price, often in the form of women's freedom and safety. Bertha observed, "The Peruvian man is more loving, but he also gets bitter quickly. If you behave well, though, everything is fine." Peruvian men were also depicted as more likely than American men to cheat on their partners, a practice that was generally expected but not condoned.[4]

My interlocutors were notably ambivalent about what they described as the typical Peruvian relationship style. Many were proud to describe the Peruvian national character as passionate, loving, emotional, and devoted to family, but this pride was attenuated by the association of these characteristics with irrationality, irresponsibility, and potential family disintegration. *Celos* played an important role in this ambivalence. Although most dictionaries translate *celos* as "jealousy," it means much more than that. *Celos* signals an intense love and potentially violent possessiveness. For instance, the first time I walked into Milagros's house, a cage of small yellow birds at the entrance caught my eye briefly before Milagros's mother interrupted my gaze. "They just had babies, but don't look directly at them," she said. "If you look at them, the parents will kill them. They start pecking at their heads, kill them, and eat their brains . . . because they are *celosos*. If you look at the babies too much, they get *celosos* and they kill them."

Mothers would talk about how they were *celosa* with their children, signaling that they cared for them deeply but were potentially overprotective. Romantic partners were also supposed to be *celosos*. Although *celos* was cited as a common reason that relationships failed—"She was very *celosa*. A person simply can't live like that"—*celos* also coded for the seriousness of a relationship. During an initial flirtation, men would often follow the question "Do you have a boyfriend or husband?" with "Y él está celoso?" (Is he possessive?) in an effort to gauge just how far a flirtation could go.

The practice of "marking," calling your partner's mobile phone to check in, was similarly associated with the tangled nexus of love, possessiveness, and mistrust through which many Peruvians interpreted their romantic relationships. When one of my interlocutors' partners called them at work, a colleague would inevitably jibe, "Oy, te está marcando" (Ohhh, someone is marking you), suggesting the caller was trying to control them but also that the caller cared enough to do so.[5]

In newspapers, *celos* was most often depicted as an irrational, unmodern emotion that led to violence and femicide and had to be stamped out for the purpose of healthy, loving relationships.[6] In quotidian conversations, *celos* was often associated with the oppression of women and cited as something that impeded their lives outside the home; their husbands were *celosos* and wouldn't let them go out. *Celos* was the distorted underbelly of national values that included passion, emotional attachment, and family devotion. Despite the drawbacks, my interlocutors indicated that these traits not only characterized them as Peruvians but also made them more human.

FAMILY POVERTY

Diana, the head of Pachacútec's INABIF after-school program, offers a striking example of how women might negotiate these different dimensions of modern intimacy and the ways official ideologies linking women's intimate lives to national poverty are reproduced in everyday life. Diana was a short woman in her early forties with lightly toasted skin and curly brown hair that she harnessed into a tight braid. In every interaction I had with her, she took great care to present herself as mature, educated, and morally virtuous. She was official discourse incarnate, the Christian, social welfare version of the good Weberian bureaucrat, fully inhabiting her post in an organization charged with overcoming "poverty, extreme poverty, and social risk by strengthening the capacities of children, adolescents, and their families in ways that prepare them to confront life."[7] Echoing the official messages of INABIF, Diana contended that poverty and social risk were the consequences of "unprepared" and "incapable" families and asserted this position in her interactions with Pachacutanos and in the ways she narrated her own life story.

Her account of why she decided not to have children intertwined with her understanding of what couple and family relationships should be.

> I never wanted to be one of those women who gets divorced or who has one husband after another. No, . . . I didn't want to bring a child into the world if it wasn't going to have a stable mother and father, if it wasn't going to be the product of a true love that lasts. I never wanted any of that where you get married and then he cheats on you, you separate, there's fighting. What kind of environment is that for a child? . . . That's why I decided long ago that no, that I wasn't going to have children.

In marked contrast to her professed ideal of family life, most of the parents Diana dealt with in Pachacútec were single mothers, "or if not," she said, "the children live with their grandparents or aunts and uncles or what have you." Diana attributed much of the poverty she encountered in Pachacútec to a "cycle of poverty" in which immature or unstable relationships played a critical role.

> This is all the product of immature sexual relationships, young people who fall in love. Well, it is not really love. It is all illusion and sex. Afterwards, they get pregnant, and young people are not capable of

> raising [their kids]. They don't have anywhere to live. . . . Poverty brings more poverty. It's that they want the easy life. They want to go out to the discotheque, meet their little partners, dance, cause trouble, and like that they get pregnant. And they are not thinking about their duties as parents. They don't think about how to formalize a home, how to have a place to live, a job, or how they are going to feed the child later. . . . They are not ready to form a home.

As Diana spoke, I was struck by her focus on "forming" and "formalizing" a home. Particularly in a context where "formalization," official recognition and inscription, was closely associated with development and modernity, I wondered what it meant to "formalize" a home as opposed to formalizing a house, business, or identity. Diana explained, "To formalize a home means to marry civilly in front of the municipality. To formalize is to be decided. . . . If you don't have that, the children end up living with godparents, aunts and uncles, grandparents."

Diana said that being decided and formalizing the home were important for economic reasons: "Girls who have babies at thirteen years old, all of them end up the same way. How are they going to manage after breastfeeding the child? At six months old you have to supplement that with food, with special purées, and how are they going to buy it? Parents can't give the child something they don't have." However, in Diana's account, the formalized home was also important for combatting poverty in its own right. For her, the poorest of the poor, those most in need of assistance, were children who did not live in two-parent households or who were not cared for primarily by their biological mothers.

Diana's understanding of poverty became evident when, on my first visit to INABIF, she tried to convince me to be a *madrina*, a godmother, for either the entire INABIF after-school program or at least for the neediest children there. "Here, we are like siblings. . . . All of the children know each other quite well. But most of the kids already have lots of siblings at home. Elvis has six. Alice has four. Mirian, well, Mirian has fewer, only three." By describing the number of siblings each student had, Diana sought to index their premodern demographic identities and send me a message about the extent of each child's poverty without making it obvious to the students.

Concerned that the kids would pick up on what Diana was saying about them, I tried to counter the insinuation by responding positively to the high numbers, saying aloud that it was nice that the children had lots of people to play with at home. Diana tried again, this time hinting at poverty more forcefully: "Many of them are orphans. They live with their aunts and uncles, a few with their older siblings. . . . We have one student here who is part of a family of five orphans. The youngest is four, the oldest is seventeen. And the oldest works so the others can study."

On another occasion Diana took me to visit an INABIF branch several kilometers down the road that provided lunches for local children. When we arrived, Diana prompted the site administrator to tell me about the orphans who ate there. "Yes," the woman affirmed, "there are a lot of abandoned children here. . . . They stay with their aunts and uncles, or with their siblings." The administrator went on to explain that many of the children who ate there lived with their parents, but their parents couldn't provide them with lunch at home because they were out working during the day. "Even when the parents work far away, it is a type of abandonment. It is a moral abandonment," she said. The use of the term "abandonment" here reflects the high expectations placed on mothers as primary caregivers and the ease with which mothers can be found to fall short in this capacity. It likewise reflects the importance of feeding and the sharing of substance for constituting relatedness in Peru and the pervasive belief that biological mothers, who have already nurtured children through the sharing of blood in utero, are best suited to continue nurturing by nourishing and that failing to do so weakens existing filial bonds (Van Vleet 2008; Weismantel 1995).

Diana suggested that two-parent family structures and a mother cooking at home were critical to a child's well-being. When I asked her to explain what she meant by the term "nuclear family," she referred to behaviors rather than structures: "people who don't drink, who don't swear, who aren't violent." For Diana, nuclear family structures were associated with particular behaviors but were not coterminous with them. While the challenge of realizing this familial vision had purportedly prompted her decision to remain single, she nonetheless perpetuated this vision of proper families in the children she helped care for.

As we walked back to the civic center from the food-service INABIF, we were trailed by a ten-year-old boy named Bryan, whom Diana cited as an example of how the INABIF's perspectives on family could improve lives.

> Before, he was very disobedient. But now he's calm. Goodness came to his heart. . . . The problem is that kids now are very exposed to bad influences. . . . They shouldn't be watching movies, news, telenovelas. . . . A telenovela teaches you about sex, about cheating, about jealousy.

> And all of this is bad. In the INABIF we give lectures to parents to try and teach them how to improve their home environment, but there is only so much we can do. And it's a shame, because it's all a chain. If the parents are drunks, the children are also going to be. It's a chain.

Bryan dutifully repeated Diana's lesson, saying, "Yes, it's all a chain."

THE CURIOUS CASE OF SINGLE MOTHERS

In a context where family is understood as a critical site for the elaboration of modern citizens and a developed nation and women are identified as singularly responsible for its maintenance, single mothers occupied a complex and contradictory moral position. They were understood simultaneously as the poorest of the poor and as immoral "reproducers of poverty" (Boesten 2010). In their everyday negotiations of this identity, women vacillated between presenting themselves as icons of virtuous struggle and as separated beings, permanently parted and perpetually incomplete.

The association of single-motherhood with poverty was common sense in Peru. In a speech delivered by the mayor of Ventanilla at a local rally I attended, the percentage of single mothers in the district was cited as one of several demographic features that contributed to and were constitutive of area poverty: "Of the population in Ventanilla, 70 percent live in settlements; 50 percent lack water. . . . As the population increases, so does the delinquency. Many come from destroyed families. Seven of ten mothers here are single mothers or abandoned."

The relation between single mothers and poverty was likewise codified in bureaucratic practices of targeting social assistance. To identify eligible recipients, social workers at the Catholic charity soup kitchen used a point system in which belonging to a female-headed, single-parent household—identified in the records as a *familia disfuncional* (dysfunctional family) in contrast to a *familia nuclear* (nuclear family) with the father and mother present—and having a large *carga familiar* (family obligation, number of dependents) carried substantial weight. The single-mother identity was so salient in determinations of deserving poverty that some interlocutors presumed certificates of single-motherhood would be required to receive state assistance, although no such requirement, and indeed no such document, exists.[8]

In encounters with state agents, the deservingness of single mothers hinged on their ability to present themselves as blameless in their singleness; their partner had to either abandon them or abuse them to the point that leaving the relationship was the only viable course of action. At the same time, the women had to appear hyperagentic in fulfilling their obligations as mothers. As one interlocutor explained when I asked why she thought single mothers were always considered the neediest: "It's because they must care for others when there is no one to care for them." Yet the image of being both agentic and blameless was hard to maintain for single mothers who were also always shadowed by specters of sexual impropriety. A female functionary in charge of food assistance programs in Pisco alluded to promiscuity as a cause of poverty even in the aftermath of disaster: "Since the earthquake, there is more poverty. There are more single mothers, and it seems like people have more children. Many women got pregnant after the earthquake despite not having houses. I don't know where they did it, but that's how it was. But poverty like that you see everywhere."

The specter of sexual impropriety likewise came up when I inquired about the ubiquity of single mothers at the site of a recent invasion. When a group of women said they deserved recognition for their land claims because almost all of them were single mothers, I clumsily asked why there were so many single mothers there. One quick-witted woman responded, "Porque se dejan" (because they let them, meaning they allowed men to have sex with them), leading to uproarious laughter from all the women in the group.

The moral marginalization of single mothers has a long history in Latin America, where single mothers have on various occasions been officially deemed unfit to care for children they birth out of wedlock (Fonseca 2009; Milanich 2002). For instance, in describing a nineteenth-century court case in Chile, Gabriel Salazar (1985, 290) quotes an official who states, "I have been ordered to investigate those women vagabonds who live in our district without means of subsistence; principally those who maintain illicit relations and have many illegitimate children. . . . The local inspector has ordered that the children of those women be deposited in homes of respectable individuals."

In Peru, single mothers are often depicted as constitutionally unable to fulfill the requirements of good mothering, which demands an all-consuming commitment. The intrinsic impossibility of the morally unambiguous single mother emerged in Anita's description of the "problemática de la mujer pachacutana," the problem of the woman from Pachacútec: "The problem is that 70 percent of the women in Pachacútec are single mothers. Heads of household. That is, they are mother and father for their children. And because they are working, they have to leave their children alone in the house."

The phrase "mother and father for their children" was typically used to depict single parents in a favorable light, as selflessly taking on a double burden and devoting themselves entirely to their children. Yet what followed from this double burden—"leaving their children alone in the house," leaving them in someone else's care, or leaving them to be fed by someone besides the mother—was often framed through the language of abandonment. This was where all mothers, and especially impoverished single mothers, readily lost the moral high ground and became (re)producers of poverty, failing in their naturalized duties to mold their children into proper citizens and defend them against the entropic forces of vice and criminality to which unprotected children are believed susceptible.

The term *abandonado* in Peru has connotations of permanence, as an irreparable severing of bonds of care and concern, and has important legal implications, as declarations of abandonment allow the state to take control of a child's well-being (Leinaweaver 2008). Yet in practice, "abandonment" is used to refer to even temporary shortfalls in expected but perhaps unspoken obligations of care. Thus, gendered expectations that tie women to the household mean that women who migrate for work or simply work outside the home can be accused of socially and legally abandoning their children, while men can disappear for months at a time and still be deemed good fathers (Campoamor 2016; Wilhoit 2017).

The ease with which mothers are deemed to be failing in their care duties, and the discursive gymnastics women must deploy to construct themselves as moral beings while struggling to provide for children in precarious circumstances, are related in part to the hypervisibility of mothers in the discourses of international development, Latin American nationalism, and Andean kinship, all of which circulate and intertwine in urban Peru, informing everyday ideals of moral motherhood. Krista Van Vleet (2008, 128) suggests, "Tracing the ways in which multiple texts speak to each other, sometimes reinforcing and at other times contesting particular meanings, enables a fuller though not a complete rendering" of experience and helps us to interpret silences that may be "suggestive of social constraints and contradictions, in which and through which, individuals must still act and live."

Since the mid-1990s, global development agents have emphasized the feminization of poverty, the increased likelihood of poverty in female-headed households, and what Sylvia Chant (2008) describes as "the bold and largely untenable claim" (172) that fully "70% of the world's poor were female" (166). To redress this feminized poverty, development agents construct programs to empower women, facilitating their participation in political and market spheres so they can care for their families and promoting an imaginary of female household heads as entrepreneurial and autonomous caregivers.[9] Yet programs to empower women as mothers have had perverse effects, translating into "a generalized bid to alleviate poverty primarily, or even exclusively through women" (Chant 2008, 172), thus increasing women's responsibilities while providing limited support and invisibilizing other dimensions of female identity and other actors who might assume care and development duties (Lind 2009).

Women as mothers are likewise hypervisibilized in national discourses in Latin America that promote and politicize Marianist understandings of mothers as chaste, self-sacrificing figures who manage clean and virtuous homes in service of the nation. In Chile, Clara Han (2012) notes, "women's roles in reproduction and domestic labor have been a central aspect of imaginations of political community since the emergence of the liberal Chilean state" (131). The nineteenth-century " 'woman-mother' of the popular classes" was a critical point of "intervention for a scientific and philanthropic approach to poverty" (65), and the twentieth-century "mother-militant" was praised for being a class leader "without abandoning their home and children" (132). Likewise in Peru, women's political participation has been predicated on the extension of their maternal roles into the public sphere as managers of food-assistance cooperatives and child care centers or as more honest and socially minded variants of male politicians (Blondet 1999; Blondet and Trivelli 2004; Boesten 2010; Mannarelli 1999). The focus in these discourses is not so much on single mothers as on mothers in their singularity. Their political agency and unassailable moral status are predicated on an ostensibly singular devotion to children that eclipses other relations and axes of identity. Paradoxically, the singular fixation on mothers reaffirms heteronormative national scripts while naturalizing the absent father such that, "even if physically present in the household, the father is not expected to occupy a productive or even morally authoritative role" (Campoamor 2016, 159).

Andean marriage and kinship patterns similarly affirm the normalcy of heteronormative two-parent households and make space for singularly powerful mother figures in the form of *cholas* and market women. Early ethnographic descriptions of Andean gender and kinship emphasized the "complementarity" of men and women, an understanding that the full social person was the man-woman pair (*quariwarmi*),[10] and that adulthood was constituted by marriage and the formation of neolocal households that engaged in reciprocal relations with the rest of the community (Harvey 1994; Van Vleet 2008; Weismantel and Wilhoit 2019). At the same time, there is precedent for powerful lone mothers in the figure of Andean *cholas*. Unlike Latin American national frames in which women's political clout comes from reasserting their properly domestic function in public space, Andean *cholas* arrange "working, sleeping, eating, and loving in ways that cannot readily be reduced to a single dichotomy of public and private" and thus are often viewed as "dirty" and lower class by formal government standards (Weismantel 2001, 74). Nonetheless, these women proudly embrace identities as *macha* (a feminist appropriation of masculine toughness) and as "madre y padre para mis hijos" (mother and father for my children), fulfilling care duties by creating reciprocal relations with other women, not necessarily without men but regardless of them (Seligmann 2009; Weismantel 2001; Wilhoit 2017).

In Peru's urban settlements, these different understandings of uniquely empowered lone mothers intertwine as women constitute their identities in dialogue with others and in relation to broader societal discourses. I most often heard women speak of themselves as single mothers and as mothers and fathers for their children when they were presenting themselves to bureaucrats and potential patrons as people deserving of assistance or when narrating life stories in which they saw themselves struggling valiantly to care for children without a clear sense of whom they might call on for assistance.

In other contexts, the heteronormative and companionate background for these lone-mother identities would dominate. Women would describe themselves not as single but as separated, an identity that invoked the lively and ever-present absence of a lost companion and a failed companionate relationship. This deep sense of loss and familial incompletion, which was made possible by the value placed on intimate and familial love in everyday life, was evident in Peruvians' dramatic narratives of abandonment as well as in clipped responses that pointed to things they remained silent about.

NARRATING SEPARATION

One particularly memorable instance of a separation narrative came out of a community brainstorming session run by an international NGO seeking a novel, compelling, and contextually sensitive way to frame its child-focused development work in Pachacútec. One of the internationals running the meeting laid out the challenge the NGO faced: "We are looking for the biggest problems, but we would like to work on an issue where there hasn't been much attention. The problem is that the biggest problems are already being worked by everyone."

The organizers began the meeting by asking participants to offer *testimonios* (testimonies) of their "greatest joys and sorrows," with particular reference to early childhood, which they would film for funders back in Europe. To justify this approach, one said, "Generally, the reports they get are in the form of numbers and documents. We hope the video will give them a fuller understanding of the situation in Peru." Although it was likely unintentional, the NGO's use of the term *testimonio* for the responses they elicited opens intriguing avenues for analysis. *Testimonio* is a Latin American literary genre in which a "witness portrays his or her own experience as a representative of a collective memory or identity" (Yudice 1991, 17). John Beverley (2008) describes *testimonio* as a metonymic and authentic "emergency narrative—involving a problem of repression, poverty, marginality . . . or simply survival" that disrupts intellectual hegemony by giving subaltern populations an opportunity to voice truth from their vantage (572). *Testimonio* carries connotations of bearing witness and, Beverley contends, obligates readers to respond in some way: "We can act or not on that obligation, but we cannot ignore it" (574). Yet *testimonio* can also establish hierarchical relations between the narrator and the listener or reader, reproducing the inequalities of gender, class, race, and cultural authority that determine the urgent situation of the narrator to begin with (573). Indeed, after the meeting, several attendees told me they felt this opening activity was exploitative and voyeuristic and that sitting around reflecting on personal tragedies wasn't going to accomplish anything for poor children in Pachacútec.

But that was afterward. During the meeting, attendees were all to listen and share alike. I exited briefly at the start of the meeting to greet some children I knew who were waiting for their parents outside. By the time I returned, three women were already in tears and another woman was about to begin her *testimonio*. She gave her name and slowly began to reveal that the hardest time in her life was when she separated from her partner.

> I wanted to commit suicide. I wanted to kill my two children and then myself. But then I thought, "And if I die and they don't? Or they die and I don't?" . . . But sometimes when it got bad, . . . I even got to the point of buying the poison. . . . Then I got sick and my mother arrived to help

> and things started to get better. . . . Now my mom has passed and the only joy in my life are my two children, being at home with my children. One is eight and the other is five.

In response to a question about how she retained optimism in her household, she replied, "I tell my kids 'I love you,'" then quickly admitted, "I am a bit possessive of them" (*Tengo un poco de celos con ellos*).

When she finished, one of the internationals running the meeting asked if anyone remembered the woman's name. No one did. The testimony had eclipsed the teller, standing in more broadly for women's experiences of poverty and suffering in which children are simultaneously reminders of women's separated state and their only salvation from it. "Verónica," the woman said softly. "My name is Verónica."

Speech acts occur and have meaning in context, meanings that are negotiated between speakers and hearers and that are productive of particular relations. Heard in real time rather than read or watched later, Verónica's *testimonio* resembles what Van Vleet (2008) identifies in the Bolivian Andes as *llakikuy*, a discursive act of sorrowing that "expresses a gap between the expectations of relatedness and the actualities" (80) and a performance that "enacts connection, points to ruptures in the social fabric, and influences an audience" (81). Like *testimonio*, *llakikuy* calls on hearers to respond in some way, perhaps by offering comfort that seeks to repair the broken relation and in so doing, generates other relations of care. In this instance, the NGO organizer responded by telling Verónica, the rest of the room, and the camera that the first thing he noticed about her was her smile and how happy she looked. His comment was an effort at repair that emphasized her resilience and valiance as a single mother, offering a model of selfhood that seemed intrinsically complete and was recognizable to international development agents and Pachacutanos alike.

For her part, though, Verónica left the wound open, holding in view both the pain of her intimate loss and her capacity to endure. "Of course," she said, "I always smile on the outside, but on the inside sometimes . . ." She trailed off, leaving us to imagine what her smile obscured, highlighting the gap between appearance and reality, overtly reaffirming the cultural logic that a person's interior world was ultimately unknowable, hinting that internal pain and external persona were woven together, and then retreating into a silence that would allow all of us to get on with things. It was another instance of unruly domestication; things were patched over but not resolved, under control yet somehow still threatening in its intimate unknowability.

As participants continued around the circle, the different narratives of joy and sorrow seemed to track Verónica's template. Sorrows revolved around intimate loss, typically separation from a romantic partner that transected shortfalls in expectations of care from other family members. And people's greatest joys were invariably their children. Given the extent to which women's life projects were bound up with partners and families, it made sense that the loss of this ideal would constitute people's greatest sorrows.

In more quotidian circumstances, this sadness was expressed in subtler ways, often in short clips of conversations as the issue of romantic partnership and separation touched down in people's everyday lives, intersecting with stories about how they had come to live in a settlement or what they had done yesterday or would be doing today or tomorrow. I remember distinctly when Patricia mentioned that she came to Pachacútec to escape an abusive partner, her tone making clear that she did not wish to discuss their history further. I was also struck by the small ways Liliana would reference but quickly back away from talking about her romantic life, correcting me that the man I thought was her husband was really the father of her children, identifying her current boyfriend as merely someone she hung around so she "didn't get rusty," or openly ignoring a phone call and joking, "It's not the one I want." And then there was the time some Pachacutanas were comparing notes on their partners' romantic efforts or lack thereof on Valentine's Day. My longtime acquaintance, Ana, said simply that she was separated and preferred not to talk about love because it depressed her. "Now I dedicate myself to my children," she said, a common refrain that erected a personal boundary that, as friends and neighbors, people respected.[11]

Though these separation narratives played an important role in constituting experiences of poverty, in practice, separation was rarely permanent or complete. The diverse ways legal, local, and lived understandings of relationships aligned in the everyday complicated the nature of relational identities and related determinations of deserving poverty, while also creating spaces, cracks in the state's categorical schema, that women either fell between or used to their advantage (Scott 2005).

RELATIONS IN LAW AND PRACTICE

The first time I met Dr. Brennan, a lawyer the regional government had sent to supervise the distribution of land titles in Pachacútec's Special

Project, he was eager to convey that he was different from most government functionaries, more compassionate and benevolent: "It shouldn't matter to me if they [title applicants] are poor or not. I could . . . attend to the legal part and that's all. But I have a hard time ignoring the larger context. One becomes sensitive to the hardships people face."[12] Yet as soon as he finished this statement, he launched into an example of how his compassion had led him astray.

> This woman came in and she took me for a fool. She came in and said she had nowhere to live, and she had these kids and asked me for help. "Look, look at my kids," she said. So I felt bad for her and I found her a plot of land. Later there were problems. . . . The *dirigente* of the neighborhood kicked her out and told me why. It seems that she has a husband who is a [land] trafficker. . . . I should have been smarter. She said, "Look at my kids," . . . but then I find out it's not just her and her kids. She has a husband. That's why generally if you want to find out who is truly needy, you have to monitor them [*hacer un seguimiento*]. That's when the lies come out.

Although many of my interlocutors said monitoring and surveillance would help pin down identities and ensure that people were who they said they were, my own experiences in maintaining contact with interlocutors over years suggest otherwise. When it comes to relational identities—especially civil status identities such as single or married but also kin identities such as mother, child, and sibling—surveillance does less to reveal who people really are than to highlight how social identities change over time and across contexts. On the one hand, an individual's movement through the life course is partially constituted by the accumulation of relations and relational identities. People begin life as children, siblings, and cousins and over time accumulate other relational identities, becoming spouses, parents, aunts or uncles, in-laws, and compadres. Yet this progression is less linear than the term "life course" suggests. People draw on relations at different moments, and the strength of any tie or relational identity depends on particular life circumstances. Thus, while single mothers feature prominently in Peruvian ideologies of poverty, which is why Brennan categorized the female land applicant as deserving of special assistance, what it means to be single in Peru is not entirely clear. Legal definitions align with neither folk categories nor lived experiences of couple formation and dissolution. Moreover, although narratives of separation and abandonment are crucial for gaining resources from the state and the sympathies of neighbors and for constituting oneself as a decisive and empowered individual, these narratives are belied by the elasticity of relationships in practice.

Despite declaring their relationships to be over for various audiences, people remain tied together by different relational threads that can be weakened or reinvigorated in particular moments. My point here is not to unmask performances of single-motherhood but instead to consider how ideals and everyday experiences of single-motherhood are produced through layerings of law, discourse, and affect. By examining the interplay between legal and folk categories of coupledom, the possibilities for advancement and entrapment that exist in the space between formal designations and lived realities of kinship, and the ramp-up in state efforts to formalize individuals' civil status, I show how singleness is constituted in practice and illuminate the moral economy of relational flexibility in sites of poverty.

According to Peruvian ID cards, only four relational identities are possible: single, married, divorced, or widowed. These categories imply and instantiate a particular life trajectory. People are meant to go from single to married and then exit the state of marriage through divorce or death. Although remarrying is possible in this schema, one can never go back to being single. After being legally partnered, a person remains a special type of social entity whose present relational identity invokes the loss of a previous state. The normative implications of official civil status categories inform and reflect Peruvian conceptions of marriage and singledom, even if the civil status recorded on one's ID card has little to do with one's lived relational identity. Indeed, a Peruvian Ministry of Health report from 2013 indicated that 78 percent of births in Peru's public hospitals were to women in informal unions who described themselves as *convivientes* (Andina 2014). This striking figure highlights the uneven ways law permeates intimate relationships.

For most of my interlocutors, civil and religious marriages were tacked onto unions after they had already been constituted in practice. This custom is reminiscent of Andean "trial marriages." Far from mere marital experiments, in the Andean tradition the marriage trial period was used to establish a large "network of kin relations of permanent importance to both families" and allowed adults to mediate the young couple's "transition from adolescence to adulthood" by providing economic and moral support (Price 1965, 320). William Carter (1977, 212) characterizes this transitional stage as a long series of "intricately interwoven rituals, each of which sanctions a given stage of marriage and a given ontological level of growth on the part of the marriage partners." During this period, the various transitional or intermediate stages of marriage were themselves recognized as particular social entities.

In Peru's urban settlements, partners generally move in together, sometimes prompted by pregnancy, and then become tied to each other over time and through various life events such as having children, building houses, and constructing relations with in-laws. Milagros and her mother, Patricia, were kind enough to explain the relational order of things to me over lunch one day. Patricia began, "Once they sleep in the same bed, they're not *novios* [sweethearts] anymore. They are only *novios* when one has their apartment and the other is in their parents' house. . . . Once you sleep in the same bed, you have to say *conviviente* [cohabitant] or *compañero* [partner]." Although *convivientes* often referred to their live-in romantic partners as *esposos* (spouses), Milagros and Patricia explained that they are not officially *esposos* until they are married in either civil or religious ceremonies. The final term that Patricia and Milagros felt warranted explanation was *padre de mis hijos* (father of my children). In the company of her family, Milagros explained that *padre de mis hijos* is what a woman calls her partner after they have separated, suggesting that a mutual child was all that still tied the couple together. In private, though, Milagros revealed some of the messier affective dimensions of her own relationship with her former partner. Although she and her former *conviviente* had been separated for ten years, she said, "he still comes back from time to time, and I receive him. I shouldn't receive him. My family judges me for this, . . . but what am I going to do? He's the father of my children." Importantly, the terms *conviviente* and *compañero* were more than folk categories. Even if a couple had no government-issued marriage certificate to officialize them as a singular social entity in government registries, *conviviente* had become a civil status option listed on the national census, and certificates of *convivencia* could be obtained and notarized to allow partners to process documents for one another. Still, popular and quasi-official recognition of *convivencia* did not make marriage obsolete. When interlocutors talked about their romantic partners, they would frequently emphasize the seriousness and formality of their relationships by saying they had been married civilly and/or religiously. Milagros's grandmother proudly noted that she had been civilly married to her husband for fifty-two years and religiously married for eighteen years before he passed away.

> We were [first] married *civil* rather than *religioso* because there wasn't enough money for both, and they say that being formal under the law

> of man is worth more . . . because the law of man, civil marriage, is what you need to document anything as a couple. What's more, if you're not legally married, if your partner dies, you don't count as a widow and you have no right to the goods that you shared. . . . There are cases of children throwing their moms out onto the street and leaving them with nothing because there was no document that verified she was ever married. We've seen that sort of thing on the television.

In theory, without a civil marriage, partners were still technically single, and this single status was recorded on their national ID cards. Charo argued that, in these cases, ID cards were a lie, and that acting based on them would make the bearers liars too. She remarked, "My ID says I'm single, but I've had my *conviviente* for years already." In the year that I had known Charo, I had never once seen her *conviviente*, the man she typically referred to as her *esposo* and who spent most of the week living in the south of Lima so he could be closer to his job. When I asked Charo why she hadn't been formally married, she offered a half-joking response that I had heard from many others: "Because we want to stay in love." Charo's relationship points to the patchwork of law, affect, and folk categories that characterize conjugal relations in practice in urban Peru. Different components of coupledom, such as economic cooperation, legal obligation, sexual intimacy, affect, coresidence, shared ownership, and child-rearing can be disaggregated and stretched across time and space, keeping people tethered together despite their apparent singleness. Charo's analysis also points to the potential for disjunctures between how relationships are viewed by government agencies, neighbors, and the individuals who live with and are made by them.

Convivencia represents the most common misalignment between lived and legal relational categories in urban Peru. The second most common misalignment occurred among people who had been formally married but were now de facto separated. Many of these separations occurred suddenly, prompted by abuse or infidelity. In other cases the separation process was more gradual, drawn-out, and fuzzy at the edges. This is how Vicky's marriage ended. In the mid-1990s, when Fujimori's administration deployed economic shock therapy to revive the Peruvian economy, consumer prices rose along with unemployment. Vicky, her husband, Pedro, and her four children had no choice but to move out of their rented apartment in Lima and into a house in Ventanilla they had purchased several years earlier with a government subsidy. Prior to the Fujishock, moving to a place so far from centers of employment seemed foolish. But when jobs dried up and they could no longer afford rent, moving was the only option.

Vicky kept the family afloat by doing piecework embroidery at home while her husband searched for formal employment that never materialized. Eventually he decided to start an interprovincial transportation company with his brothers in his natal province of Arequipa. At first, he sent money home to Vicky when he had it, and he called often. Over time, though, the money and phone calls became less frequent until they finally petered out entirely. A decade went by before Pedro returned to Lima to celebrate the marriage of his eldest son, Nico, to the mother of Nico's newborn child. At the wedding, Pedro mentioned that he now had a baby the same age as Nico's child back in Arequipa.

With their children grown and Vicky supposedly happier living without Pedro, the birth of a child from another *compromiso* (commitment) would have been the last nail in the coffin of that relationship, were it not for Vicky and Pedro's legal and property ties. Vicky never even considered getting a divorce. Like others I spoke with, she said it would look ugly on her ID. She and Pedro remained legally tied and had to coordinate any time Vicky wanted to apply for a loan or put an addition on her house. It wasn't until 2010, fifteen years after their initial separation and seven years following Pedro's announcement of his other *compromiso*, that they severed their joint property ties by putting the house in the name of an adult son. He was applying for a visa to the United States, and everyone in the family was transferring assets to his name. In another instance of the ways legal, economic, and affective ties can be tangled together and stretched across space, it was only by drawing on his kin that Vicky's son could officially present himself as an autonomous and upstanding citizen with enough ties to Peru to get a visa to leave it.

Vicky and Pedro's relationship remained amicable enough that they could cooperate on legal matters; other women, however, found their formal civil status was a terrible impediment. This was the case for several women trying to obtain housing assistance in Pisco. Within the neighborhood, they were recognized as single mothers and socially considered to be among the neediest earthquake victims. But because they figured as married on their national IDs, they needed husbands' signatures to apply for certificates of property loss and new government-subsidized homes. A *dirigente* said, "This is especially bad because they are the people who are most needy. They are abandoned. They have kids, but they don't have a husband to support them." If they managed to get further along in the formalization process, de facto single mothers also worried that their husbands might come back to claim the properties as partially theirs. This was one of Nelly's big concerns. An agent of the property formalization commission, COFOPRI, suggested that, in these circumstances, applicants could gain some legal protection by writing declarations of de facto separation to be processed along with the land title. It was an impromptu version of the certificate of single-motherhood that some interlocutors felt should already exist. Nelly was relieved. "That's good," she said of the declaration, "because you know how it is. After you formalize [a land claim], suddenly the men come back to get what they think is coming to them."

CERTIFYING CIVIL STATUS

During my fieldwork, local governments and state organizations in Peru were working hard to rectify these social-legal misalignments by offering communal marriages and rapid divorces. Twice a year, every year, municipal governments in low-income districts offered free community marriages in an effort to encourage *convivientes* to concretize their unions through ceremony and legal certificates. Political promoters were temporarily transformed into legalistic matchmakers, trying to convince reluctant friends and neighbors to formalize their companionate relationships by describing how romantic the ceremony would be and how their jobs as promoters depended on them recruiting as many couples as possible. For communal marriages, municipalities waived administrative processing fees, and functionaries endeavored to make the ceremonies meaningful by drawing freely on religious, cultural, and civic motifs.[13] Tents were set up on asphalted recreation courts that were cordoned off with diaphanous gold curtains, white bouquets, and municipal police. A stage was built so that the mayor and the Peruvian celebrities chosen as *padrinos* (godparents) for the ceremony could offer advice to the new couples and a judicial official could pronounce their legal rights and obligations as spouses. Finally, a reception was provided to celebrate the couples in their newly officialized lives together.

A promoter from Pachacútec described the communal marriage as "a social service, something nice that the mayor does for the people." This simple description framed formal marriages as goods that Peruvians required or desired, while the ceremony itself positioned presiding politicians within the moral sphere of the family and the formalization of its foundational union. Another Pachacutano, however, suggested that formal marriages were primarily encouraged to "avoid the wiliness of the people" (*evitar la viveza de la gente*), that is, to keep people from exploiting the distance between the official image and lived realities of family. Until their unions were formalized, he surmised, people could continue to receive benefits from the state as heads of different households, unfairly multiplying their total household benefits. In a place where poverty was figured as a domestic affair and social assistance was distributed by household, identifying and stabilizing the composition of households was critical to ensuring proper benefit distribution.

For Peruvians struggling to access state resources, documenting separation was often more important than documenting marriage. In 2008 the Peruvian congress passed Law 29227, popularly known as the *ley de divorcio rápido* (law of rapid divorce), which allowed couples who had been married for at least two years to obtain no-contest divorces in three months for 150 to 400 soles, depending on the official socioeconomic status of the presiding district. Like laws governing land titles and other documents and bureaucratic procedures that permeated everyday life, the rapid-divorce law was reprinted and sold in individual copies on newsstands throughout Lima. The Catholic Church came out against the law, claiming it would undermine the sanctity of the family institution. However, the law had broad support from legislators who argued that barriers to divorce encouraged parallel families, which threatened not only the sanctity of families but also their governability (Comercio 2008).

Interestingly, even people who had never been married seemed to have an interest in formally constituting separation. I stumbled upon this phenomenon while looking through police intake reports in Pachacútec to investigate the frequency of domestic violence claims, which was a major focus of government and NGO workshops offered to area women. To my surprise, by far the most common intake entry was not for domestic violence but for *abandono de hogar* (home abandonment), followed by *retiro voluntario de hogar* (voluntary home departure). The local police chief interpreted their predominance as a symbol of family disintegration and the lack of love in poor Peruvian homes. However, this moralistic account did not explain why people would report these events to police in the first place. The reason for reporting was documentation.

A report of home abandonment triggered a police investigation. Officers would go to the claimant's house and look for evidence of abandonment, typically the absence of a partner, his clothes, his toothbrush, and so forth. The officers would then sign the report to show that the claim had been verified. For the bargain price of five soles plus "gas money" for the home visit, a common idiom for petty bribes, officers would give a copy of the report to the claimant, certifying their identity as a single or abandoned parent. An acquaintance of mine went through this process when she was being scrutinized for entry into a new settlement in Pachacútec. She had told *dirigentes* that she needed land because she was a single mother, and the *dirigentes* wanted proof. The verified report of home abandonment served as a popular certificate of single-motherhood. Given the emphasis on decisiveness and formality for a modern identity, this practice likely had emotional and ontological value as well; it constituted the official condition of separation even absent documentary evidence of the union.

When I shared these thoughts with DEMUNA attorney Rebecca, she brushed them off.

> I'm familiar with that theme already. What happens is that couples fight, go down to the police station to file an official complaint of voluntary home departure or home abandonment, and then a week later they are back together. . . . It happens to us too. Couples come down here to mediate a child support plan while they are still angry at each other, and then within a week they reconcile. We try to make sure couples are good and separated before we go through our process. We are not going to produce reports *por las puras* [for the hell of it]! And couples are capricious. . . . Out of every twenty cases, we get maybe two or three that are this kind of couple.

For Rebecca, this on-again-off-again relational style, particularly when accompanied by the pursuit of formality, was the most damning evidence of someone's distance from modernity and identity as a member of the undeserving poor. Her perspective reflects the ways that state legibility projects ultimately depend not on totalizing knowledge, but on strategic ignorance of the many ways life outruns officialdom. Her perspective also reveals how, for the poor, efforts to pursue modernity, decisiveness, and formality by inviting the state into the messy, ambiguous, and ambivalent world of intimate relations can be refigured in ways that reassert their marginality.

TRUTHS AND CONSEQUENCES

In Peru, poverty is indelibly entangled with state-sanctioned domestic ideals, the ways women experience their failure to achieve these ideals, and the marginalizing misalignments between official visions of relational identities and their everyday, elastic realities. Importantly, efforts to identify the definitive truth of these relations amid their tangled lived and legal realities have social and economic consequences for people striving to make their lives in contexts of material scarcity. I remember distinctly what happened with Edith, a self-reported single mother who applied for and was slated to receive construction assistance from an NGO in Pisco. Edith's neighbors later approached the NGO and accused her of misrepresenting her single status. They said Edith was romantically involved with a man who owned his own home on a lot adjacent to his mother's house and that his mother was already receiving construction assistance. Because they viewed Edith as a member of this larger, benefit-receiving household, they described her to the NGO as "una persona viva," a wily, crafty, and calculating individual donning the image of a single mother to get more than she deserved. The potential complexities of Edith's case—the quality or security of her relationship with her partner, the need for land farther from his family, the reasons neighbors might have had for approaching unprompted to denounce her—didn't matter to the registrar. She simply took Edith off the rolls with the explanation "We don't want to give to someone who lies to us." These relational and domestic complexities and official ignorance of them have important consequences for Peruvians seeking social assistance. They also intersect with housing policies in ways that perpetuate the physical and ideological landscapes of poverty that characterize Peru's urban peripheries.

« SIX »

Housing, Kinship, and Landscapes of Poverty

My heart leaped into my throat when I saw the neighborhood we had been assigned to survey in Pachacútec: Los Heroes. The first time I went to Los Heroes for a prearranged interview in 2008, I was chased out by women wielding large wooden sticks. Unsure where my loyalties lay, the residents were concerned I would tell police I had witnessed them setting fire to wooden houses belonging to an absentee *dirigente* and alleged land trafficker.[1] My Peruvian friends gloated that they had warned me about doing research in a place like Pachacútec, a place that they described as *movido* (turbulent, unsettled). Though typically used to indicate an area plagued by crime and vice, when applied to Peru's peripheral settlements, the term *movido* signaled something more literal: a place where intracommunal conflicts could prompt violent shakeups in the residential landscape, lines between the legal and illegal were difficult to discern, and situations could turn bad quickly. A year later when a functionary I was shadowing brought me to Los Heroes a second time, the absentee *dirigente* and alleged trafficker accused me of being a municipal spy and threatened to "eat me for breakfast with rice and fried egg." With this threat looming, I did my best to avoid the area. But now, another year later, I feared that my four-week stint shadowing surveyors from the ENAHO national survey would bring me back to a place I was clearly unwelcome.

It wasn't until I examined the official sketch of our survey area that my heart settled back into my chest. The site that I knew to be *movido* was left blank on the map; the designated survey area appeared on the other side of the highway, clearly marked with a neatly laid grid. Each numbered square corresponded to a distinct house and, in theory, a distinct household. These official demarcations and the presence of a few brick-and-mortar buildings suggested that this more established area of Los Heroes would be calmer and more settled. Academic geographers suggest that the most exciting and revealing social dynamics occur at the edges of maps, where sociospatial orders are in flux and the foundational violence of property—by which I mean physical appropriation and exclusion backed up by threat of force—is closer to the surface (Blomley 2003). Given how my previous ventures on the edge of the map in Los Heroes had gone, I was relieved to be spending some time on the grid.

It quickly became clear, though, that life on the grid was less predictable than the survey map suggested. The ENAHO surveyor and I asked a neighborhood shopkeeper to point us toward the first name and address on our list: Flora, Block A, Lot 4. The shopkeeper said Flora had moved away almost a year earlier and had lent the house to her recently married daughter. But the daughter and her partner had problems, "violent problems," she added. Neighbors often heard cursing and crashes from inside the house. Thankfully, the daughter had left about six months prior to live with her sister. Soon after that, the husband's brother moved in. The two cohabited until the husband found a job in the south of Lima the previous month. Now the brother lived in the house by himself. The shopkeeper described him as a nice young man who worked as a street clown in the center of Lima. He sold candy, put on impromptu shows, and playfully mocked young couples in the street in the hopes of earning a few soles.

Because the property was listed as a "nonpanel" household and therefore was not part of ENAHO's longitudinal study, we could survey whoever happened to occupy the house at the time of our visit. So, at 11 a.m. on a Thursday we knocked on the clown's door. A sleepy voice groaned inside, and we called out our introductions through the gray wood paneling. Despite his evident exhaustion, the young man opened the door to the floorless shack and stood shirtless and shivering in the doorway as we completed the lengthy interview. When he said he was the only member of the household, the raspy voice of a half-sleeping woman yelled curses at him from inside the house. He responded by grabbing a sweatshirt and closing the door behind him so we could complete the rest of the interview outside. There, he reiterated that he was a bachelor who lived alone, the house had no water or electricity, and he ate all of his meals out in the street. With so little household consumption to report, the interview ended relatively quickly.

The next interview was with Viola, Block A, Lot 22. Viola was a "panel respondent," meaning we had to gather information on *her* household at whatever address might contain it. This task took us three visits over the course of two weeks to complete. According to ENAHO information from the previous year, Viola was a single mother of three who owned her home in Los Heroes. Yet when we arrived at her address, all we found were a few dilapidated straw mats on an otherwise empty plot. Neighbors told us that Viola and her youngest child had gone to a northern province to care for her sick parent. The neighbors did not expect her back for eight weeks. Although they assured us that we had the correct address, that the plot with the collapsed straw hut belonged to Viola, the neighbors encouraged us to visit the house across the street, where Viola and her three children typically lived with Victor and his two children from a previous marriage. As far as we could tell, in the year between surveys, Victor had gone from being Viola's neighbor to being her romantic partner. Since they shared meals and living quarters, for the purpose of the survey, Viola went from being a single mother of three to a partnered mother of five.

Although Viola was the official head of household, the surveyor obtained most of the required information from Viola's sixteen-year-old daughter, who lived in Victor's house and regularly managed household expenses. We supplemented her responses with information from Viola's partner, Victor, although he was adamant that we should interview Viola directly. He explained that although he and Viola lived together, they each had their own land and were heads of different households. On our third visit, we found Viola on the all-but-vacant lot, planting flowers and leveling the sand so she could install a concrete floor. Like Victor, Viola insisted that she and her children really lived on this lot and that Victor and his children were a family apart. The surveyor nodded as though she agreed but ultimately retained the two-parent, five-child version of the household. We had visited this household three times and acquired in-depth information on seven individuals. It would be a shame, she said, to annul all that work.

These different encounters at Los Heroes—the violence of the ungridded settlement area, the rapid turnover in the clown's house, and the tensions over how and where Viola's household should be recorded—can best be understood by examining how Peruvian housing policies have shaped and intersected with Peruvians' intimate aspirations and strategies of living over time. In Peru, the house is a site where law, electoral politics, and grand political visions for the nation intertwine with personal life projects and domestic relations. The house is indissolubly public and private, marking these socially constructed realms while also shaping and mediating between them.

Housing plays a particularly important role in constituting kin relations. Janet Carsten and Stephen Hugh-Jones (1995, 39) contend that, in many sites around the world, "the process of kinship and the process of the house are so thoroughly intertwined as to be one process." Relations between coresidence and kinship are especially marked in Latin America, where relatedness is typically conceptualized not as a biological fact but as something made over time through coresidence, reciprocity, processes of nurturance and shared substance, and temporally elongated acts of growing accustomed (Kuznesof 2005; Leinaweaver 2007; Van Vleet 2008). Houses can also be conduits through which relations are made at a distance as migrants enhance their status in origin communities and reinforce their relational identities as spouses and parents by contributing to household construction and maintenance (Leinaweaver 2009; Pribilsky 2007). Additionally, houses provide a means through which the state is folded into kinship processes throughout the life course (Han 2012). Official ideologies shape the kinds of homes people desire, and policies and political regimes inform the techniques people deploy to realize these desires as they use homes to provide for kin and constitute themselves as particular types of persons.

The Peruvian state's efforts to fight poverty through housing have contributed to the unruly domestication of poverty, ideologically positioning the house as the site of poverty's reproduction while also facilitating livelihood strategies that deploy peripheral homes in unorthodox and morally ambivalent ways. National censuses and other survey technologies in Peru intersect with official and everyday discourses in ways that perpetuate discriminatory attitudes as houses discursively slip from markers of poverty to sites for its reproduction. The ideological entanglement of housing and poverty has emerged alongside policies that have sought to fight poverty through the home, first through self-help housing programs in the 1970s and then through the distribution of land titles under neoliberalism in the 1990s. As enacted, these policies have had complex effects. They have accentuated the multifaceted and contested nature of landed property in urban settlements, integrated illegality and purportedly temporary poverty into the life course of many Peruvians, and facilitated important kinship and security strategies that, paradoxically, reproduce the apparent poverty of Peru's urban peripheries.

COUNTING (NON)MODERN HOUSEHOLDS

For surveyors and census takers, the most difficult questions to answer are the ones that come first: Who are the members of this household, and can you, the surveyed, speak for them? In Pachacútec it was as common to find multiple generations, adult siblings, in-laws, and compadres behind a single door as it was to find husbands, wives, and their children occupying multiple houses. The diverse ways family relations aligned with these physical structures made clear that the idea of a "household," which conflates the physical structure with the social relations it supposedly contains, was untenable in this context. Nonetheless, surveyors found creative ways to contort what they saw on the ground to fit official categories, making it possible to maintain this convenient fiction.

The idea of the nuclear-family household is a powerful official misapprehension that reflects and shapes normative ideals of family and how the Peruvian state seeks to govern its population. For most of Peru's history, ideals of family were shaped by the Catholic Iberian Peninsula. However, by the twentieth century, kinship and gender values originating in Protestant northern Europe had become a new global civilizing force, initiating a new "onslaught on notions of relatedness and sexuality" and "another project to recategorize personhood" (Harris 2008, 294). Modernization theory associated nuclear families, companionate marriages, and low fertility rates with economic development, and many scholars saw the components of this demographic transition as both a developmental inevitability and an ideal to be regarded as appropriate and right (Kuznesof 2005, 860). While anthropologists have been skeptical of the inherent value of the conjugal system and the inevitability of a global demographic transition, they have shown that the pervasive association of the nuclear family with modernity has itself been a powerful source of change (Thornton 2001). In Latin America and across the globe, government policies have focused on reducing family size and instantiating particular living arrangements in pursuit of development (Boesten 2010; Greenhalgh 2003). Meanwhile, popular media have encouraged individuals to idealize companionate relationships and corollary forms of emotional intimacy (Hirsch 2003).

In Peru, the association of particular family forms with modernity has made family form an important marker of class. Poverty is associated with unstable partnerships and having too many children, whereas upper-class status is associated with "duly constituted families," a watershed category in Peru that alludes to "stability, regularity, fidelity, resources, educational capital and often Catholic religious practice" (Anderson 2009, 193). Social theorists and historians have further argued that states prefer discrete, clearly identifiable family units because they provide clear lines of responsibility for all of society's members. Elizabeth Anne Kuznesof

(2005, 859) observes, "From a historical and legal perspective, the family in Latin America is represented consistently as the fundamental unit of society." Jacques Donzelot (1979, 48) calls the family simply "the smallest political organization possible." As a political organization, the family ideally has a territorial component in the house. One of the major long-term projects of the Peruvian state has been to align residential arrangements with government-sanctioned ideals of family. This is a project that can be read in successive national censuses. Far from neutral technologies that record natural facts about the population, censuses play important roles in constructing the populations they purport merely to describe (Arel 2002; Scott 1998).

In 1940 Peru conducted its first modern census of the twentieth century, that is, its first census with the explicit intent of elaborating scientific information that could be used to improve the welfare of the population.[2] This census can be understood as an exercise in modern nation-building; it was a demonstration of state control over a national territory preemptively framed through geographic and racial hierarchies. Peruvian statisticians decided that it was best to use different methodologies to count residents of Peru's jungle, mountain, and coastal regions and of its rural and urban areas because of the different cultural characters and the distinct "cultural levels" (*niveles culturales*) that they imagined dominated these spaces. One statistician explained that they opted to rely on reports from traders and missionaries to construct estimates of Amazonian populations, rather than counting inhabitants directly, because the Amazonian Indian was "unlike the rest of the country (mountains and coast) in every respect"; the Indian "keeps his freedom" and "accepts no other rule than that of his own community" and thus would be "useless to try and count" (Parró 1942, 8). In coastal and mountain regions, enumerators were instructed to treat respondents differently based on spatialized presumptions about their social distance from modernity. In Lima and a few other select cities, enumerators acquired information about households as reported by the household head. In rural areas, enumerators were to use their own best judgment regarding whether to go through the head of household or simply enumerate individuals and relations as they saw and understood them (Parró 1942, 17). Although partially motivated by language considerations, these different methodologies index and reproduce distinctions between the urban citizens whom state agents imagined they could work through while upholding dominant divisions of public and private space and the subjects who occupied the state's sociospatial margins and thus required more heavy-handed intervention (Donzelot 1979).

Using these different techniques, enumerators recorded ostensibly basic demographic information such as age, sex, and race (options were white/mestizo, indigenous, black, and yellow) as well as information about the type of house respondents inhabited, including building materials, number of rooms and occupants, and any other observations they deemed relevant to understanding where the house ranked in the sociocultural hierarchy of the day (Meltzer 2013). Enumerators were further instructed to assign addresses to houses where they were not already present, an effort by the Peruvian state to impose a governmentally rational spatial order that might help to convert irrational Indians into enlightened citizens (Degregori and Sandoval 2008; Rose-Redwood and Tantner 2012).

In 1961 statisticians officially named Peru's census as one of "Population and Housing." It was a historical moment in which Peru's expanding *barriadas* were becoming a critical government concern and a marker of marginality. Census forms from this date evidence officials' dual preoccupations with measuring housing quality and degrees of indigeneity. Enumerators recorded housing characteristics such as construction materials, water connections, number of rooms, number of occupants, and tenure status. Questions relating to family form such as "civil status" and "relationship to head of household" were fill-in-the-blanks, allowing for significant variation among respondents and potentially creating challenges for officials who needed standardized information to effectively categorize and compare households. The census no longer asked about "race" but rather sought to determine degrees of indigeneity by asking about "mother tongue" and "if the respondent spoke Spanish." Additionally, the census form included a table where enumerators could record respondents' "Physical Defects," "Illnesses," and "Uses and Regional Customs." In this table, regional customs such as "walks barefoot," "wears *ojotas*" (sandals made of leather or tire rubber), "wears a poncho," and "chews coca" were placed on the same level as blindness, warts, goiter, and mental retardation. In other words, indigeneity was positioned as a debility that warranted increased state attention to overcome.

The 1972 census repeats many of the questions from 1961 but eliminates the table of debilities and evidences a refinement of the household concept. In 1961 the census form asked the surveyor to fill in information about the total number of occupants in the residence after the interview. In 1972 the question was reframed in terms of the relation of houses to homes, asking enumerators to determine how many "homes" were present in this single residence.

The 1981 census invited respondents to be a part of making this determination, educating them about the difference between houses and homes in the process of asking the question: "If the census home is the number of people who eat from the same pot and sleep in the same house, HOW MANY HOMES ARE IN THIS RESIDENCE?" The 1981 census further systematized the question of occupants' relationships to the head of household. In contrast to the fill-in-the-blank format of 1961, the question was now multiple choice among these options: (1) wife/partner, (2) child, (3) son-in-law/daughter-in-law, (4) grandchild, (5) parents/in-laws, (6) other relative, (7) domestic worker, (8) renter, (9) other non-relative. Here the census conceptualized households as primarily linear, intergenerational families consisting of spouses, children, and grandchildren. Siblings, compadres, cousins, and other affinal relations were lumped together and their specificities rendered invisible under "other relatives" even as middle and upper-class household relations mediated by monetary exchange, like "domestic worker" and "renter," are granted their own categories. In tiny print, the 1981 census instructs enumerators to record the characteristics of household members in a particular order. The head of household should go first, followed by his wife, his unmarried children, his married children and their partners and kids, then "all the other members of the census home." It is a subtle indication of an emerging official preoccupation with household nucleation.

This official interest in household nucleation is more pronounced in the 1993 census, which instructs enumerators to ask the household head the total number of individuals in the home and to create a registry that lists their full names in the following order: household head, spouse, single children without kids, married children and their families, parents or in-laws, other relatives, domestic workers, renters, and other non-relatives (friends, compadres, and their families). By explicitly distinguishing between each family nucleus in this list, the 1993 census reinforced a normative model of the nuclear family and helped to create a proxy by which to measure the "housing deficit."

The 2007 census enumerated family members in much the same way as the 1993 census and likewise reinforced the normative belief that each nuclear family should occupy a single house.[3] The prevalence of households that did not conform to that model was popularly read as evidence of Peru's national failings and underdevelopment. A nineteen-year-old census taker who lived with her child, mother, and two older brothers and their wives in a single house in Pachacútec told me, "The whole point of this census is to help make sure that each house has just one home in it, so that the houses with lots of families in them, like mine, can be divided up so each family gets their own, and the people who already have a house don't take more than they need." This view was echoed by another interviewee who said, "The big problem in Peru is that there are too many people in one house. The children get married, have kids, and don't move out on their own." When I asked this interviewee how one might explain this phenomenon, he offered both economic and cultural reasons: "They don't have jobs so they can't afford it, . . . [but it is also] a problem with the mothers who don't know how to let go of their kids. It is not like in your country, where mothers encourage independence. That is a big problem in Peru." Such statements suggest that the family model articulated in the census helps to perpetuate ideals of autonomous nuclear-family households and, in so doing, bolsters explanatory frames that attribute national failings to problematic mothers and improperly structured domestic spaces.

HOUSING CULTURES OF POVERTY

Government technologies like censuses and surveys further facilitate the domestication of poverty by making the household the smallest unit of poverty analysis. To fight poverty, the Peruvian government endeavors to target its interventions ever more precisely, making finer and finer distinctions between different levels of poverty within spaces. Since poverty is measured at the level of the household, the home becomes the finest unit of poverty available. When government officials and settlement residents spoke of the need to target antipoverty interventions even within designated extreme poverty zones, they referred to household-level targeting. When NGO representatives solicited community comments at a meeting about programs that might be useful in Pachacútec, community members insisted first on the need for enhanced targeting: "Each part of Pachacútec has a distinct reality"; "You all should figure out which zones [within Pachacútec] have extreme poverty and work on the violence there"; "Up high on the *cerro* [mountain] we know a woman with five children, a single mother who lives in *pura estera* [a structure composed entirely of straw mats]. We want to help her, but we can't."

Similarly, individual households were the smallest possible level of distinct cultural realities. Various interlocutors told me that every household experienced *su propio realidad* (its own reality) and that no one could know the reality that existed inside another's household. The repeated use of the term *realidad* struck me as significant for the way it signaled otherworldliness, invoked the possibility of extreme alterity and alternative phenomenologies, and acknowledged the limits of interpersonal knowledge. Of course, recognition of this unknowability did not stop people from speculating.

A primary way my interlocutors assessed *cultura*, a term meaning simultaneously culture, class, education, and upbringing, was by looking at the houses people inhabited. These houses readily slipped from being described as an index and container of poverty to being a force that generated it. People whose houses were made of sturdier materials such as bricks or concrete, which are collectively termed "noble materials," were officially defined as wealthier and unofficially understood as belonging to modern, stable, and duly constituted families. By contrast, people whose homes were made of precarious materials such as straw, plywood, and plastic were deemed poor and typically imagined as belonging to more precarious families. District governments operationalize these assumptions by only taxing houses or the portions of houses that are made of noble materials. Although homes deemed precarious are still represented on cadastral maps, they are demarcated with dashed lines that index not sources of tax revenue but sites of irregularity and social conflict that may be readily erased or altered in response to the whims of politicians and planners.

In the assessments of many psychologists, social workers, and settlement inhabitants, the physical precariousness of homes was itself a source of familial violence, abuse, and sexual predation, all likely to impede children's full and autonomous development. Ideas about connections between housing, family structure, and modernity can be discerned from the sorts of educational programs offered to women in settlements. One of the few long-standing NGOs in Pachacútec ran a program known variously as Vida Saludable (Healthy Life) and Vivienda Saludable (Healthy Home). The confusion over the program name was understandable, given that most of the workshops discussed how women could create healthier family dynamics by modifying the physical structures and organization of their homes. A program promoter described the workshop series to me.

> The first theme we covered was the rights and good treatment of the child. We explained the importance of personal space for the child's development, which many people here don't provide. Many people have just one room that everyone sleeps in. That's not okay. So, we have a month of workshops about the development of the child. Then we verify if the moms implement [what they learn] . . . or if they still need

> to move some boxes or whatever . . . and if they apply the workshops in their homes, they are given an incentive, like *calamina* [corrugated tin] or something else to separate their house [into rooms].

Ideas about the kind of physical space required for healthy child development transform middle-class norms into psychosocial imperatives in ways that disadvantage and discriminate against settlement residents. These prejudices are exacerbated by rumors of rampant domestic and sexual violence in Pachacútec and in peripheral settlements more generally. In several speeches, Ventanilla's district mayor cited a jaw-dropping statistic that 70 percent of domestic violence cases in metropolitan Lima came from Pachacútec. DEMUNA employees further suggested that all of Ventanilla's rape cases came from Pachacútec. After speaking with local police and representatives from the Women's Emergency Center in Pachacútec and central Lima and conducting extensive online searches, I am convinced that these perceptions and the statistics cited to support them have no basis in official or state-manufactured records.[4] Nonetheless, when I asked experts and laypeople their opinions of this statistic, many readily hypothesized that these alarming numbers might result from the sort of housing available in Pachacútec.

Martín, a state psychologist who mediated disputes between separated or separating couples in Pachacútec, was initially dubious about the supposedly high incidence of domestic and sexual violence there. "If there's a greater amount here than elsewhere, it has to simply be because there are more people here," he said. However, he soon began positing a household-level explanation for the allegedly high rates of domestic violence.

> Maybe it's because of the close quarters that there is more domestic violence and incest. . . . Of course, everyone has personal space that belongs to them and should be respected. . . . Imagine [being] in a one room house with six people. You have to change your clothes in front of the rest of your family, and so your space is violated. What's more, since everyone is living so close to each other, there is less to detain the sexual violence from happening.

Drawing on his university education in psychology and sociology, Martín went on to explain that the taboo against incest was a sociocultural construct rather than a biological imperative. "It's culturally problematic," he said. "There's a social sanction against it. . . . Whatever education and culture the people who do those sorts of things have, somehow they haven't absorbed these sanctions." Martín's analysis reveals how well-meaning academic and social-psychological discourse can be used to reinforce culture-of-poverty narratives that pathologize particular household structures as indicators of inadequate socialization and mechanisms through which deviance and violence are reproduced.

HOUSING POLICY AND THE MAKING OF PROPERTY

Hegemonic ideas about the relationship between housing, cultural formation, and poverty in Peru have prompted numerous policies designed to fight poverty through housing. Paradoxically, these policies have institutionalized the building of precarious, often illegal, and ostensibly poverty-inducing homes as part of the individual life course and a normal stage in both family and urban development. They have also critically informed the ways Peruvians understand property and inhabit the periphery.

In 1961 Peru's congress passed Law 13517 on Marginal Settlements as part of an effort to meet the housing needs of growing numbers of rural-to-urban migrants while asserting some control over Lima's urban expansion. The law prohibited the formation of extralegal, squatter-initiated settlements, often termed "invasions," yet promised to help existing communities upgrade and regularize their settlements through a process of *saneamiento físico-legal* (physical-legal cleansing), which involved installing essential urban infrastructure in situ; eliminating garbage, debris, open sewage, and other manmade environmental and health hazards; officially recognizing settlements in public records; and distributing individual land titles to occupants. Still, the illegal settlements continued. As Peru's government fell behind in its obligations to support infrastructure upgrades, it passed new laws allowing settlements to be legalized prior to complying with physical urbanization norms. A pattern emerged in which illegal occupation was followed by legal recognition with infrastructure installed after the fact. Although this dynamic of urban growth created homeownership opportunities for Peru's poor, it also condemned many to live for years in "pockets of poverty" defined by their lack of basic urban amenities and perpetuated the insalubrious housing conditions that Peru's congress originally sought to eliminate (Fernández-Maldonado 2007).

Settlements continued to be demonized as illegal urban aberrations, but the norm of legalizing land appropriations was bolstered by both revolutionary and conservative political discourses. On the revolutionary side, land redistribution was increasingly seen as key to undoing centuries of colonial and postcolonial oppression. Urban land takeovers could be framed as spontaneous acts of redistributive justice, taking from people who had left land fallow because they had more than they needed so that the poor might put the land to good use. It was in the question of what constituted "good use" that squatters aligned themselves with conservative values. Squatters endeavored to strengthen the moral legitimacy of their land claims by describing themselves as hardworking mothers and fathers seeking dignified homes in which to properly raise their children.

British architect John Turner was conducting research in Peru's urban settlements as these property dynamics were taking shape. Inspired by what he saw as the grassroots initiative of the poor, Turner extolled the virtues of "self-help" housing sites and argued that squatters were enacting the most logical solutions to Lima's housing shortages: building their homes progressively in ways that responded flexibly to the changing needs and economic capacities of their families over the life course. Young families might begin by occupying precarious homes in underserviced shantytowns, which at the time Peruvians were calling *pueblos jóvenes* (young towns). As their families grew and their economic conditions improved, they would progressively consolidate their homes, moving through what Peruvian housing scholars describe as stages of "incipient" and "partial" consolidation until they ultimately occupied finished, middle-class homes in upgraded, modern neighborhoods.[5] As Turner's ideas circulated internationally and were inscribed in the United Nation's first Declaration on Human Settlements in 1976, they further legitimated Peru's progressive housing approach as a reasonable way to meet the needs of impoverished growing cities and helped to cement a new morally inflected temporality for Peruvian settlements. Rather than being viewed dichotomously as either nonmodern urban aberrations or modern, dignified urbanizations, settlements could be placed on a virtuous trajectory of progress as settlers mobilized to transform sites of abject poverty into dignified suburban neighborhoods in a process that both reflected and effected an economic and moral transformation in their families.[6]

Behind official laws and public discourses, these urbanization processes were also being sustained by the everyday workings of populist politics and opportunism, generating informal norms for how to acquire houses in the periphery. In a 2005 article tellingly entitled "Recipe for a House," Ayacucho-born writer Mercedes Torribio recounts her role in a 1968 land takeover in Lima's district of San Martín de Porres in a way that underscores the harrowing yet formulaic nature of so-called self-help housing in Peru. In her description, the recipe goes something like this: first, collaborate with a group of neighbors to organize an overnight takeover of vacant land. Second, enact your land claim by building a shack—often beginning with a single straw mat curved into a tent that resembles a turtle shell—and remain on the land for twenty-four hours. After twenty-four hours, Peru's civil code grants you legal protections for your claim and authorities are no longer allowed to remove you by force.[7] The next step, if not done already, is to secure the support of a local politician who agrees to officially recognize settlers as needy citizens deserving of assistance in exchange for the promise of political support.[8] Finally, legally fortify your land claim by accumulating documentary proof of residence and eventually a national land title, and at the same time, lobby for infrastructure and physically fortify and upgrade your house.

In 2009 a *dirigente* summarized the dynamics of physical presence and progressive legality this way:

> The law says that after twenty-four hours, you have a right to stay. . . . So when twenty-four hours pass, you can begin to negotiate so the regional, municipal, or the provincial government will give certificates of possession. Once you have the certificate, you have something more secure to file for the property title, which you get with time.

Peru's history of land appropriations has created a situation in which property emerges not as a thing to be definitively possessed but as a claim that must be constantly enacted through a multifaceted performance that shantytown residents call *vivencia*. This term can be translated simply enough as "residency," "inhabitance," or "lived experience." But in Peru's urban peripheries, *vivencia* also implies a range of activities and attributes derived from the political history of self-help housing. On the one hand, claims to poverty, gendered familial virtue, and an immediate need for space to raise a family give people moral claims to property. However, as one *dirigente* articulated, *vivencia* is not just about need or occupancy but also about contributions to community life.

> *Vivencia* is not just to live there, to be stuck in your house day and night. Living also means to collaborate, to participate in a meeting, to give your input. When there's a chore to do, you go out and do the chore. When it's necessary to protest, you go out and protest, and you work hand in hand with the *dirigentes*. . . . That's what living is for me. . . .

> Whether or not you're in your house twenty-four hours a day, you have to *be there*.

Despite the fixation on appropriate use and active community participation for securing land rights, squatters still covet documents, particularly national-level land titles, as components of this property enactment and expect these documents to have some power to keep other claimants at bay. While documents of all sorts can materialize relations of recognition between officials and residents and communicate those relations to others, Kregg Hetherington (2018, 706) suggests that people may pursue national land titles because they represent the possibility of receiving the protections of the state and thus of participating "in a form of power veiled in uncertainty, whose vague threat allows owners to transcend local squabbles" and avoid some of the everyday obligations that would otherwise be required for them to enact their property claims. Yet Peruvians also recognize that the value of documents, and the significance of the relationships they materialize, are themselves unstable.

Between 1961 and 2002 the administrative responsibility for titling lands in Peru shifted between national and local governments four times, and the particular government office responsible for titling changed thirteen times (Calderón Cockburn 2002). Each political and administrative change could render previous authorizations invalid and require settlers to pursue new political relations and recognitions. Complicating matters further, processes of legal recognition were often cumulative (Webb, Beuermann, and Revilla 2006). Settlers needed the authorizations of various political entities, from neighborhood associations to district and regional governments, that might disagree about whether to endorse settlers' technically illegal land claims. During my longest fieldwork period, in 2009–2010, titling powers officially lay with regional governments, though the specific requirements for obtaining these titles varied depending on the particular legal history of the settlement, the circumstances of property acquisition, and whether the area was currently under a state of emergency that transferred titling authority to the national government.

The only constant in this legal morass was that obtaining and retaining land rights in the periphery required demonstrating continued occupation over time in a way that was legible to various audiences and officials. Settlement occupants responded accordingly, continually accumulating documentary proof of residency from as many organizations as possible and ensuring that they were recorded as occupants in various official lists and registries. This visible performance of occupancy and official recognition enacted property as a form of persuasive communicative practice for onlookers (Blomley 2003). It also produced an archive and trace inscriptions that Peruvians hoped would protect them from rival land claims.

In the 1990s President Fujimori attempted to streamline titling processes, temporarily cloaking clientelist titling practices in neoliberal ideologies. Around the time of Fujimori's first election, right-wing economist and Peruvian neoliberal ideologue Hernando de Soto was receiving worldwide attention for his assertion that legal land titles could eliminate poverty in the Third World (de Soto 1989). He argued that formalizing the poor's property claims would give life to their otherwise "dead capital." Once their claims were formalized through titles, de Soto theorized, the poor could use their land as collateral to obtain credit from banks that in turn could be used to finance business ventures to alleviate both individual and national poverty through a kind of popular capitalism.[9] Multilateral development institutions promoted this policy of "financial enablement" around the world. In 1996, as other social programs were being slashed and state assets privatized to repay national debts, Peru received a six-million-dollar loan from the World Bank to follow de Soto's recommendations and establish COFOPRI, an agency to formalize the poor's informal property claims. By 2009, COFOPRI had issued approximately 1.8 million urban land titles (Fernández-Maldonado and Bredenoord 2010). At least 5,500 of them were distributed in Pachacútec's Pilot Project in 2002.[10]

According to many Pachacutanos, these titles had important effects on the community. Some spoke proudly about how titles had turned them from mere *posesionarios* (land possessors) to respectable *propietarios* (property holders). Others, however, indicated that titles had undermined community development. A baseline data report produced by Pachacútec's *dirigentes* in 2005 stated that community solidarity had waned following the distribution of land titles and that numerous lots were now "inadequately occupied."[11] One Pachacutana went so far as to describe neighborhoods with a higher percentage of titled lands as "pueblos fantasmas," ghost towns only vaguely populated by formal shadows. The effect was a landscape that was both sprawling and full of holes.[12]

Though Pachacútec's emergence in the year 2000 at the height of Peru's neoliberal titling fervor make it tempting to see it as an exceptional case, mentions of "tourists," "free riders," "poachers," "pirates," and "traffickers" in research on Peru's urban settlements prior to the 1990s suggest that this phenomenon was not unique to Pachacútec or to neoliberal Peru

(M. Davis 2006; de Soto 1989; Irigoyen, Chipoco, and Cheng 1988; Smith 1994). Rather, it seems that neoliberal titling policies accentuated existing settlement strategies, revealing how Peruvians integrated documentary ghosts into kinning and livelihood strategies and how the commercial dimensions of shantytown homes were entangled with family obligations and aspirations. Together, these strategies reproduce what I describe as "landscapes of poverty" in Peru's urban peripheries, spaces that aligned with a particular poverty aesthetic and were frequently interpreted by both Peruvians and outsiders as homogeneously poor and correspondingly uncultured.

CONSTRUCTING HOMES, CREATING KIN

In Lima it is standard for children to live with their parents until they marry or, more precisely, until they form what they intend in that moment to be a stable conjugal union. At that point, they aspire to move out of their natal households and form new ones. In this framework, the couple as a social entity becomes the foundation upon which new households are built. When I asked interlocutors why they decided to move to the *barriadas*, they often responded with the aphorism "Casada casa quiere," married people want their own house. This phrase highlights the shared etymology of *casada* and *casa* (marriage and house), illustrating the extent to which marriage is intimately tied to and partially constituted by household formation. It also demonstrates that the desperate need for urban housing, vividly represented by the proliferation of impoverished squatter settlements, is linked to state-sanctioned ideals of family and coresidence. My interlocutors in Pachacútec described this as the "Peruvian dream."

"You know how you all have the American dream, where the immigrant arrives and makes himself a success from nothing?" a prominent *dirigente* inquired. "Well, we also have a Peruvian dream, where we have our own house and our own things." Importantly, this dream is not only about material possessions but also about particular patterns of ownership and autonomy that relate to ideals of public and private life.

Although the Peruvian dream was unrealized for many people, household autonomy and neatly nucleated families remained normalized ideals that indexed personal responsibility and modernity. Marisa shared with both pride and astonishment that she was the only one of her five siblings to have moved out of her parents' home.

> Can you believe it? All of them have partners and kids, but I'm the only one who has moved out. I don't know how they can stand living for so long in *casa ajena*, a house that isn't theirs. For example, you can't invite friends over because the house isn't yours. What if the grandma doesn't like them? No, it's better to have something that's your own. When I go back to visit, my nephew tells me how responsible I am and how his mom isn't responsible at all. He tells me, "You're responsible because you have your own house, your own things. You manage everything that is yours." And it's not easy to buy your house, but it is possible.

For people without the financial resources necessary to rent or purchase housing in urbanized neighborhoods, settling in a *barriada* via an invasion or *traspaso* (purchase of settled but untitled land) became a practical way to realize ideals of couple autonomy.

Building a home and neighborhood from scratch was a trying process, and many of my interlocutors spoke with pride about having built their homes from nothing. They offered dramatic narratives about living miles from civilization without transportation, clean water, or electricity, with nothing but straw mats, plastic, and cardboard to protect them from the cold. "When we arrived there was nothing. All of this was sand," was a common refrain in these descriptions. Interlocutors would wax nostalgic about the community solidarity that had existed in these periods and spoke fondly of good leaders who had fought or worked with politicians to acquire legal titles and infrastructural services for the community.

But the recollection of past hardship is qualitatively different from hardship endured in the present. Hardship in the present is often slow and tedious. In the case of Peru's urban settlements, these hardships involve sitting on barren land with little to do or being at the beck and call of politicians. They involve poor sleep, sore muscles, and persistent wet coughs. They involve asking neighbors to pick sand fleas out of your hair and later fighting bitterly with them about how much water they consumed from the collective supply. More distressingly still, there was no guarantee that these efforts would succeed. The neighborhood might fail to gain legal recognition, or individual families could be disqualified from receiving housing for various reasons and be forced to try again. And yet, people who persevered through this stage often spoke of it as a rite of passage into adulthood.

Sicha initially described his move to Pachacútec as a constrained choice made to retain his dignity but later reformulated it as a necessary step in the transition to adulthood. Apparently, the move was spurred by his irritation with his mother-in-law. He recounted, "It was horrible. . . . I don't want anyone telling me how to act as a father, in my relationship with my wife. . . . What I do with my partner is my problem. . . . It's a totally intimate and private universe, and no one has any reason to get involved. . . . I'll take advice, but I won't tolerate commands."

Although Sicha loved the middle-class district in which he had been living, he traded it for a chance at autonomy in Pachacútec. It took him six months to set up his house and convince his wife that the move was worthwhile. After living in Pachacútec for more than a decade, they were now helping younger relatives strike out on their own. Sicha gave an example. "I'm helping my niece move into the new invasion, the settlement expansion on top of the mountain. It's hard, of course. They don't have water or electricity, and the cold is horrible. But we've all had to go through that. We've all had to suffer like that."

In this way, the apparent poverty of urban settlements, sometimes termed "young towns," has a generational component. According to popular wisdom, young couples, only just beginning to establish their families, occupy young towns. Policemen in one of Pisco's relocation sites suggested that the abundance of young couples contributed to high rates of crime and domestic violence in these areas. In their view, younger spouses were more emotionally volatile and had to make do with fewer economic resources than more established families. During these incipient stages, the families and the precarious houses they occupied were both seen as more likely to fall apart.

If couples made it past the foundational stages of the "domestic cycle," the new family would proceed "through stages from no or few small children present to a stage in which the founders of the domestic group are elders and their children are adults" (Anderson 2000, 3). During this process of maturation the household expands, adding members through biological reproduction and fostering, incorporating nieces, nephews, or younger siblings who contribute to the household economy until they are ready to form a family nucleus of their own (Anderson 2009). We can visualize this growth as amoebic. Households expand and segments are progressively distanced from the center until they split off to form their own expanding cells in a continual process of growth and estrangement.

Although beliefs about domestic cycles, nucleation, and rites of passage shaped many Peruvians' expectations for young couples, it does not necessarily follow that one household is entirely separate from another. In his discussion of genealogical relations and social systems, Radcliffe-Brown (1952, 51) argues,

> The existence of the elementary family creates three special kinds of social relationships, that between parent and child, that between children of the same parents (siblings) and that between the husband and wife as parents of the same child or children. . . . When a man marries and has children he now belongs to a second elementary family, in which he is husband and father. This interlocking of elementary families creates a network of genealogical relations, spreading out indefinitely.

Carsten and Hugh-Jones (1995, 39) likewise contend that in "house-based societies" the house represents both siblingship and marriage: "Siblings share common substance but when they grow up, marry and live separately, these bonds progressively weaken as their own substance merges with that of their respective spouses . . . [and] they produce children of their own . . . [in a] continuous process of transformation." Over their lifetimes, Peruvians occupy many social and kin positions. Although at different life stages some roles may be more important to their identity and status than others, the transition from one stage to another is rarely clean or complete.

When my research took me to more rural areas of Peru's coastal region, I often came across what a Peruvian colleague described as a "typical coastal house," an unassuming façade that opens onto a single parlor and then winds back in a labyrinth of doors and partitions. Architects do not dream up these designs. Instead, these constructions follow an intergenerational logic. As my colleague explained, "Every time a child gets married, when they have a partner and kids, they add another room."

Similar intergenerational patterns are at work in urban settlements, but in these areas, population density, the real estate market, and government involvement make the grid more tyrannical. Rather than expanding original structures indefinitely, families must find other ways to provide for one another. One common strategy is to settle or gain de facto use of adjacent lots. A *dirigente* remarked, "You know how it is, someone wants two lots, so they put one in the name of a cousin or an in-law who is always working or on a trip somewhere." On any given block, a few individuals might be responsible for maintaining numerous houses that legally belong to other family members and go to great pains to ensure no one outside their immediate social network moved in.

When adjacent plots were legally held in the names of absent family members, residents often had de facto use rights. This gave them greater capacity to respond to their own changing circumstances and to assist various friends and family members in need. When Marisa came to Pachacútec she took over two plots, one for her and one for her then five-year-old daughter, because, she explained, "You can't leave your kids with nothing." At age fifteen her daughter still had no reason to move out, so Marisa's friend Miguel was occupying the plot. Miguel was a young man from Huancavelica who worked with Marisa and had fallen in love with a woman in Marisa's neighborhood. "He was suffering a lot living in [his girlfriend's parents'] house, so I lent him my daughter's land and now we're neighbors. Plus, now that our bathrooms are right next to each other, we have so much more time to converse," she joked.

By lending Miguel the plot of land adjacent to hers, Marisa ensured that the land was actively occupied by someone who aligned with dominant ideals of rightful land recipients in the moral economy of Peru's urban settlements. This in turn helped to secure the land for her or her daughter's future while also strengthening her ties to Miguel as their residential proximity transformed them from friends to extended kin. Over the years, Miguel and his wife babysat for Marisa's children, collaborated with her on community development initiatives or district government activities, and eventually became godparents for her son, helping him finance his university studies.

When plots within the existing settlement were not available for kin, relatives found solutions in settlement expansions (*ampliaciones*). Officially, land settled after 2004 was not eligible for formalization through COFOPRI. However, with expansions, the antiquity of the initial invasion was extended to include newly constructed houses so that they might be grandfathered into the legislation. By design, most people with use rights in expansions were relatives of residents in nearby settlements. In this way, sprawling urban settlements come to reflect the intergenerational spatial logic of the typical coastal house, with settlement expansions becoming important sites of intergenerational connection.

It is not unusual to find that title-holding residents of established *barriadas* are the primary protagonists in the physical and legal development of the expansion. A COFOPRI official commented that, although Peruvians are legally only entitled to one plot of land from the government, "many people invade more than once because they need something for their kids. Once they do, it's the responsibility of the state to give them access to property . . . so they have a right to other benefits like loans or constructing with stable materials."

Rodrigo was a retired schoolteacher who owned a well-constructed concrete house with a foundation two meters deep. Yet when I met him, he and his wife were literally in the trenches, trying to build another foundation for their son's family. He explained that since his son and daughter-in-law both worked, they didn't have time to be at the house all day, attend community meetings, or do many of the other things required of residents in self-help communities. "We're helping our kids now to set an example so that someday they'll do the same for their kids," Rodrigo said, "maybe not with a house but perhaps supporting them with an education, a degree, who knows. It's a matter of having a good relationship with your kids, doing things for them."

The relative equivalence of education and housing as ways to provide for a child's future was made especially clear when a *dirigente* tried to sell me a house, by which he meant a plot of land containing a precarious one-room structure that he said he had claimed for his sixteen-year-old son. He justified his asking price by calculating the cumulative cost of sending his son to Peru's naval academy. Either as a home or an asset exchanged for education, the house was a means of fulfilling his parental obligations to help secure his son's future.

In addition to expanding the legal boundaries of the neighborhood and helping relatives build homes, title-holding residents often took charge of the everyday management of settlement expansions in their initial stages. As Lina explained while screening residents for a new expansion, "I live in [a different settlement], but since my kids are here and they don't know the process, I am guiding things." Lina's knowledge of the settlement process gave her de facto control over who settled in the expansion. "These lands are for the people from [the settlement below] or for the family of the people, not for outsiders." In clear reference to the gendered moral economy that drives views about rightful homeownership in Peru's urban settlements, Lina went on to state that they could make exceptions. "We can allow single mothers who really need the land or working families, but we don't want any bachelors. They should be out working."

As if on cue, a woman emerged from an unauthorized shack to ask about settling in the expansion. She carried a baby in a blanket on her back and wore a knee-length skirt with wool stockings that marked her as someone originally from the sierra. She spoke slowly and began by saying that she had slept there the night before to indicate that she was already performing residency. "And who told you to do that?!" Lina barked. The woman continued, saying that she was a single mother, that her husband beat her, and that she couldn't live with him anymore. Initially, Lina maintained that the land was reserved for the children of the settlement below, but she eventually gave in. "Fine, you can put yourself there and we'll support you. But you better live there permanently. And don't you dare bring that disgraceful husband of yours around. We don't want that around here."

BROKEN HOMES AND CATCH-ALL CONSTRUCTIONS

The prevalence of young families in young towns and settlement expansions and the constant displacement of poverty qua precariousness to the outskirts of self-help housing sites reveal how poverty and illegality are integrated into the life course of many Peruvians. Yet, as indicated by the priority given to single mothers in invasions and settlement expansions, family growth is only part of what is inscribed in the landscape. People also used shantytown homes to cope with ruptures in their domestic lives, seeking not necessarily to break family ties but to control the nature of these connections. The need to manage intrafamilial ties and tensions was what initially prompted Pablo's family to move to Pachacútec. He told his story this way:

> I have a brother-in-law who is a homosexual and a son who is in the military. One day, my in-law . . . arrived home drunk and began to give my wife problems, being offensive. . . . He threw a brick from the third floor down at my wife. . . . So my son went up and they started hitting each other. Well, my mother-in-law didn't like her son and my son fighting . . . that is, the uncle with the nephew. . . . So before things got worse and created lasting problems in the family, I decided to leave for my father's house. . . . But the space there is very small. . . . So, the next morning I came to Pachacútec. . . . I left everything I had behind. Everything. . . . And that's no small thing, because my house was tiled, it had a first-class bathroom, it had chandeliers just like in ballrooms. . . . But I did it because I had to. The thing was to distance myself from everybody so that there was no reason for a permanent visit, . . . you know, when a family member comes for one visit, then another, then another, just like that, constantly.

In other cases, people moved to control the influence other family members had over their spouses, presuming that proximity to those relatives altered their partners' character. After escaping an uncomfortable family situation in Trujillo, Pilar and her partner moved in with his cousins in Lima. "But," she said, "they were very *machista*. They drank a lot, and I didn't like how my partner was around them. So when I got the chance to invade Pachacútec, I took it." Though the physical distances she traveled were smaller, Elisa had a similar story. Her partner had a plot of land adjacent to his mother's. Elisa stayed with him there for a while, but eventually demanded that they move. She explained, "He mistreated me more when we were close to his family. . . . He gets angrier more, yells more freely. . . . So I made him move into my lot. . . . It's still close to his family, just a few blocks away, but he treats me better when we're in my house." In these instances, people's experiences of their partners were affected by their physical distance from other family members and by the power dynamics that came with homeownership.

In other instances, partners moved to settlements seeking distance from each other. This phenomenon was so common that some locals considered Pachacútec a land of broken homes and second marriages. When Marisa was first married, her in-laws helped her and her husband move into a fully consolidated concrete house in Lima's northeastern cone. Yet when I met her fifteen years later, she lived in what officials would term a provisional or incipient dwelling in Pachacútec; it was a two-room structure with a concrete floor, wooden walls, and a large enclosed area in the back that she could build up later. She made this transition to get away from her husband.

> It's that my husband was a womanizer. . . . I caught him with another woman and I left. . . . I found my plot here in Pachacútec. I didn't have to invade because there were still plots available, so I sat down with the *dirigentes* and they sort of interviewed me. They ask many things, if you're going to live there permanently, if you work. They make you sign a roster every day and attend monthly meetings. It's demanding, but that's what I did. And since I was a single mother, they gave me the land. . . . Later my husband found me to yell at me, "How could you abandon your home?! I'm your husband." . . . But I told him, "No. You have no right to yell at me. I have pictures [of his infidelity]. . . . You treat me with respect because you didn't find me in the street. You took me out of my house. You asked permission from my parents. I am not just some loose and anonymous woman [*una mujer cualquiera*] that you have license to treat like that.

I had heard variations of this story many times from self-described single mothers in Pachacútec. In some cases, women were escaping physically abusive relationships, but for the most part cheating husbands were cited as the cause of the separation. The prevalence of single mothers in Pachacútec is in many ways an effect of informal policy and ideology. Land in peripheral settlements is supposed to go to the poorest of the poor, and in the Peruvian imaginary, this means single mothers. Women in Marisa's situation are therefore given extra consideration when it comes to determining who should be allowed to settle these areas.

But Marisa's story did not end with her as a single mother, at least not then. She recounted that, after she left her husband, her daughter fell sick from asthma "because she missed her father so much." She continued, "When she was in the hospital I called my mother-in-law and told her to tell her son to come to the hospital for his daughter. And since then, we're back together." Despite discourses to the contrary, for Marisa and many of my other interlocutors, "married" and "separated" were not permanent conditions, and the fluctuations in their relationships were partially reflected by their housing conditions.

As a corollary, my interlocutors tended to presume that fully consolidated houses made of sturdier noble materials were more likely to contain duly constituted families. When I mentioned to Marisa that I would be moving to Techo Propio, the only fully serviced housing development in Pachacútec, she told me this was a good choice. "In Techo Propio they are a different class of people. They come from well-formed families. . . . The rest of Pachacútec, those are people *más sueltos* [loose, untied], men who have abandoned their wives, single mothers, you know the type." Official records might corroborate Marisa's presumption. Techo Propio, a state program dedicated to supporting homeownership for low-income Peruvians, had sponsored an eponymous housing project in Pachacútec and distributed homes to families who could substantiate, on paper, that they were poor. Applicants had to present bank statements demonstrating their low incomes and provide legal marriage and birth certificates to prove they had *carga familiar* (family burden, dependents). This meant that only the privileged poor, people with formal wage-labor jobs and access to state formalization procedures, qualified for homes. As a result, the occupying families officially appeared to be stable, duly constituted, and as Marisa had termed it, "well-formed."

Inside the Techo Propio development, however, things looked different. Many houses were empty or on loan, and inhabitants had been lobbying for years to have houses redistributed to people who truly needed them and would live in them full time. Melisa was a single mother living in a house that legally belonged to her mother. Her mother had applied for the house years earlier when she was married to her second husband.

By the time the paperwork was in order and the house constructed, she had separated from her husband and moved to the provinces to live with her son. So Melisa, recently separated from her partner and with a new baby, moved in. Troubled by the lack of neighbors and the ways their absence disadvantaged the community, Melisa was now leading the charge to have the houses expropriated and legally redistributed to needy individuals who would actively inhabit them. When I asked if expropriation and redistribution could cause her mom to lose her house, Melisa assured me she would not let that happen. She said the government would only redistribute empty houses, meaning houses that had no one present to advocate for the owner.

Yet even empty houses have complex stories and play important roles in people's lives. Ada, a psychologist for the Women's Emergency Center in Pachacútec, owned a house in Techo Propio that she was not living in but that, in her view, was not empty either. "I had always intended to live there," she said. "That's why it has furniture in it." But because her children had asthma and could not tolerate Pachacútec's damp climate, for the time being, Ada and her family lived with her parents in another district. This solution, though, came with its own challenges.

> The problem is that when you don't live there, the neighbors complain. They think if you don't live there, you must not need it, that you should sell it to someone who really does need it because they don't have anywhere to go. And they're right. But the thing is, I don't have another house. This is the only house where I have title.

Ada said she very well might need the house someday, particularly since her husband did not get along with her parents. She attributed this in part to his "very strong character" and to the "different type of formation" he had. "I had both my parents, and they're still together," she said. "Meanwhile, my husband's father wouldn't recognize him. He denied he was his. So, he grew up in a house with a single mother and therefore has another type of formation."

She added that her parents also disliked her husband because of how he had treated her in the past.

> He abandoned me, and we were separated for three years. We were married, both civilly and religiously, and were married for a year before I got pregnant. But when I had my daughter, he left me for another woman. But we also had problems. We were fighting a lot . . . and he

abandoned us. . . . I felt awful being separated. It was like, here I am a psychologist, how can I be separated?! It just felt wrong, like I was living a lie. . . . But then he started coming back to visit my daughter, and from that, we had our son, and since then, we've been together.

Contrary to discourses that associate well-formed families with consolidated homes and untied individuals with progressive housing, the accounts of Techo Propio residents reveal that both constructions are used to accommodate fluctuating lives and relationships. Although I met Marisa and Ada at times when they were with their husbands, their familial trajectories may not end there, in which case their extra properties may help them constitute different domestic lives.

Under the right circumstances, the established homes of friends and relatives can similarly serve as refuges for separated individuals such that these established homes are constantly under construction. This was the case for Milagros and her mother, Patricia. Milagros lived in a small prefabricated wooden module with approximately ten meters of straw matting extending behind it to enclose the rest of the plot. On one memorable visit, Milagros led me behind a wooden wall, past the kitchen, through a maze of straw and plastic partitions with cloth curtains, up a stepladder, left at the bathroom, and into a room with a dirt floor and straw mat walls that was exploding with clothes at every stage in the laundry cycle. Milagros washed clothes for the eleven people who lived in the house: her two kids, mother, grandmother, two uncles, one younger brother, one cousin, two half siblings, and herself. She said she didn't mind all the washing or living with so many people. "Here, I don't get bored or lonely. What's more, when I need help with something, like a fundraising activity, all of them support me. . . . Before, when I was living . . . with the father of my children, . . . I spent practically all day by myself. I'm much happier here."

Though Milagros said she had been lonely and unhappy for a while, she only moved in with her mother after her husband ran off with another woman. It was as though the rupture in her identity as a spouse made it easier to residentially assert her identity as Patricia's daughter. In contrast, Patricia had moved to Pachacútec to escape a violent partner, falling back on sibling ties until an opportunity emerged for her to have something of her own. Patricia glossed over the story quickly.

The father of my youngest son . . . would drink, talk big, and hit. That's why I left. . . . And I came to Lima because I had siblings I could live with. My brother lived in a rented apartment, and I lived there for two years until my *comadre* told me there were lots in Pachacútec and we could come and live here.

That was in 2000. Since then, the number of family members living with Patricia or in houses nearby has increased almost every year. Her house, with its unruly extensions and temporary partitions, is where family members come when they have nowhere else to go, and with each addition, the house and family are remade.

The only person I knew whose relationships seemed to be neatly contained within a single house was Ismael, a former administrator of the civic center and the first person I met in Pachacútec. In 2007 Ismael was living in an under-construction household as the semipermanent guest of one of his compadres. Over time, though, he increasingly slept in his small windowless office in the civic center, saying this arrangement made it easier to perform his administrative duties and protect the building from delinquents. During this transition, I also increasingly found Ismael in the early mornings glassy-eyed and smelling of rum. On mornings like this it was a challenge to get him back to his office; even in this state, he was eager to introduce me to friends and *dirigentes* and to show me around Pachacútec's burgeoning education facilities. Soon, rumors began to circulate about Ismael's drinking and supposed interest in children. When a teacher accused him of trying to lure kids into his office with candy, Ismael relocated from the civic center to "the matchbox," the fully consolidated model home built by the Ministry of Housing around 2005. Far from the endpoint of a positive progression that symbolized the consolidation of his family relationships, in this case, the finished house was a symbol of his ostracism.

PERFORMING RESIDENCY AND PRODUCING LANDSCAPES OF POVERTY

In a context of material scarcity and inadequate and unstable employment, having access to multiple plots of land enhanced Peruvians' abilities to adapt to changing life circumstances and to care for one another. This was especially true for women. They could fall back on settlement homes when other aspects of their lives fell apart and subsequently use hard-won cultural competencies about how to secure land and make a life in the periphery to provide for kin, all while fulfilling gendered obligations that tethered them to the home. Yet these forward-thinking, family-oriented livelihood and security strategies were viewed unfavorably by many in Pachacútec. Abstracted out to the level of the community and the nation, Pachacutanos saw these strategies as reproducing poverty; they enabled the unjust accumulation of property by a select few individuals and perpetuated the impoverished conditions of the urban periphery.

I remember vividly a conversation with Pablo, when he asked me how I would evaluate "the cultural level of Pachacútec." I responded as a relativist, saying that rather than rank generalized cultural levels, I preferred to consider how knowledge aligned with life in particular cultural milieus. Pablo was visibly unsatisfied by my response, so I elaborated. I explained that I knew a more typical response would be to say that residents of Lima's upper-class districts had a higher cultural level than people in Pachacútec, but my view was that upper-class residents probably knew little about securing land in a settlement or building a dwelling from almost nothing in an invasion. My question to Pablo was that if those people came to Pachacútec and had to make a life for themselves, who would have a greater cultural level then?

Pablo clearly thought I was talking nonsense and decided to set me straight: "Knowing how to invade is not an indicator of culture! Invading is illegal. Taking something that isn't yours? Robbing? That is something illegal. Knowing how to do illegal things does not increase your cultural level!" I resisted the temptation to bring Pablo's own circumstances to bear on the conversation. I said nothing about how he had knowingly purchased untitled land and was therefore technically an illegal squatter. Nor did I mention that his capacity to move from one space to another and make his way in both formal and informal Lima had helped him cope with challenging family circumstances and secure his job as a political operative for the municipality. Instead, I challenged his framing of illegality and spoke more broadly about the complexities of legality and rightful ownership in settlements like Pachacútec. I argued that it was one thing to own a piece of land, to have full legal title making it one's own in the eyes of the national government, but that it was quite another thing to *hacer vivencia*, to contribute to the life of the community, to support one's neighbors, and help the community *salir adelante* (progress). I went on to describe more complex cases in Pachacútec when people effectively fulfilled the duties of active residents without living on a plot full time or performed their community duties with such zeal that they maintained rights to multiple plots of land. I suggested that they did all the work of living there, which created the appearance of fully inhabiting the plot and gave them social rights to the space.

More nonsense. Pablo corrected me as calmly and forcefully as he could. "A wily person who doesn't live there but who makes their garden pretty as if they lived there? That is a selfish and calculating person who isn't truly needy."[13] He went on to say, "The truly needy are the people who don't have anywhere else to live. If they needed the house, they would inhabit [*harían vivencia*] full time. They would sleep there. They would remain there."

As we continued the conversation and picked it up again on subsequent occasions, it was clear that Pablo recognized that not all Pachacutanos fit neatly into his dichotomy of "truly needy" residents (the archetype of which was a parent who inhabited the land continuously and contributed fully to infrastructural development and community life) and "selfish and calculating" people who did not need the house. There were people who owned no other home but worked far away and only came to Pachacútec on weekends and holidays. Others typically slept elsewhere, such as in more established households in nicer districts, but participated actively in community development. Still others, often with economic means and large social networks, built nice houses in Pachacútec and worked with neighbors to ensure that the house appeared occupied when this appearance mattered most. Yet when pressed, Pablo continued to fall back on the moral framework of rightful recipients and those exploiting the system to take more than they needed.

On another occasion, Pablo summarized his view of the land invasion system this way: "It has its good and bad points. On the good side, it gives truly needy people access to land who would not otherwise have it. But on the bad side it gives these same opportunities to people who aren't needy."

I had indeed encountered people who seemed to be benefitting from a system not intended for them. The clearest example was Claudia, though in some ways even her situation was fuzzy at the edges. The first time I met Claudia she was holding a crowbar and leading a group of neighbors in an effort to knock down the only brick house on their block. I had haplessly stumbled upon the event when taking a shortcut to Pachacútec's lower avenue. Interpreting me as a reporter or a social worker, the owner of the damaged house roped me into the encounter: "They say they want development, but here they are knocking down houses!" As I tried to continue down the hill, Claudia and her companions surrounded me, metal tools in hand, and demanded to see my camera. They wanted to make sure I hadn't taken any photographs. Out of context, they said, images of what had transpired could be misinterpreted. After seeing that my camera had been off and there were no relevant pictures on it, Claudia invited me to her house for a cup of instant coffee. Sitting in her large wood-paneled house, which doubled as a restaurant, Claudia explained how this apparent act of destruction served community development. That same week, regional government surveyors were coming to register houses, and district-level cadastral surveyors were measuring lots. The neighbor's brick house extended over the would-be street line and did not conform to the map drawn by urban planners. If the district or the region, in the form of their different vest-wearing agents, saw the neighborhood that way, it could delay plans to asphalt roads, which would be detrimental to the rest of the community by making it harder and more expensive to bring construction materials, potable water, and other goods into the community.

Claudia invited me back several times. During these visits, it became clear that Claudia bore little resemblance to intended beneficiaries of self-help housing in places like Pachacútec. In addition to the house and restaurant in Pachacútec, Claudia and her husband owned a large, fully consolidated house in one of the wealthiest districts in Lima, a summer home in a rural resort town, and a wholesale pasta business. Yet she was clearly quite competent when it came to performing the duties of *vivencia* and ensuring that her settlement developed efficiently.

I happened to visit Claudia a few days after our first encounter when her four sisters, all of whom had claimed plots of land in the neighborhood, were also present. During that visit, the regional registrar also arrived to inscribe Claudia and her four sisters into the regional property ledger. They gave him their names and ID numbers and told him where they lived on the block. They also handed over copies of the identity documents of their adult children and indicated which lots on the block belonged to them. Collectively, Claudia's family had claimed seven lots in the neighborhood. When the registrar commented that they were all from the same family, Claudia responded, "Yes, we're all the same family. But we're also individuals."

Claudia's statement illustrates the nature of family as a composite entity, comprising many individuals who can come together or remain strategically separate for different purposes and who may themselves be fractured into their physical and legal parts. Dominant policy frameworks suggested that houses were supposed to be containers for growing families and people had to demonstrate family obligations (i.e., dependents) to be eligible for these homes both formally and informally. Nonetheless, ownership by way of documents and legal titles was frequently an individual matter. This gave tight-knit families an edge in securing land and informed the ways kinship was made and how it materialized in the landscape. Contrary to visions of progressive development in which homes expand and solidify in accordance with a predictable domestic cycle, people like Claudia, Marisa, and Ada demonstrate the ways land can be partially and strategically inhabited, allowing it to play a role in multiple projected futures. However, in the institutional context of Peru's *barriadas*, this pattern of inhabitance and the sprawling, pockmarked landscape it produced were read visually and statistically as poverty. These partial forms of inhabitance also in many ways increased the hardships of those people who did fully inhabit their lots, even when they themselves were complicit in maintaining this landscape.

In 2000, Amelie had been living in her parents' home along with her children and several of her adult sisters. When the opportunity arose for her to have land of her own in Pachacútec, she took advantage of it and dutifully complied with the requirements for full-time residency. She spoke at length about the number of times she had to reregister her land claim during her first few years in Pachacútec to certify her need. She feared that if representatives from the Ministry of Housing or another state agency knocked on her door and did not find her at home, they would give her land to another person. She recounted that "many people lost houses this way," even if they had already been registered.

Once titles were distributed and the original surveillance died down, many registered inhabitants left, including members of Amelie's family who relied on her to perform the official image-work of inhabitance for them.

> The people have left and now there are many abandoned properties, . . . and on these abandoned lands, what happens? Because there aren't many people that live here, we can't ask for many things. . . . Also at one time there were many delinquents who moved onto those empty lots, and it was dangerous for people. . . . There were rapes, . . . robberies. . . . *Vivencia* is important because we help each other, [but] look here on this side, I have my neighbor who doesn't live here. My sister also doesn't live here. . . . Almost all the land up the hill belongs to my sister. . . . Gosh, I wonder how many properties I have now.

Amelie clearly recognized the detrimental effects that absentee neighbors had on development and on her everyday experience of community. Nonetheless, her remark "I wonder how many properties I have now" alluded to the way she herself was complicit in maintaining these conditions. When household surveyors came to her block for any reason, she would rush through shared courtyards and answer doors, offering copies of the identity documents of the supposed resident along with an explanation as to why they were not present at the moment. She was performing official inhabitance for nearly everyone on her block, a technique that protected the land claims of loved ones, infuriated others who said they could put the land to better use, and for the moment, perpetuated the physical and experiential impoverishment of her neighborhood.

These strategies are critiqued from afar as forms of self-serving accumulation that undermine community development. But they also evince community and familial solidarity and support for neighbors' efforts to bet on particular kinds of futures while hedging against unknown eventualities. This insight can be extended to the experience of Viola and Victor, the couple in Los Heroes who insisted that they be registered as heads of different households. Their insistence can be read as evidence of their capacity to collaborate as a couple while holding onto multiple potential futures. However, their capacity to collaborate in this way also depended on community solidarity. When neighbors affirmed Viola's residency on the underdeveloped plot, they also affirmed their connections to her as a social being and member of their community; Viola was someone whose future they were willing to protect despite her physical absence.

The diverse strategies of claiming and retaining land in settlements like Pachacútec produce kinship, opportunities for advancement, and security in the face of unknown futures. Yet they also reproduce what are commonly interpreted as landscapes of poverty: settlements where the foundational violence of property remains close to the surface, where precarious and unconsolidated homes predominate, and where the infrastructure required for modern and dignified urban existence remains elusive. Moreover, the various ways lived occupancy deviates from idealized understandings of *barriada* residency helps to reproduce perceptions of a society overrun by dishonest players and a sense that Peru is a nation of systemic injustice, self-interest, and moral impoverishment, even as most of these deviations occur in the name of kinship, care, dignity, and development.

DOMESTICATED POVERTY

As poverty has come to be figured in relation to the household in Peru, Peruvian settlement strategies have evolved in ways that, ironically, perpetuate the sprawling and pockmarked peripheries conventionally read as materializations of poverty. Since the mid-twentieth century, government policies and technologies have framed nuclear-family households as normal and proper and demonized deviations from this norm as unhealthy. Peruvians have pursued these government-endorsed housing ideals by claiming land and constructing homes in the urban periphery and by accumulating documents that tenuously transform their claims into property. Yet even as people idealize nuclear-family households built of so-called noble materials, they use houses in other ways as well, not simply to shelter growing families, but to help constitute kin relations and prepare for uncertain futures. As long as these houses remain precariously constructed or inadequately inhabited, they can be read, statistically and colloquially, as sites of poverty and family breakdown; yet they can also be understood as materializations of growth, care, in/security, and aspiration. While state policy and discourse seem to have succeeded in domesticating poverty, houses and the relations they materialize continue to defy containment or easy definition.

Conclusion

A DIFFERENT POVERTY STORY

Toward the end of a fourteen-month fieldwork stretch in 2010, another episode of *Extreme Lives* caught my attention. A former Miss Peru, Jessica Tapia, spent three days embedding herself in the extreme life of a woman named Gloria who made fifteen soles a day doing backbreaking agricultural work in the south of Lima. During the episode, Gloria is shown as a single mother of three whose partner abandoned her just before her second child was born. Her fifteen-year-old daughter, Bélgica, had recently left home because she and her mother had been fighting. "No teníamos comunicación" (There was no communication between us), Bélgica tells the cameras as she sits, isolated and exposed, in the town's central square. Gloria's home is made of disintegrating plywood panels and has no water or electricity. However, her missing daughter and the implied familial disintegration is the central drama of the story. Alone at night with the cameras, Gloria pleads, "Bélgica, I want you to come home. Where could you be? I feel so alone." By the end of the episode, Jessica Tapia has refurbished Gloria's house and brought her daughter home in time for Christmas. Bélgica emerges from a giant Christmas box to hug her mother, saying, "For you, Mamá, on Christmas . . . we are going to be more united as a family."

As the characters recount their experiences of the past few days, it is clear the family has changed in other ways as well. Gloria describes with gracious melancholy how the show's producers and celebrity guest star "have fought so much for me. I am so grateful for what they have done for me. . . . They are leaving me with a changed home. She [Jessica Tapia] has baptized us with her last name. Now we belong to her." The episode ends with them chanting a variation on a classic protest call to arms: "¡El pueblo, unido, jamás será vencido!" (The people, united, will never be defeated!) becomes "¡Los Tapia, unido, jamás será vencido!" (The Tapia family, united, will never be defeated!). With the help of wealthy and generous strangers, the home is at once fortified for the fight against poverty and reshaped as loyalties are built across class lines.

The dominant narrative promoted by the program hosts, the celebrity protagonists, and the featured family was one of selfless charity and family solidarity in recognition of a *mujer luchadora*, a hardworking "woman warrior," struggling valiantly to pull her family out of poverty. Yet having spent many months swimming in the poverty narratives that emanated from state agents and single and working mothers in urban Peru, I surprised myself with my own double reading of the episode. A single working mother with three children and a runaway adolescent daughter could easily be accused of abandoning her children in their home. The lack of love in the household resulting from their precarious economic circumstances drove the adolescent daughter into the street, where she would repeat the cycle of poverty. Moreover, if Gloria's husband had abandoned them as a complete and permanent event before her second child was born, it raised questions about where her third child came from and, relatedly, how singularly devoted she was to her role as a mother.

Though I didn't hear any critique like this from my interlocutors in Pachacútec, likely because of their distance from the episode's protagonists, the episode did have an afterlife. It was followed by a week of tabloid battles between different poverty-related reality television shows. The disputes centered on which shows exhibited genuine solidarity with the poor and which were simply exploiting them to pull in higher ratings. These arguments were interspersed with accusations that Jessica Tapia was romantically involved with the male host of *Extreme Lives* and was partially responsible for breaking up his marriage. Tapia, meanwhile, remained steadfast that she had done nothing wrong. The host was already separated when their relationship began, she argued. She had no reason to feel guilty or apologize to anyone. And so the tale of a virtuous and struggling single mother and the heroic poverty assistance she received was tied together with a back-and-forth about poverty exploitation and dissimulation and celebrity gossip about alleged home wreckers and the questionable finality of romantic separation.

There are many stories told about poverty in Peru. There are the dramas that dominate news and reality TV shows, programs that pan precarious homes and impoverished landscapes, then zoom in on individuals as they suffer through critical moments in their intimate lives. There are the official and authoritative explanations that frame poverty as a cycle, locating its origins and most dire effects in the disintegration of home and family. There are the public secrets about how poverty is exacerbated by the self-interested schemes of politicians or maintained by those who have found ways to profit from its existence, which collectively produce a background hum of cynicism and suspicion. Some stories focus on sites of poverty and situate these spaces temporally, naming them either "progressive housing sites" that the concerted efforts of citizens are transforming into dignified urbanizations or "slums of despair" that have either stagnated or decayed because neighbors have not remained vigilant (Chambers 2005; Duhau 2014). Others focus on individuals and populations using descriptions in which different dimensions of poverty—often framed through the present-future grammar of risk and vulnerability—bleed into one another as part of the language of need that people use to make claims on the state and each other. In many of these stories, poverty emerges as a visible, self-evident entity, hyperreal and omnipresent, yet also always elsewhere, as people are warned that claims to either individual poverty or public progress cannot be taken at face value.

I am aware that this ethnography is in many ways just another poverty story, one that assembles and overlays many others in a way that recalls some of the state formalization projects I have described. Indeed, the charge that ethnography can become just another legibility project, an effort to give more coherent form to worlds often deemed "informal" because their logics elude bureaucratic frames, needs to be taken seriously.[1] Yet because narratives run ahead of "social practices to open a field for them" (Certeau 1988, 125), I remain hopeful that an ethnographic retelling that challenges conventional poverty geographies, that permits some eraser marks, smudges, and inconsistencies, and that figures state-society relations as woven tapestry rather than as nested spheres or overlain institutions, can arouse a slightly different awareness of poverty as a problem that mobilizes us and facilitate new ways of thinking, being, and acting in the world.[2] Though such provocations must remain open-ended, here I offer some reflections on the central insights of this ethnography and the new orientations they might imply.

REMAKING POVERTY

The global effort to attack poverty suggests that there is such a thing as "global poverty," a poverty that is the same the world over, for which there are unitary explanations and universal solutions, and whose fluctuations can be measured with the proper analytic tools. Yet globally comparable poverty does not simply exist, but rather is continually (re)produced by the metrics, media, discourses, and documents that purport merely to represent it. An entire industry has grown up around these productive poverty-monitoring activities, an industry that incorporates myriad actors, from high-level World Bank officials and university professors to the settlement inhabitants who will supposedly benefit from these activities. The role of impoverished settlement inhabitants in the production of global poverty knowledge mimics their role in global capitalism more generally; they are the unskilled labor of low-level data manufacturing and the consumers of emotionally engrossing statistics and poverty performances.

At the same time, global audit culture, of which poverty monitoring is only one component, has an important counterpart in the production of skepticism. Arjun Appadurai (2006, 6) describes this as a central irony of modernity: the perpetual pursuit of procedure and predictability through "highly regimented bureaucratic-legal orders" paradoxically generates pervasive uncertainties. These uncertainties are often tied to census concerns regarding how many persons of a particular type exist in a given territory and how anyone can be sure a person is who they claim to be. Although Appadurai refers principally to ethnic categories, his insights can be applied to any group marked off for special legal treatment or entitlements, including the ever-contested number of Peruvians in poverty or extreme poverty whom officials invoke to justify myriad social and economic policies and assert their own legitimacy as state actors.

The pervasive uncertainty about whether recipients of poverty assistance are who they claim to be results in part from the ways images, maps, and statistics combine to create a construct of deserving poverty that is so grandiose, temporally bounded, and impossibly precise that no real individual could be expected to align with it. In describing household poverty-assessment techniques in urban Chile, Clara Han (2012) argues that the categorical requirements for poverty assistance transform "the state's social debt to the poor . . . into the poor's debt to the state" (68), forcing the poor to conform to undignified imaginaries of poverty to receive aid and then obliging them to exit poverty quickly to regain moral standing. Likewise, in Peru's urban peripheries the poor are forced to conform to impossible imaginaries of poverty to receive state assistance and often the sympathies of neighbors. These performances, and the broader statistical and documentary productions of deserving poverty, reinforce ideals of what deserving poverty looks like while also provoking a generalized mistrust of appearances.

Importantly, Peruvian imaginaries of deserving poverty are predicated on notions of stable relational identities, that is, one's identity as a parent, a partner, or someone who has been abandoned and is thus defined by relational loss. As a result, the real-life tenuousness and flexibility of relationships can undermine a person's identity as a member of the deserving poor. Although single mothers are also daughters, sisters, and cousins and may wish to pursue life projects that involve romantic relationships, careers, political interests, or community-development activities outside the home, their designation as "deserving" hinges on the extent to which they refuse relations and identities that might ease their sense of material and relational deprivation (Van Vleet 2019). In this sense, deserving poverty can be a performance, but also a prison.

Poverty discourses that emphasize lone and previously unseen individuals who ostensibly exist outside political and social networks also inform the temporal framing of virtuous poverty. Short-term assistance may be framed as either charitable or extractive, depending on how visibly the giver benefits from the gift. Meanwhile, protracted assistance and the construction of stable distribution networks are often demonized as political, and the beneficiaries of these networks are described as *vivos* (wily) or mafiosos (corrupt). Put another way, the very formalization processes involved in making recipients both politically visible and deserving of assistance in Peru also place these recipients outside conventional imaginaries of the deserving poor. Moreover, because the status of "truly needy" is reserved for unseen individuals, the targeting efforts of social programs often focus less on socioeconomic criteria than they do on ensuring that recipients have not previously received aid. Ensuring that recipients only receive aid once is an especially problematic endeavor when those recipients are families whose size, composition, and internal dynamics are constantly shifting.

In line with other research on poverty and development, this ethnography suggests that flattened portrayals of the poor can exacerbate social distances, transform the suffering of others into something unreal, and make "deserving poverty" an impossible ideal (Kleinman and Kleinman 1996; Strathern 2004). Simmel (1965 [1908], 132) argues that "poverty" as a social category is something other than the individuals who supposedly occupy that category. He contends that just as people may desire an abstract love rather than a beloved, they may seek to end or ameliorate an abstract poverty rather than assist real impoverished individuals (132).

Researchers have shown that this abstract poverty remains the object of concern even in the case of child sponsorship and microloan programs in which individual recipients—as complex, multifaceted, and changeable real-world beings—often become mere sites onto which abstract notions of poverty are projected (Bornstein 2005; Englund 2015; Strathern 2004). These findings suggest that rather than means testing, categorical requirements, or matching recipients to the imaginaries of poverty that donors have in their heads, development agents might do more good by fostering more encompassing imaginaries of aid recipients, allowing them multiplicities, imperfections, and uncertainties.

We might begin this process by trying to understand people as deserving of assistance not because they are a special case or an exception to the rule, but because people's circumstances are products of global patterns in which we are all enmeshed, and it is worthwhile to support everyone in leading their best lives. It is also possible that what we really need is a new way to conceptualize poverty or perhaps to "forget the poor" altogether (Englund 2015). Scholars have argued that social concepts of "poverty" and "the poor" function primarily as othering labels that position people outside the "we" of society (Biehl and Eskerod 2007; Brown 2005). It may therefore be time for us to find new frames that permit genuine connection and solidarity.

UNGOVERNABLE FORMALITIES

The specific government programs I have examined in these pages—the Right to Identity Campaign, women's workshops, communal marriage and rapid divorce initiatives, and the provision of housing and land titles—all endeavor to fight poverty through formalization. By inscribing individuals, relationships, and property claims in state registries and distributing documentary proof of these inscriptions, state agents aspire to create a more legible and governable society. The association of poverty with disorder and ungovernability in urban Peru allows state agents to frame formalization as both a route to receiving state assistance and the substance of development itself, producing virtuous citizens and a more capable state in one fell swoop (Mosse 2013).

From the perspective of transnational development organizations, these formalization programs are doing exactly the right thing, ensuring that people are included in the state and creating empowered yet governable citizens in the process. From a Foucauldian perspective, which is more circumspect but not necessarily at odds with the international development vantage, these formalization efforts exemplify the work of governmentality; they endeavor to align governance of the self, family, and society in a way that makes it easier to conduct the conduct of the population, choreographing people's relations with things and one another toward whatever ends the state deems advantageous (Foucault 1991). Peruvian formalization programs are based on a normative vision of sovereign, civic-minded individuals who are embedded in and formed by stable, nuclear families that mediate members' integration into the state and public sphere (Kuznesof 2005). In the worldview perpetuated by Peruvian policy discourse, these individuals and families are connected to an ostensibly disinterested, technocratic state through documents. Keeping these documents up to date and maintaining an alignment between real-world relations and official records becomes the principal and never-ending project of government.

Yet as I've shown in this book, rather than creating governable societies from "government-naïve" populations, as much formalization discourse suggests, these programs are often enacted in marginal areas already inundated with paper and statelike practices that have marked socioracial meaning. As a result, formalization programs can end up perpetuating and exacerbating the very inequalities, illegibilities, and unruliness they seek to redress. In the context of Peru's racialized postcolonial state, formalization programs become civilizing projects, and the distinction between formality and informality becomes a guise through which long-standing patterns of racial discrimination persist. Beyond this, there are moral connotations and identities associated with the manner and extent to which people engage documents. People who lack sufficiently updated documents are deemed *dejado*, apathetic and irresponsible subjects who are undeserving of assistance or citizenship. Meanwhile, those who know too well how to navigate Peru's labyrinthine bureaucracies and turn the system to their advantage are deemed *vivos*, wily and unscrupulous beings whose very existence mocks Peruvian aspirations to orderly modernity.

Documents also bring new things into being. These include lauded sociolegal entities such as citizens, property holders, and social base organizations, but also maligned beings like ghosts (documents unhinged from lived realities) and the mafia (exclusionary networks of people and paper). These maligned entities muddy the clean bureaucratic landscape to which good governance programs aspire and ultimately produce a state that is illegible to much of the population. Moreover, while formalization programs are conventionally framed as technocratic and apolitical, in contexts where the identity of the state is woven together with the identities of specific politicians, documents can also produce partisan political networks. The provision of formal documents and their attendant promises of inclusion in a technocratic state are not the antithesis of politics but can be a guise through which politics happens and a mechanism by which the political networks that constitute the inclusionary and exclusionary nature of the state are built.

Understanding how policies are experienced by the people subject to them requires beginning with a more clear-eyed view. This view should recognize marginal areas not as products of state absence but as the results of previous policy interventions, and it should see documents not as tools of immediacy and transparency but as productive of new entities and relations.

SINGULAR MOTHERS AND WOMEN'S WORK

When poverty is measured, conceptualized, and attacked through the household, the structural causes of poverty become harder to discern and thus harder to rally against or reform. These domestic and domesticating frames, however, also generate unruly phenomena that defy state control, from the public proliferation of urban sprawl to the intimate and gendered experiences of suffering and social incompletion that refuse repair. Critically, one of the first-order effects of these poverty-domestication projects is the centering of mothers as both objects and protagonists of antipoverty initiatives.

In Peru, mothers are deemed responsible for the poverty or development of the nation based on the kinds of child-citizens they form in and through the homes they manage. Close examination of RENIEC's Right to Identity campaign reveals how the responsibilization of women is at the heart of state identification projects and the associated identity projects of the state (i.e., efforts to represent and constitute the state as omniscient, technocratic, administratively competent, and modern). Just as women are integral to statecraft, they are also central to the everyday work of politics. Women's association with the ostensibly apolitical sphere of the home makes them powerful political symbols and agents. The gendered divisions of labor that tether women to the household also make them principal protagonists in grassroots development and social assistance work that is figured as an extension of domestic care. The women who prove themselves adept at this work are also those most likely to be recruited into the ranks of local political administrations that reimagine this community clout as *fuerza política*, political force that can move people to action. Ironically, women who take paying jobs as political promoters or who move too far into the public or political sphere can tarnish their reputations as devoted mothers and community servants, which in turn can cost them their community esteem and perhaps ultimately their jobs.

The themes of responsibilization, impossible ideals, and reputational tightropes emerge again in my analysis of single mothers who are central to Peruvian poverty discourses both as archetypes of the truly needy and as social threats who might reproduce poverty by improperly "forming" their children. I have explored the real-world experiences of single mothers who are too often caricatured as simultaneously two-faced and one-dimensional. In the process, I have shown that single mothers are placed in impossible moral positions vis-à-vis child-rearing. Working outside the home is viewed as abandoning their children, yet single mothers who devote themselves to their children and rely exclusively on state programs, even participatory ones, are viewed as *dejados*, people who would rather wait for a handout than work to change their circumstances. State-sponsored development programs emphasize women's roles as spouses, but women who remain in troubled unions or try to rekindle romances are framed as lacking self-esteem or being uncommitted to their children. Moreover, women who draw on their identities as sisters, daughters, and cousins to provide for their children can be accused of exposing their children to unhealthy domestic dynamics and failing to create proper homes for them.

Indeed, for all the moral complexity embedded in single-motherhood, relational instability or uncertainty is even more problematic. One of the biggest fears state agents had when it came to single mothers was that they might not be single at all. Even tenuous connections to partners were taken as evidence that a woman's single status was not complete and that she was somehow gaming the system by presenting herself as poor while receiving the benefits of being partnered. While some legally single but socially partnered individuals did take advantage of the disconnect between their legal and lived identities, given the potential for relationships to fall apart, the practice can be understood more generously as reasonable hedging and a well-intentioned security strategy. In other contexts, similar future-oriented efforts to prepare for contingencies and guard against risks are viewed as evidence of a modern sensibility. Yet for Peru's poor, and specifically for poor women, these sorts of calculations are viewed as evidence of deviousness.

Having described all the work that falls to women in Peru's urban settlements, I hope to have awakened a new sensibility among readers, making them more attentive to the ways women's empowerment becomes responsibilization, blame, and burden as well as more open to women's internal multiplicities and many coexisting identities, relations, commitments, and aspirations. For without such an awareness, the war on poverty morphs all too easily into a war on the poor.

Epilogue

Much has changed in Pachacútec and its encompassing district of Ventanilla since I began working there in 2007. Major highways have been built or widened; a grand municipal palace was constructed in downtown Ventanilla along with an imposing civic square; and new businesses including a modern combination supermarket-cinema have arrived to take advantage of the growing consumer base. Cell and radio towers speckle the surrounding sand dunes, video surveillance equipment abounds, and water infrastructure is finally being installed in Pachacútec. The problems preoccupying politicians and the broader population have also morphed over the years from crime and insecurity in 2016, to the corruption scandals of 2017–2019, to the social shockwaves of the Covid-19 pandemic in 2020, to the political instability, inflation, and food insecurity of 2023. Yet for all these changes, the political and discursive patterns that underlie these problems and the struggles, ambivalences, and resentments that characterized people's everyday experiences have persisted.

I was first confronted by these evolving yet strangely familiar discourses and dynamics in 2016 following a multiyear hiatus in which I had been unable to visit. When Vicky's son picked me up from the Lima airport, he told me that citizen insecurity had become a critical issue in Callao. The entire region had been in an official state of emergency for the previous six months. "Supposedly it was only going to be for a little while," he said, "but they keep extending it. Other districts in Lima are asking for this too, asking that they too be put in a state of emergency." His description of what a state of emergency meant in practice felt mundane: "It means they put more police around, and if the police see a small group of young men gathering, they tell them to disperse." It seemed that for him, the state of emergency was primarily a way to get the government to do what it should have been doing all along.[1]

It was after midnight when we arrived at Vicky's house. She had stayed up to greet me and wrapped me in a hug. "Hola hijita! How have you been? How long it's been since I've seen you!" I had missed her too. She congratulated me on my marriage and told me to hurry and have kids before I "miss the train." Over the next few days, Vicky caught me up on family news: marriages, divorces, jobs changes, moves, land that had been bought, sold, exchanged, or built on. She focused on the big events that make up people's lives, the events that make a difference to their everyday experiences by reshaping their social identities and corresponding relations to the world around them.

Her youngest son got a job working in a province of Lima. He was making good money and only coming to the house on weekends. His income allowed them to purchase new appliances and build a brick wall to separate their front yard from the public sidewalk, an important symbol of progress and class status. But he had to quit after injuring his back and was once again living with Vicky in the house full time, doing odd jobs in the neighborhood to contribute income where he could. Her oldest son had also moved out for a time to live with a girlfriend, but after eighteen months, that too fell apart. Vicky said the girlfriend didn't like that her son's ex, the mother of his child, was still calling him regularly. "But it was [the girlfriend's] fault for not understanding that he's always going to be tied to [his ex]," Vicky contended. "Since they have a child, [his ex] is always going to be asking him for things or asking after her son. But she didn't understand that, even though she also has a kid."

That son was back in her house too but was still in touch with his recent girlfriend. "Sometimes he still buys things for the woman's son. . . . He helps where he can because he feels bad, because the kid's father doesn't come around or assume responsibility for him." It seemed we all bore marks of our experiences over the previous few years, but for the moment we were all back in a house that, while also changed, remained a place we could fall back on as we moved forward.

As for the district itself, which had grown up around and through these quotidian life-making activities, Vicky said the district mayor had been doing good work; the municipality was planting greenery, collecting garbage regularly, and maintaining clean streets. The only places that hadn't improved, she said, were those places where the neighbors didn't know how to organize. "How can the mayor know the necessities of the people if the people don't tell him?" she asked. Change, it seemed, required that citizens organize into recognizable institutional forms, making themselves legible so that their voices might be heard.

My visits to central Ventanilla revealed a more complex picture of urban growth. True, there were more parks and greenways and more buildings of glass and concrete. But there was also more crowding and congestion: 400,000 people from across the country squeezing past each other on the sidewalks and riding in the crush of minivans and mototaxis that inched along the highway, a haze of exhaust enveloping everything. In the distance, mature plants grew on the previously barren sand dune that marked the edge of Pachacútec, and beyond them, a water tower that seemed to promise the area's escape from at least one component of poverty.

The administrative center of Pachacútec had also undergone physical changes, though I was more struck by the change in my relationship to it. Upon taking pictures of the renovations to the *agencia*, including the soaring cellular tower and the new second-story video surveillance office, I was reprimanded by a doorman who explained that it was forbidden to take pictures of public institutions. Most of the promoters and administrators I had worked with a few years earlier had moved on to other things, and I would need new permissions from new supervisors if I wanted information about government activities, that is, if I wanted to be back inside the state.

However, Ximena was still there. She ran a copy kiosk across from the *agencia* and had been in the background of myriad government activities during my earlier fieldwork. She recognized me from the many times I had accompanied Pachacutanos making copies for various bureaucratic procedures, and she called me over to chat. She told me that my friend Ismael died several years earlier. "It's that he liked to drink," she said, offering this as a medical and moral-existential explanation for his passing. She did not know where he was buried.

Ximena asked if she had changed since I last saw her, if she looked more wrinkled and worn out, if she looked like she had been suffering. She explained that she separated from her husband one year and seven months earlier. "He found another woman, and now he lives with her," she said. "She lives just around the corner, so I always see them walking together. I wish they would go far away."

As we talked, people approached to ask about getting duplicates of their ID cards. For 25 soles Ximena said she could order a duplicate for them online, and they could pick it up from RENIEC at the *agencia* in three days. Later Ximena told me that the online fee was only 20 soles. She paid this with her bank card and kept 5 soles profit for each transaction. She used to only do printing and copying, but over the previous few years her business model evolved along with the bureaucratic practices of the state. Her new computer, printer, and CCTV cameras suggested that business had been good. When I asked how she came up with this business plan, she quietly replied, "The father of my children showed me." I felt bad for raising the specter of her relational loss and her continued entanglement with it, but it was a hard topic to avoid. Her successes and sorrows knotted together as she built her life through this place.

None of my primary interlocutors from Pachacútec were exactly where they were during my longest period of fieldwork, but most were still in Pachacútec and still involved in development politics, albeit in different ways.

Marisa left her job with the district government due to what she described as "gossip." She was rumored to be having extramarital affairs and neglecting her household. She said she decided to leave rather than endure slights to her character. Nonetheless, she continued to use the administrative and political skills she developed there in her work as a block-level *dirigente* and in her work with Pachacútec's Pro-district movement, a group trying to transform Pachacútec into an independent political district with administrative autonomy and budgetary control. Drawing on her fieldwork experience with the district government, Marisa was heavily involved with the information gathering required to gain district status. Before it could legally become a district, Pachacútec first had to appear as a district on paper, with its would-be geographic, infrastructural, demographic, and socioeconomic composition clearly delineated. Creating this dossier helped to produce Pachacútec as a coherent legal entity and served as evidence that inhabitants had enough governing capacity to be worthy of this political-legal status.

Pablo had been in and out of local government over the years, depending on whether the administration saw him as a political asset or a political threat in a given moment. In 2016 he was back in and working with the district's Office of Human Settlements, which was responsible for resolving land disputes and distributing proof of possession to settlers. His office was in central Ventanilla but not in the new municipal palace. As the public face of the municipality, he said, the palace was reserved for less conflictual offices. But Pablo preferred his work in settlements to the sanitized government operations that happened in the palace to which he had been previously assigned. "In settlements, you deal with issues at a higher political level, themes of land, invasions, proof of possession, physical-legal cleansing, maps. All of this is more exciting." In Pablo's view, the issues of territory and authorization that he worked on played a fundamental role in shaping the district and the future of area politics. Everything else the municipality did—citizen security, sports and recreation, landscaping—was mere window dressing.

When I asked him about developments in Pachacútec and the possible persistence of extreme poverty in the area, his response invoked both technocratic and political frames. First, he said that there was no more extreme poverty in Pachacútec. "Extreme poverty means the people who don't have enough to eat or the people who can't work. The elderly, the disabled. Currently, extreme poverty means the special cases, the special categories." If I was interested in extreme poverty, he said I needed to go to Huaycán, the notoriously poor *barriada* in Lima's eastern cone. The area predates Pachacútec by twenty years, but Pablo said, "Huaycán is the new Pachacútec because their leaders don't know how to organize, whereas in Pachacútec we do. Even though the *dirigentes* have changed, the new *dirigentes* are organizing themselves well to get things done because now they do so on a foundation that was developed by previous *dirigentes*." According to Pablo, "extreme poverty" described both the special individuals who were categorically identified as deserving and the generalized helplessness effected by community disorganization or, in Huaycán's case, produced by forgetting how to organize and self-advocate with the government. From this vantage, the fight against poverty seemed like a fight against entropy and was thus never-ending.

When I asked Pablo about the security situation in Callao, he admitted it was a problem. "Now people kill each other at very little provocation," he said, attributing the dire situation to "the lack of values taught in the home, to irresponsible parenthood. . . . There's no guidance, so the kids grow up . . . to be violent." I thought about how even if security had replaced poverty as a dominant problematic in Peru, the fixation on the household as the root of social ills continued unabated.

As we parted ways Pablo commented that marriage looked good on me. "You can read on a person's face how they live," he said, "if they are happy or sad at home. This is something you wear on your face."

I thought about Ximena.

A few weeks later I finally caught up with Anita. She had been busy working for a local councilwoman whom she described as a *mujer luchadora*, a tireless woman warrior with mayoral aspirations. As we walked from Pachacútec's market to her house, she congratulated me on my marriage before quickly advising me not to let my husband go around by himself. "As a couple, each of you has to be attentive to the other," she explained. But I needed to exercise special caution, she said, because "bad women" were everywhere.

> If you're not careful, if you don't mark him regularly—"Hello, my love. Where are you? Who are you with?"—he can end up getting involved with another woman. Even if you think he's a good man and he has no intention of cheating on you, sometimes in life, things happen. You're at a friendly gathering, drinking, and all of a sudden you lose yourself. These are things that happen to a person, that one can't control. But if the partner is there with him, it's less likely he'll be out drinking, flirting, and forgetting himself.

I saw her advice as propagating patterns of gendered discrimination and expectations, relational insecurity, and mistrust. But it was advice that she gave because she cared, because she wanted to prepare me for the possibility that my current life might fall apart and help me avoid that fate the best way she knew how. A small part of that advice cocooned itself in my subconscious.

Our conversation moved organically from bad women and untrustworthy men to empowered women without men. She reminded me of how the World Bank had picked her to attend a meeting of female community leaders from around the world so that experts could better understand women's lived experiences, get advice about what solutions would serve them best, and determine whether World Bank money was going where it should. "And it is not going where it should," she said. She went on for more than an hour about the diverse ways she and women like her were being shut out of development. Even if they were properly credentialed, she said, women like her couldn't get a job if they didn't have a patron on the inside to advocate for them. Meanwhile, programs like Techo Propio reached only the privileged poor, people who could prove with bank statements that they had stable, if low-paying, jobs.

Anita went on to describe an idea for a project she had that would include poor women and ensure that social assistance funds went to the right people. The government could train women in resilient infrastructure and issue loans for them to buy materials from local microenterprises. This would stimulate the local economy and empower women to advance themselves and *salir adelante* by building their own homes of concrete, which would be an "irreversible investment." But she said that no one was supporting the idea. "I've presented that project to the region, the district, the central government, and they've all told me there's no budget for that. . . . So, where is the budget? It's going to big projects with big companies where [the politicians] can steal." She went on to describe the major corruption scandals that had ensnared almost every well-known Peruvian politician in recent years, including four presidents and the regional and provincial governors of Callao, all of whom had received kickbacks for awarding big construction contracts to large foreign companies.[2]

> How many millions of soles destined for projects in Pachacútec ended up going to [those companies and politicians]?! All these irregularities, we are the ones who suffer. . . . The World Bank, foreign countries, they send money in good faith. . . . [But] the fathers of our country are the ones who don't want us to grow. They don't want us to develop. It's not in their interest for Pachacútec to develop quickly because if we do, in whose name are they going to ask for money? They use us. . . . They use us to enrich themselves and their people.

Anita explained that this corruption was having harmful effects on the nation and described research she had done into these issues, fluidly interweaving insights from conversations with various professionals, statistical information she found on the internet, and her own lived experience.

> I know how to navigate the internet and investigate my own country. . . . I can tell you, for example, which province has the most poverty, which provinces have chronic malnutrition. . . . And you can see that at the national level, [Peru] is low in education, low in nutrition, low in values. . . . In Peru, there's no formality among couples in households. We're deficient in formality. Forty percent of homes in Peru are destroyed, . . . formed and destroyed. . . . Peru has many poor places, and Pachacútec is one of them. . . . [At World Bank meetings] they have a big screen, and there you see maps. They say, let's see, Peru . . . Ventanilla. . . . And there is Pachacútec as a red spot. It's red! Why? Because we are vulnerable. . . . The problem of sanitation, housing, natural disasters, earthquakes, all of this. . . . The World Bank gave us money, [and] how are we? The area is the same. . . . When one lives it, one knows. The benefits don't arrive to us.

I asked Anita about the water infrastructure being installed in Pachacútec and whether that project gave her any hope that things might be improving. Her response indicated that any material progress indexed by Pachacútec's new water supply was entangled with the nation's moral deficits. Anita asserted that water was not coming to Pachacútec, at least not yet, not the way it should. The water and sanitation system was being installed in phases, and each phase was accompanied by groundbreaking and inauguration ceremonies to give politicians opportunities to show off and take credit. But there were also problems. In phase 1 the water company dug up the streets to install the primary pipelines but never repaved them, and the community was having to mobilize to get them to finish the job the right way. In phase 2 they installed individual household water meters, including on abandoned houses, which had unjustly rewarded Pachacútec's "tourists," a term she used for nonresident owners and part-time inhabitants who were profiting from the hard work of full-time residents. And they hadn't even begun the wastewater treatment plant. "Where is all the shit going to go?" Anita shouted in exasperation.

Until the treatment plant was complete, Anita said, there wouldn't be proper water infrastructure in Pachacútec, and all the ceremonies and celebrations were simply smoke. Anita compared this propaganda to what the government did when there was a natural disaster, as there had been during the rainy season in the sierra that year when mudslides destroyed entire towns. "They give the illusion that everything is fixed," she said, "but it's a lie. . . . Unfortunately, in Peru, the corruption is immeasurable."

Notes

INTRODUCTION

1. *Estera* is a term for a large woven reed mat commonly used in precarious and early-stage constructions in Peru's coastal regions. These low-cost mats are often sold in sizes of 2 x 2 meters or 2 x 3 meters. Depending on their size, rigidity, and tightness of weave, they can be used as roofs or walls or bent over in a semicircle and used as a tent. A very early-stage house might be composed of five *esteras*, four as walls and one as a roof, minimally supported by wooden poles stuck into the ground. Whenever I use terms like "straw," "straw hut," or "straw mat" in this text, I am referring to *esteras*. Due to the symbolic and aesthetic significance of this construction material, when directly quoting interlocutors I generally opt to use the Spanish *estera* accompanied by the appropriate English translation.
2. This consisted of several one- to three-month trips during academic breaks from 2007 to 2012, as well as a fourteen-month extended fieldwork trip from August 2009 to October 2010, when I conducted the bulk of this research. I then spent several years engaged in research and writing about these issues from abroad before reinitiating summer fieldwork in Peru for this and a related project from 2016 to 2019.
3. The phrase "culture of poverty" is typically attributed to Oscar Lewis who, in the early 1960s, used the term to describe sociostructural, psychological, and behavioral similarities he identified in segments of low-income populations in the United States, Puerto Rico, and Mexico. He asserted that certain traits—such as limited participation in dominant social institutions, poor social organization, matrifocality, feelings of inferiority, a present-time orientation, and provincialism—began as common adaptations to common problems in certain capitalist societies but subsequently perpetuated themselves across generations as children were socialized into these orientations. Lewis (1966) qualified his assertions by distinguishing his "culture of poverty" from economic poverty and explaining that the majority of poor populations did not exhibit this so-called culture. Nonetheless, the term is frequently invoked to provide a scientific gloss

to denigrating stereotypes about the poor and to blame the poor for their circumstances. Although there are similarities between the ways my Peruvian interlocutors depict the household heritability of poverty and the ways culture of poverty frames are invoked in the United States, the underlying logics of an ecologically tied cultural particularism, class associations of habits and mannerisms that Peruvians call *educación*, and theories of personality formation are distinctive enough to Peru that I do not engage US culture of poverty debates here. For a succinct discussion of these debates in the United States see Goode 2010.

4. Numerous scholars have argued that the "modern era" is partly defined by the emergence of a particular kind of poverty (i.e., the widespread pauperization that results when capitalism spreads, existing community relations break down, and millions are deprived of access to land and other resources) together with a particular institutional approach to addressing it (Escobar 1995; Foucault 2007; Milton 2007).
5. For instance, poverty-relief programs like conditional cash transfers versus universal basic income imply different understandings about the causes of poverty as well as different ways of thinking about the rational capacity of the poor and their relations to other citizens.
6. See Didier Fassin's 2007 discussion of W. H. Auden's "Age of Anxiety."
7. See Escobar 1995 and Rist 2008 for thorough histories of the coevolution of "poverty" and "development."
8. See Comaroff and Comaroff 2006a and Zhang 2001 for similar analyses of the "total crime fact" in South Africa and the "floating population" in China, respectively.
9. I draw the term "generic intimacy" from Comaroff and Comaroff's (2006a) description of the "total crime fact" in South Africa.
10. Celeste Watkins-Hayes and Elyse Kovalsky (2016, 199) describe the pervasiveness of tropes of the deserving and undeserving poor both in the United States and in international poverty frameworks, explaining that even though "politicians and policy makers generally do not use 'deservingness' explicitly . . . discourse and policies reflect the implicit boundary-drawing processes that parse worthiness."
11. Efforts to fight poverty through formalization gained popularity in the international development community following the English-language publication of Hernando de Soto's seminal book *The Other Path* in 1989, in which he extols the poverty-fighting power of property formalization. Later enthusiasm around fighting poverty through political inclusion can be traced to Amartya Sen's 1999 book *Development as Freedom* and the framework of "inclusive liberalism" that emerged from it. A Peru-specific application of Sen's capabilities framework can be found in Altamirano et al. 2004.
12. Colin McFarlane and Michael Waibel (2016, 1–2) argue that "formality and informality can be variously conceived as territorial formations (e.g., the slum and the city), categories of particular groups (e.g., informal labor), forms of organization (e.g., structured/unstructured; rule based/unruly; predictable/unpredictable), and as modes of knowing the city (e.g., formal and informal knowledges and practices)."

13. Malinowski (2014 [1922]) coined this phrase in describing the goals of anthropological fieldwork.
14. See Anderson 2009 and Fernández-Maldonado 2007 for further discussion of the terms "duly constituted" and "consolidated," respectively.
15. When describing childrearing, my interlocutors in Pachacútec typically used the verb *formar*, meaning to form, mold, or make, rather than verbs like *criar*, to raise. Though sometimes used in relation to children, the verb *criar* was more often used to describe raising animals for food. To best convey the worldviews of my interlocutors, in this text I generally use terms like form, formation, shape, and mold when describing the work of childrearing in Peru.
16. See Ellison 2018 for a discussion of this nationalist dimension of domestication.
17. These statistics were derived from the results of Peru's 2007 census for Pachacútec's encompassing district of Ventanilla. Given Ventanilla's pattern of spatial expansion, it is reasonable to assume that most of these "recent migrants" (i.e., people who resided elsewhere five years before the census) lived in Pachacútec. If we expand the recent migrant definition to include people who had migrated to Pachacútec during and immediately after 2000 relocation, it would likely increase the proportion of recent migrants from Lima-Callao dramatically.
18. The spread of virulent strains of MDR-TB in Lima has been discussed by Paul Farmer (2003) and in numerous public health journals; see especially Rojas et al. 2008; Shah et al. 2010.
19. Subsequent maps produced by residents working to obtain district status indicate that Techo Propio has since integrated into the Special Project.
20. According to the earthquake census, the earthquake caused more damage in the province of Chincha, where 108,408 individuals had houses that were destroyed or severely damaged by the earthquake, compared to 54,855 individuals in Pisco (INEI 2007).
21. See Briggs and Mantini-Briggs 2003 and Caldeira 2000 for how extreme cases and emergency circumstances can make ever-present social phenomena more visible.
22. By 2016, Ventanilla's civil registry had been absorbed into the national RENIEC system, but in 2010, both offices operated out of the *agencia* simultaneously.
23. See Gupta and Ferguson 1997 for a critique of the notion of "the field" in anthropology.
24. Even the most activist and engaged ethnographic fieldwork requires openness and a degree of self-effacement. Without this, I believe ethnography morphs into memoir or travelogue.
25. For examples see AlSayyad and Roy 2004; Anand 2017; Caldeira 2017; Gilbert 2007; Holston 2007; Simone 2010; Weinstein 2014.
26. Nikhil Anand (2017) similarly opts to call the Mumbai neighborhoods he studies "settlements," though he considers the connotations of settler colonialism more of a liability.
27. In Peru, "cholo" is used to refer to Andean migrants or people with mixed indigenous ancestry, most often disparagingly.

CHAPTER 1: POVERTY PRODUCTIONS

1. The nuevo sol is the currency of Peru. During my research, the average exchange rate was approximately 3.3 soles to US$1.
2. See Nading 2014 and Wilhoit 2017 for additional examples of the feminized labor of data gathering.
3. Had we gotten to the end of the survey, the ENAHO would have picked up on some of this as well, as questions intended to capture institutional trust are now included in the survey.
4. This phrase is generally attributed to the nineteenth-century naturalist Antonio Raimondi.
5. John Comaroff (2001, 306) defines "lawfare" as "the effort to conquer and control indigenous peoples by the coercive use of legal means." He discusses the concept at length in the above-quoted 2001 article, "Colonialism, Culture, and the Law: A Foreword," and in an introduction he cowrote with Jean Comaroff entitled "Law and Disorder in the Postcolony: An Introduction" (Comaroff and Comaroff 2006b).
6. Several scholars indicate that Lima's primacy as the seat of Peruvian national culture was not inevitable. Rather, during the rise of the republic, Lima competed with Cuzco for this status (de la Cadena 2000; Thurner 1997).
7. I borrow this phrase from José Matos Mar's 1984 seminal book about this period, *Desborde popular y crisis de estado*.
8. "The Washington Consensus" is a term coined in 1989 for a set of ten policies that the US government and Washington-based international financial institutions deemed necessary for economic growth in developing nations. These policies emphasized government fiscal discipline, trade liberalization, deregulation, privatization, and increasing foreign direct investment. When scholars describe the rise of neoliberalism, they are largely referring to this package of reforms, which have their ideological basis in liberal economic theory.
9. These headlines were translated from lines that appeared on the back cover of the daily paper *Peru21* in 2009 and 2010.
10. This phrase, which for many years appeared on the World Bank website (https://www.worldbank.org) under its mission statement, is repeated in numerous mission statements published by the World Bank and its subsidiary groups as well as in documents that seek to succinctly articulate the World Bank's mission. For instance, the phrase appears on the UN Environment Program website (https://www.unep.org/pt-br/node/28687) and on the World Bank's LinkedIn profile (https://www.linkedin.com/company/the-world-bank/).
11. The World Bank helped finance poverty mapping in Ecuador in the mid-1990s. Widespread global poverty mapping took off in the early 2000s, following the development of methodological innovations that combined census and sample survey data (Elbers, Lanjouw, and Lanjouw 2003). In 2006 the World Bank collaborated with researchers at CIESIN (Center for International Earth Science Information Network), a geographic research institute at Columbia University,

to publish *Where the Poor Are: An Atlas of Poverty* (CIESIN 2006). In 2007 the World Bank published *More than a Pretty Picture: Using Poverty Maps to Design Better Policies and Interventions* (Bedi, Coudouel, and Simler 2007), which draws on examples of poverty mapping from twelve countries around the world. For an example of the centrality of mapping to contemporary global poverty analyses, see the proceedings from the World Bank's "Land and Poverty Conference 2019: Catalyzing Innovation" (https://www.worldbank.org/en/events/2018/08/13/land-and-poverty-conference-2019-catalyzing-innovation#2).

12. Further supporting the notion that FONCODES's poverty maps are effectively maps of state presence, there is an overlap between officially identified extreme poverty zones and areas with high rates of narcotrafficking. I was acquainted with several Peruvians who worked in these notoriously dangerous areas specifically because of how much more money their skills and wares were worth there. In other words, conventional monetary poverty was not the major problem. When I asked a FONCODES field director what sorts of antipoverty programs they could implement there, he said that police and army officers were the first step to fighting that particular poverty variant.
13. Pierre Bourdieu (1977) coined the term "habitus" to denote embodied class and culture dispositions that are reproduced, and potentially changed, through practice over time.
14. The Spanish phrase typically used to describe these activities is *hacer seguimientos*, which literally means "to do followings" and might be translated as "follow up," "monitor," or "surveil."
15. On audit culture see Strathern 2000.

CHAPTER 2: AMBIVALENT DEVELOPMENTS

1. APRA (Alianza Popular Revolucionaria Americana, American Popular Revolutionary Alliance) is the name of then President Alan García's political party.
2. See James Ferguson's 1994 analysis of development as an "antipolitics machine" for further discussion of the ways the development apparatus ignores ground-level realities that do not match its vision or demonizes deviation from this imaginary as aberrant, such that its discourses and representations have coercive, world-shaping power.

CHAPTER 3: PAPERING THE MARGINS

1. These three quoted terms are taken from Scott 1998, MacFarlane and Waibel 2016, and Foucault 1991, respectively. The notion of bureaucratic rationality being the central characteristic of the modern state can be traced to Max Weber's book *Economy and Society* (1968, originally published posthumously in 1921).

2. New contexts may of course inform the interpretations, uses, and political significance of documents (Hetherington 2011). Nonetheless, the static representation of relations and reality in a particular moment is critical to the promise of documents and the social dynamics they engender.
3. Peru has been described as exceptional among Andean countries for its lack of an obvious indigenous identity movement. María Elena García (2005) argues that this perceived lack is a product of the ways social scientists have imagined social movements and their consequent failure to explore the alternative forms political action can take. Despite not deploying recognizable banners of indigenousness, in Peru, indigenous populations mobilize frequently and engage the state through confederations, cooperatives, unions, political parties, and grassroots and state-led mobilizations. These engagements diverge from conventional social scientific visions of social movements in that they are shot through with class relations and assume the possibility of engaging with the state on multiple levels. My argument that indigenous political engagements have also been subsumed under the label of "informals" and interpreted through the lens of popular capitalism is meant to supplement these other arguments about indigenous mobilization.
4. This argument recalls the "Two Peru" thesis put forth by historian Jorge Basadre in 1929 (published in 1947) in which he distinguishes between the official, legal Peru (*el país legal*) and what he terms "deep" Peru (*el país profundo*). Also see Mayer 1991.
5. The celebration of the informals as the real Peru was also one of former president Fujimori's most successful political strategies. According to several political analysts, he informalized the politics of the center, appealing to urban migrants and indigenous peoples as an outsider who would challenge the corrupt criollo establishment that had used the law to line their pockets at the expense of impoverished, indigenous, and informal populations (Kay 1996; Roberts 1998; Wise 1994).
6. The title *El otro sendero* invokes the name of Peru's Maoist guerrilla organization Sendero Luminoso (Shining Path) to highlight that this popular capitalism is an alternative way Peru's underclasses have sought to improve their positions. In this, it mimics W. W. Rostow's influential text on modernization theory entitled *The Stages of Economic Growth: A Non-Communist Manifesto* (1990 [1960]). *El otro sendero* was published in English in 1989 as *The Other Path: The Invisible Revolution in the Third World*. The original version was written with coauthors Enrique Ghersi and Mario Ghibellini, who later won a lawsuit they filed against de Soto for publishing editions in which he appeared as the sole author. In *Unruly Domestication* I have chosen to attribute citations solely to de Soto because he was the only listed author of the English translation and because of his status as a prominent public intellectual who has played a major role in promoting these ideas in Peru and internationally.
7. These documents showed that the *dirigentes* had been charged with assault and illegally occupying land. Many of the settlers in G4 would now have similar records

since they had been registered by the state's attorney as illegally occupying public lands. As far as I know, subsequent legalization has no effect on this police record.

8. Lima newspaper *La República* carried the story "No queremos más infiltrados en Vaso de Leche" (We don't want more infiltrators in Vaso de Leche) on August 6, 2010.
9. President García declared many states of emergency during his 2006–2011 term, but the emergencies in Pisco, on account of the 2007 earthquake, and in the Amazonian town of Bagua were among the most widely publicized and deeply politicized. García declared a state of emergency in Bagua in May 2009 after 5,000 self-identifying indigenous people blocked a highway to protest executive decrees that threatened their territorial lands and livelihoods and were made without consultation with indigenous leaders (Bebbington 2009; Rénique 2009).

CHAPTER 4: STATE IDENTITIES

1. Annelise Riles (1998) observes that texts like these are more often referenced than read. They are typically stored on office shelves, gathering dust until they are mined for preapproved phrases that might be reproduced, verbatim and uncited, in other policy documents to index ideological and political affinities between institutions. I have identified sections from the RENIEC plan reproduced verbatim in five-year identity card distribution plans for 2011 and 2017 and noticed specific phrases from the document reproduced on MIMDES web pages related to the rights of the child and in international NGO reports about identity management (CRVS Systems 2019).
2. Anthropological analyses of kinship, time, social structure, and social personhood challenge the idea that any of these traits are inherent—that is, grounded in the person rather than in the social framing of that person—or necessarily static over time and across contexts. Instead, scholars have pointed to the roles of states and colonial governments in asserting the naturalness of particular identity categories as a way to enhance their power and facilitate the administration of populations (Kertzer and Fricke 1997).
3. The centralization of information was a primary motif of Fujimori's administration. RENIEC's activities with identity and civil status paralleled COFOPRI's work with property management and FONCODES's work with poverty identification.
4. Despite these efforts, full political inclusion in Peru still depends on voting. Voting is mandatory in Peru, and Peruvians' participation in elections is marked on the back of their ID cards by a sticker. If individuals fail to vote and affix the corresponding sticker to their ID cards, the cards are invalidated. Peruvians are officially prohibited from using the cards to engage in transactions with state authorities until they acquire the stickers by paying a fine for their lack of civic engagement.
5. Biomedicine in Peru focuses heavily on organ health, particularly the liver and

kidneys. Peruvians often interpret back pain as kidney pain caused by bodily jostling and exhaustion.

6. Leinaweaver (2008) identifies exceptions to this in which "abandoned children," without activated family connections, have no last names.
7. Peru's Civil Code of 1936, title 3, articles 19–21, 362, and 392.
8. It is possible Ethel's mother was resistant to this, in part, because it might increase her sociolegal responsibility for her grandchild, who the naming practice would now suggest was her daughter. Several of my interlocutors expressed concern about older adults having to raise their grandchildren when their own children were not up to the task of parenting.
9. Details of Law 28720 and the corresponding diffusion campaign "Now I Have My Two Last Names" can be found in Aragonez 2008, Defensoría del Pueblo 2017, and LP Pasión por el Derecho 2020.
10. By 2016 genetic testing had become a frequent practice for determining or contesting legal paternity, particularly as it related to felony incidences of failure to pay child support. Stickers affixed to sidewalks and telephone poles advertised genetic paternity testing. These stickers were as common as those advertising "Prestamos Sin DNI" (loans without ID), though not yet quite as common as those suggesting support for women experiencing "Atraso Menstrual," delayed menstruation.

CHAPTER 5: DOMESTIC IDEALS, SINGLE MOMS, AND ELASTIC RELATIONS

1. Paco, one of my host-brothers, was helping a nurse for a public health institution clean out a storeroom and came upon her personal archive: a collection of books, pamphlets, and other public health paraphernalia that she had accumulated over the previous thirty years. Paco had seen me collect these kinds of political ephemera before and received permission to give me the archive for my studies.
2. When Peruvians initiated conversations with me, they frequently began with questions about whether I was married, single, or had children. I later realized that these questions helped Peruvians situate me socially and anticipate the kind of sociality they might expect from me. As a *soltera*, a single woman, I was told I could do as I pleased, didn't have to be home at a certain hour, and was free to pursue my studies and goals. I was also told that I should enjoy this because once I was fully partnered, this freedom would disappear. This attitude resonates with findings by Norma Fuller (2003) showing that in Lima, young single women are encouraged to pursue professional lives and identities and even some limited sexual exploration. However, once they are married or have children, their individual freedoms are curtailed and they are expected to take on adult gender roles that tether them to the home and demand complete devotion to family and children.

3. Open discussion of premarital sex could mark me as immoral, while aligning too closely with Christian-derived values and heteronormative family ideals could foreclose more candid conversations about family realities.
4. See Fuller 2001 for a discussion of how masculine identities are constituted and understood over the life course in Peru.
5. Although both men and women took pride in their autonomy and were readily critiqued by friends and colleagues when they allowed this independence to be curtailed by partners, the practice of "marking" coded slightly differently for men and women. When women were marked by male partners, their friends critiqued them for taking part in lower-class and less modern gender relations. When men were marked by female partners, critiques were grounded in the idea that control over men's social liberties and sexuality was emasculating (Fuller 2001).
6. Numerous news articles name *celos* (jealousy) as the motive for intrafamilial homicides. Examples from the Lima daily newspaper *Perú21* (https://peru21.pe/) are "Una mujer asesina hija por celos," November 5, 2013; "¿Eres celoso pero deseas cambiar?" January 25, 2014; "Mi pareja no me deja ver a mis amigos," February 14, 2014.
7. This quote was acquired and translated from the "Vision" section on the INABIF website in 2010. INABIF's official function as articulated in its operations manual in 2012 was "to contribute to the holistic development of families in situations of vulnerability and risk, with an emphasis on children, adolescents, senior citizens, and the disabled in situations of abandonment and to promote their inclusion in society and the full exercise of their rights."
8. The preoccupation with single mothers as both socially dangerous and uniquely deserving of assistance is evident in the Global North as well. Since the 1970s, anthropologists working in the United States and England have pointed to the political importance of single-parent families in welfare regimes as well as the inadequacy and destructive effects of these paradigms (Fitchen 1995; Stack 1974). William Wilson (1987) offers an example of the fixation on single mothers as a defining feature of poverty.
9. Microfinance initiatives that target women are one prominent example of international efforts to fight poverty by empowering women (Kar 2018; Schuster 2015).
10. Gender scholars studying the Andes have suggested queering the *quariwarmi*, indicating it may refer less to the man-woman pair than to the idea of complementary energies present in a single person (Weismantel 2001; Weismantel and Wilhoit 2019).
11. See Han (2012, 89) on how women living in poverty strive to achieve "dignity along the lines of speech and silence" and how respecting boundaries of private life can be an act of care among kin and neighbors.
12. Brennan used the Spanish phrase "uno se sensibiliza," meaning that one becomes more aware of a context or issue and correspondingly becomes more receptive to

people's requests and more willing to help. It was the same phrase that Carla used to describe her work with the Right to Identity campaign.

13. Processing fees ranged from 140 to 450 soles, depending on the district. Couples also incurred costs for prenuptial medical certificates, birth certificates, juridical declarations of residence, copies of updated IDs, counseling sessions on sexually transmitted diseases, and announcements of marriage licenses in newspapers.

CHAPTER 6: HOUSING, KINSHIP, AND LANDSCAPES OF POVERTY

1. See Goldstein 2004 for a discussion of how the dynamics of state surveillance in shantytowns generates mistrust and makes residents wary of the gaze of outsiders.
2. A modern census in this sense was conducted in Peru sixty years prior, in 1876, as part of an effort by the Bourbon state to supplant the governing power of the Catholic Church (INEI 2017).
3. In 2007 the census form's registry of household occupants also distinguished between different kinds of family nuclei, instructing enumerators to list single children, single children with children, and married children and their families.
4. Official statistics at the level of metropolitan Lima do not generally exist because statistics are elaborated based on political jurisdiction. Metropolitan Lima is a construct of urban planners and academics, not a political entity. Likewise, incidents tallied for Ventanilla do not distinguish Pachacútec from other areas because Pachacútec is not an independent political entity. It is also not clear where these statistics were supposed to be coming from, as neither the police nor Women's Emergency Center workers had any knowledge of this claim. Additionally, I could find no information online from police, other state entities, or area NGOs that indicated anything close to the numbers cited by the mayor.
5. The continued salience of Turner's progressive housing framework can be seen in the work of other housing scholars such as Fernández-Maldonado and Bredenoord 2010 and Tokeshi, Noriega, and Quiñónez 2005, who coined terms like "incipient consolidation" and "partial consolidation" to describe distinct stages of construction for houses in Lima's *barriadas*.
6. Later research on progressive housing sites contended that these settlements could also stagnate and, in failing to progress, end up resolving the quantitative housing deficit only to replace it with a qualitative one (Duhau 2014; Fernández-Maldonado and Bredenoord 2010).
7. On July 12, 2014, Peru's congress passed Law 30230, modifying article 920 of Peru's civil code such that authorities now have fifteen days to forcibly remove squatters before they receive legal protections as de facto property claimants and the property dispute must go to court. My observations from 2016 to 2019 suggest that this legal change has done little to curb the rate of land takeovers in Ventanilla, but more systematic empirical research is needed to evaluate this.

8. In practice, enlisting political support is often the first step in initiating the land takeover, highlighting the complicity of elites in these grassroots mobilizations. See Collier 1976 and Holland 2016 for further discussion of this dynamic.
9. For an analysis of the actual effects of titling policies on formal credit availability in Peru see Calderón Cockburn 2002.
10. This figure was taken from a report entitled "Diagnóstico social del Macro Proyecto Pachacútec, Distrito de Ventanilla, Región Callao." The report was produced in 2009 by a group calling itself the Consorcio Macro Proyecto Ingenieros in preparation for a massive water and sewage infrastructure project in Pachacútec to be undertaken by SEDEPAL, Peru's state-owned water utility.
11. This report, entitled "Linea de base Social Proyecto Piloto Nuevo Pachacútec," was produced by *dirigentes* in Pachacútec's Pilot Project in consultation with the Peruvian NGO Alternativa. It was emailed to me by one of the authors in 2007.
12. See Dosh and Lerager 2006 on the relation between land titles and urban development.
13. Pablo's Spanish wording is significant for the way it deploys many of the key terms that arise in relation to Peru's war on poverty and the way it materializes in Pachacútec: "Una persona viva que no vive, pero que hace su jardín bonito como si viviera allí? Esa es una persona viva que no verdaderamente necesita."

CONCLUSION

1. See Millar 2018 for a critique of the informality concept.
2. See Isabelle Stengers's 2005 essay "The Cosmopolitical Proposal" for more on the value and potential political potency of arousing "a slightly different awareness of the problems and situations mobilizing us" (994).

EPILOGUE

1. We could also interpret this mundane attitude as part of the subversive rise of the carceral state in everyday life. For more on this framework see Wacquant 2008 and his broader oeuvre on the penalization of poverty in the twenty-first century.
2. On Peru's corruption scandals see Zarate and Casey 2019.

References

Abrams, Philip. 1988. "Notes on the Difficulty of Studying the State (1977)." *Journal of Historical Sociology* 1, no. 1: 58–89.

Aguirre, Carlos, and Charles F. Walker, eds. 2017. *The Lima Reader: History, Culture, Politics*. Illustrated ed. Durham, NC: Duke University Press.

Allen, Catherine J. 2002. *The Hold Life Has: Coca and Cultural Identity in an Andean Community*. 2nd ed. Washington, DC: Smithsonian Institution Press.

AlSayyad, Nezar, and Ananya Roy, eds. 2004. *Urban Informality: Transnational Perspectives from the Middle East, Latin America, and South Asia*. Lanham, MD: Lexington.

Altamirano, Teofilo, James Copestake, Adolfo Figueroa, and Katie Wright-Revolledo. 2004. "Universal and Local Understanding of Poverty in Peru." *Global Social Policy* 4, no. 3: 313–336.

Anand, Nikhil. 2017. *Hydraulic City: Water and the Infrastructures of Citizenship in Mumbai*. Durham, NC: Duke University Press.

Anderson, Jeanine. 2000. "Gender and Generations in Shanty Community Development. Lima, Peru." Paper presented to the annual meeting of the Global Development Network, Tokyo.

Anderson, Jeanine. 2009. "Assembling and Disassembling Families." *Journal of Latin American and Caribbean Anthropology* 14, no. 1: 185–198.

Andina. 2014. "El 78% de madres que alumbra en Perú tiene estado civil de conviviente." January 4. http://www.andina.com.pe/agencia/noticia-el-78-madres-alumbra-peru-tiene-estado-civil-conviviente-489033.aspx.

Appadurai, Arjun. 1996. *Modernity at Large: Cultural Dimensions of Globalization*. Vol. 1: *Public Worlds*. Minneapolis: University of Minnesota Press.

Appadurai, Arjun. 2006. *Fear of Small Numbers: An Essay on the Geography of Anger*. Durham, NC: Duke University Press.

Aragonez, María Ynés. 2008. "Boletín Informativo" 47. Lima: Mesa de Concertación para la Lucha contra la Pobreza. https://www.mesadeconcertacion.org.pe/sites/default/files/archivos/2015/documentos/08/boletin_informativo_ano_vi_no_47-marzo-abril_2008.pdf.

Arel, Dominique. 2002. "Language Categories in Censuses: Backward- or Forward-Looking?" In *Census and Identity: The Politics of Race, Ethnicity, and Language in National Censuses*, edited by David Kertzer and Dominique Arel, 92–120. Cambridge, England: Cambridge University Press.

Aretxaga, Begoña. 2005. *States of Terror: Begoña Aretxaga's Essays*. Edited by Joseba Zulaika. Reno: University of Nevada Press.

Arguedas, José María. 2002 [1941]. *Yawar Fiesta*. Translated by Frances Horning Barraclough. Prospect Heights, IL: Waveland.

Arriola, Aurora. 2001. "El caso Zarai." *Caretas* (Lima), March 8.

Asad, Talal. 2002. "Ethnographic Representation, Statistics, and Modern Power." In *From the Margins: Historical Anthropology and Its Futures*, edited by Brian Keith Axel, 66–94. Durham, NC: Duke University Press.

Auyero, Javier. 2000. "The Logic of Clientelism in Argentina: An Ethnographic Account." *Latin American Research Review* 35, no. 3: 55–81.

Baiocchi, Gianpaolo. 2005. *Militants and Citizens: The Politics of Participatory Democracy in Porto Alegre*. Stanford, CA: Stanford University Press.

Balibar, Etienne. 2007. "Is There a 'Neo-Racism'?" In *Race and Racialization: Essential Readings*, edited by Tania Das Gupta, 83–88. Toronto: Canadian Scholars.

Bambarén, Celso. 2010. "Legal Issues of Humanitarian Assistance after the 2007 Earthquake in Pisco, Peru." *Prehospital and Disaster Medicine* 25, no. 3: 203–206.

Banerjee, Abhijit V., and Esther Duflo. 2020. "How Poverty Ends: The Many Paths to Progress—and Why They Might Not Continue the Future of Capitalism." *Foreign Affairs* 99, no. 1: 22–29.

Basadre, Jorge. 1947. *La multitud, la ciudad y el campo en la historia del Perú: Con un colofón sobre el país profundo*. Lima: Huascarán.

Bayart, Jean-François. 1993. *The State in Africa: The Politics of the Belly*. London: Longman.

Bebbington, Anthony. 2009. "The New Extraction: Rewriting the Political Ecology of the Andes." *NACLA Report on the Americas* 42, no. 5: 12–20.

Bedi, Tara, Aline Coudouel, and Kenneth Simler, eds. 2007. *More than a Pretty Picture: Using Poverty Maps to Design Better Policies and Interventions*. Washington, DC: World Bank.

Benjamin, Walter. 1978. "Critique of Violence." In *Reflections*, edited by Peter Demetz, 277–300. New York: Schocken.

Beverley, John. 2008. "Testimonio, Subalternity, and Narrative Authority." In *A Companion to Latin American Literature and Culture*, edited by Sara Casro-Klarén, 571–583. Malden, MA: Blackwell.

Biehl, João, and Torben Eskerod. 2007. *Will to Live: AIDS Therapies and the Politics of Survival*. Princeton, NJ: Princeton University Press.

Blomley, Nicholas. 2003. "Law, Property, and the Geography of Violence: The Frontier, the Survey, and the Grid." *Annals of the Association of American Geographers* 93, no. 1: 121–141.

Blondet, Cecilia. 1999. *Las mujeres y la política en la década de Fujimori*. Lima: Instituto de Estudios Peruanos.

Blondet, Cecilia. 2004a. "Las organizaciones de mujeres: Capital social del estado y para las mujeres." In *Cucharas en alto: Del asistencialismo al desarrollo local; fortaleciendo la participación de las mujeres*, edited by Cecilia Blondet and Carolina Trivelli, 10–18. Documento de Trabajo, no. 139. Lima: Instituto de Estudios Peruanos.

Blondet, Cecilia. 2004b. "Los comedores populares: 25 años de historia." In *Cucharas en alto: Del asistencialismo al desarrollo local; fortaleciendo la participación de las mujeres*, edited by Cecilia Blondet and Carolina Trivelli, 36–46. Documento de Trabajo, no. 139. Lima: Instituto de Estudios Peruanos.

Blondet, Cecilia, and Carolina Trivelli, eds. 2004. *Cucharas en alto: Del asistencialismo al desarrollo local; fortaleciendo la participación de las mujeres*. Documento de Trabajo, no. 139. Lima: Instituto de Estudios Peruanos.

Boesten, Jelke. 2003. "Poor Women in Peru: Reproducers of Poverty and Poverty Relievers." *Women's Studies Quarterly* 31, nos. 3–4: 113–128.

Boesten, Jelke. 2010. *Intersecting Inequalities: Women and Social Policy in Peru, 1990–2000*. University Park, PA: Penn State Press.

Bolton, Ralph, and Enrique Mayer. 1977. *Andean Kinship and Marriage*. Washington, DC: American Anthropological Association.

Borneman, John. 1992. *Belonging in the Two Berlins: Kin, State, Nation*. Cambridge, England: Cambridge University Press.

Bornstein, Erica. 2005. *The Spirit of Development: Protestant NGOs, Morality, and Economics in Zimbabwe*. Stanford, CA: Stanford University Press.

Bourdieu, Pierre. 1977. *Outline of a Theory of Practice*. Cambridge, England: Cambridge University Press.

Briet, Suzanne. 2006. *What Is Documentation? English Translation of the Classic French Text*. Translated by Laurent Martinet, Ronald E. Day, and Hermina G. B. Anghelescu. Metuchen, NJ: Scarecrow.

Briggs, Charles L., and Clara Mantini-Briggs. 2003. *Stories in the Time of Cholera: Racial Profiling during a Medical Nightmare*. Berkeley: University of California Press.

Butler, Judith. 2008. "Sexual Politics, Torture, and Secular Time." *British Journal of Sociology* 59, no. 1: 1–23.

Caldeira, Teresa P. R. 2017. "Peripheral Urbanization: Autoconstruction, Transversal Logics, and Politics in Cities of the Global South." *Environment and Planning D: Society and Space* 35, no. 1: 3–20.

Caldeira, Teresa P. R. 2000. *City of Walls: Crime, Segregation, and Citizenship in São Paulo*. Berkeley: University of California Press.

Calderón Cockburn, Julio. 2002. "Property and Credit: Property Formalization in Peru." Working paper. Cambridge, MA: Lincoln Institute of Land Policy.

Cameron, Maxwell A., and Philip Mauceri, eds. 1997. *The Peruvian Labyrinth: Polity, Society, Economy*. University Park: Pennsylvania State University Press.

Campoamor, Leigh. 2016. "'Who Are You Calling Exploitative?' Defensive Motherhood, Child Labor, and Urban Poverty in Lima, Peru." *Journal of Latin American and Caribbean Anthropology* 21, no. 1: 151–172.

Capelo, Joaquin. 1902. *Sociologia de Lima*. Lima: La Industria.

Cáritas. 2008. "Emergencia del sur del Perú, EA 19/2007. Informe final." Callao, Peru: Cáritas. http://www.caritas.org.pe/terremoto_ica_atencion.html.

Carsten, Janet, and Stephen Hugh-Jones. 1995. *About the House: Lévi-Strauss and Beyond*. Cambridge, England: Cambridge University Press.

Carter, William E. 1977. "Trial Marriage in the Andes." In *Andean Kinship and Marriage*, edited by Ralph Bolton and Enrique Mayer, 177–216. Washington, DC: American Anthropological Association.

Castells, Manuel. 1983. *The City and the Grassroots: A Cross-Cultural Theory of Urban Social Movements*. Berkeley: University of California Press.

Certeau, Michel de. 1988. *The Practice of Everyday Life*. Minneapolis: University of Minnesota Press.

Chambers, Bill. 2005. "The Barriadas of Lima: Slums of Hope or Despair? Problems or Solutions?" *Geography* 90, no. 3: 200–224.

Chant, Sylvia. 2008. "The 'Feminisation of Poverty' and the 'Feminisation' of Anti-Poverty Programmes: Room for Revision?" *Journal of Development Studies* 44, no. 2: 165–197.

CIESIN (Center for International Earth Science Information Network). 2006. *Where the Poor Are: An Atlas of Poverty*. New York: CIESIN, Earth Institute at Columbia University. https://documents1.worldbank.org/curated/pt/470061479454835343/pdf/110240-WP-Box396329B-PUBLIC-Where-The-Poor-Are-An-Atlas-of-Poverty-2006.pdf.

Collier, David. 1976. *Squatters and Oligarchs: Authoritarian Rule and Policy Change in Peru*. Baltimore, MD: Johns Hopkins University Press.

Collins, Daryl, Jonathan Morduch, Stuart Rutherford, and Orlanda Ruthven. 2009. *Portfolios of the Poor: How the World's Poor Live on $2 a Day*. Princeton, NJ: Princeton University Press.

Comaroff, Jean, and John L. Comaroff. 2006a. "Figuring Crime: Quantifacts and the Production of the Un/Real." *Public Culture* 18, no. 1: 209–246.

Comaroff, Jean, and John L. Comaroff. 2006b. "Law and Disorder in the Postcolony: An Introduction." In *Law and Disorder in the Postcolony*, edited by Jean Comaroff and John Comaroff, 1–57. Chicago: University of Chicago Press.

Comaroff, John L. 2001. "Colonialism, Culture, and the Law: A Foreword." *Law and Social Inquiry* 26, no. 2: 305–314.

Cookson, Tara Patricia. 2018. *Unjust Conditions: Women's Work and the Hidden Cost of Cash Transfer Programs*. Oakland: University of California Press.

Corbridge, Stuart, Glyn Williams, Manoj Srivastava, and René Véron. 2005. *Seeing the State: Governance and Governmentality in India*. Cambridge, England: Cambridge University Press.

Coutin, Susan Bibler. 2003. "Illegality, Borderlands, and the Space of Nonexistence." In *Globalization under Construction: Governmentality, Law, and Identity*, edited by Richard Warren Perry, 171–202. Minneapolis: University of Minnesota Press.

Crabtree, John. 1992. *Peru under García: An Opportunity Lost*. Pitt Latin American Series. Pittsburgh, PA: University of Pittsburgh Press.

Creed, Gerald W. 2000. "'Family Values' and Domestic Economies." *Annual Review of Anthropology* 29, no 1: 329–355.

CRVS (Centre of Excellence for Civil Registration and Vital Statistics) Systems. 2019. "Compendium of Good Practices in Linking Civil Registration and Vital Statistics (CRVS) and Identity Management Systems." Ottawa, Canada: International Development Research Centre.

Das, Veena. 2007. *Life and Words: Violence and the Descent into the Ordinary.* Berkeley: University of California Press.

Das, Veena, and Deborah Poole, eds. 2004. *Anthropology in the Margins of the State.* Santa Fe, NM: School of American Research Press.

Das, Veena, and Shalini Randeria. 2015. "Politics of the Urban Poor: Aesthetics, Ethics, Volatility, Precarity; an Introduction to Supplement 11." *Current Anthropology* 56, no. S11: S3–14.

Davis, Kevin E., Benedict Kingsbury, and Sally Engle Merry. 2010. "Indicators as a Technology of Global Governance." *Law and Society Review* 46, no. 1: 71–104.

Davis, Mike. 2006. *Planet of Slums.* London: Verso.

Defensoría del Pueblo. 2017. "Cómo tramitar una pensión de alimentos." Blog post, February 20. https://www.defensoria.gob.pe/blog/como-tramitar-una-pension-de-alimentos/comment-page-2/.

Degregori, Carlos Ivan. 1997. "The Maturation of a Cosmocrat and the Building of a Discourse Community: The Case of Shining Path." In *The Legitimization of Violence*, edited by David E. Apter, 33–82. New York: New York University Press.

Degregori, Carlos Iván, and Pablo Sandoval. 2008. "Peru: From Otherness to a Shared Diversity." In *A Companion to Latin American Anthropology*, edited by Deborah Poole, 150–174. Blackwell Companions to Anthropology 6. Malden, MA: Blackwell.

de la Cadena, Marisol. 1995. "Women Are More Indian: Ethnicity and Gender in a Community near Cuzco." In *Ethnicity, Markets, and Migration in the Andes: At the Crossroads of History and Anthropology*, edited by Brooke Larson, Olivia Harris, and Enrique Tandeter, 329–348. Durham, NC: Duke University Press.

de la Cadena, Marisol. 2000. *Indigenous Mestizos: The Politics of Race and Culture in Cuzco, Peru, 1919–1991.* Latin America Otherwise. Durham, NC: Duke University Press.

de la Cadena, Marisol. 2001. "Comments: Ambiguity and Contradiction in the Analysis of Race and State." *Journal of Latin American Anthropology* 6, no. 2: 252–266.

de la Cadena, Marisol. 2015. *Earth Beings: Ecologies of Practice across Andean Worlds.* Durham, NC: Duke University Press.

de Soto, Hernando. 1989. *The Other Path: The Invisible Revolution in the Third World.* New York: Harper and Row. Originally published as *El otro sendero: La revolución informal* (Lima: El Barranco, 1986) with coauthors Enrique Ghersi and Mario Ghibellini.

de Soto, Hernando. 2000. *The Mystery of Capital: Why Capitalism Triumphs in the West and Fails Everywhere Else.* New York: Basic Books.

de Waal, Alex. 2005. *Famine That Kills: Darfur, Sudan*. Oxford, England: Oxford University Press.

Diaz A., Juvenal. 2006. "Focalización geográfica: Nuevo mapa de pobreza de FONCODES." Presentation, October. Lima: Ministerio de Educación. https://repositorio.minedu.gob.pe/handle/20.500.12799/222.

Dietz, Henry. 1998. *Urban Poverty, Political Participation and the State: Lima 1970–1990*. Pittsburgh, PA: University of Pittsburgh Press.

Donzelot, Jacques. 1979. *The Policing of Families*. London: Heinemann.

Dosh, Paul, and James Lerager. 2006. "Surprising Trends in Land Invasions in Metropolitan Lima and Quito." *Latin American Perspectives* 33: 29.

Douglas, Mary. 2002. *Purity and Danger: An Analysis of Concepts of Pollution and Taboo*. Hoboken, NJ: Taylor and Francis.

Duhau, Emilio. 2014. "The Informal City: An Enduring Slum or a Progressive Habitat?" In *Cities from Scratch: Poverty and Informality in Urban Latin America*, edited by Brodwyn Fischer, Bryan McCann, and Javier Auyero, 150–169. Durham, NC: Duke University Press.

Echegaray, Eduardo de. 1887. *Diccionario General etimológico de la lengua española*. Vol. 2. Edited by José María Faquineto. Madrid: Álvarez Hermanos.

Edelman, Marc, and Angelique Haugerud. 2005. *The Anthropology of Development and Globalization: From Classical Political Economy to Contemporary Neoliberalism*. Malden, MA: Blackwell.

Elbers, Chris, Jean O. Lanjouw, and Peter Lanjouw. 2003. "Micro-Level Estimation of Poverty and Inequality." *Econometrica* 71, no. 1: 355–364.

Ellison, Susan Helen. 2018. *Domesticating Democracy: The Politics of Conflict Resolution in Bolivia*. Durham, NC: Duke University Press.

Englund, Harri. 2015. "Forget the Poor: Radio Kinship and Exploited Labor in Zambia." *Current Anthropology* 56, no. S11: S137–145.

Escobar, Arturo. 1995. *Encountering Development: The Making and Unmaking of the Third World*. Princeton Studies in Culture/Power/History. Princeton, NJ: Princeton University Press.

Ewick, Patricia, and Susan S. Silbey. 1998. *The Common Place of Law: Stories from Everyday Life*. Language and Legal Discourse. Chicago: University of Chicago Press.

Farmer, Paul. 2003. *Pathologies of Power: Health, Human Rights, and the New War on the Poor*. Berkeley: University of California Press.

Fassin, Didier. 2007. *When Bodies Remember: Experiences and Politics of AIDS in South Africa*. Berkeley: University of California Press.

Ferguson, James. 1994. *The Anti-Politics Machine: "Development," Depoliticization, and Bureaucratic Power in Lesotho*. Minneapolis: University of Minnesota Press.

Ferguson, James. 2007. "Formalities of Poverty: Thinking about Social Assistance in Neoliberal South Africa." *African Studies Review* 50, no. 2: 71–86.

Ferguson, James, and Akhil Gupta. 2002. "Spatializing States: Toward an Ethnography of Neoliberal Governmentality." *American Ethnologist* 29, no. 4: 981–1002.

Ferme, Mariane. 2004. "Deterritorialized Citizenship and the Resonances of the Sierra

Leonean State." In *Anthropology in the Margins of the State*, edited by Veena Das and Deborah Poole, 81–115.

Fernández-Maldonado, Ana María. 2007. "Fifty Years of Barriadas in Lima: Revisiting Turner and de Soto." In *ENHR 2007 International Conference "Sustainable Urban Areas"* (June 25–28), edited by P. Boelhouwer, D. Groetelaers, and E. Vogels, 1–17. Rotterdam: European Network for Housing Research.

Fernández-Maldonado, Ana M. 2010. "Recent Housing Policies in Lima and Their Effects on Sustainability." Paper presented at the 42nd ISOCARP Conference on Sustainable City/Developing World, Nairobi.

Fernández-Maldonado, Ana María, and Jan Bredenoord. 2010. "Progressive Housing Approaches in the Current Peruvian Policies." *Habitat International* 34, no. 3: 342–350.

Fischer, Brodwyn. 2014. "A Century in the Present Tense: Crisis, Politics, and the Intellectual History of Brazil's Informal Cities." In *Cities from Scratch: Poverty and Informality in Urban Latin America*, edited by Brodwyn Fischer, Bryan McCann, and Javier Auyero, 9–67. Durham: Duke University Press.

Fitchen, Janet M. 1995. "'The Single-Parent Family,' Child Poverty, and Welfare Reform." *Human Organization* 54, no. 4: 355–362.

Fitzgerald, Edmund V. K. 1979. *The Political Economy of Peru: 1956–1978*. New York: Cambridge University Press.

Forero, Juan. 2002. "Piura Journal: At 14, the Girl's Indomitable (Just Ask Her Father)." *New York Times*, December 6. https://www.nytimes.com/2002/12/06/world/piura-journal-at-14-the-girl-s-indomitable-just-ask-her-father.html.

Fonseca, Claudia. 2009. "Family Belonging and Class Hierarchy: Secrecy, Rupture, and Inequality as Seen through the Narratives of Brazilian Adoption." *Journal of Latin American and Caribbean Anthropology* 14, no. 1: 92–114.

Foucault, Michel. 1991. *The Foucault Effect: Studies in Governmentality with Two Lectures by and an Interview with Michel Foucault*. Edited by Graham Burchell, Colin Gordon, and Peter Miller. Chicago: University of Chicago Press.

Foucault, Michel. 2007. *Security, Territory, Population: Lectures at the College de France 1977–1978*. Edited by Michel Senellart and Graham Burchell. New York: Palgrave Macmillan.

Franco, Jean. 2006. "Alien to Modernity: The Rationalizaiton of Discrimination." *A Contra Corriente: A Journal on Social History and Literature in Latin America* 3, no. 3: 1–16.

Fujimori, Alberto. 2005. "A Momentous Decision." In *The Peru Reader: History, Culture, Politics*, edited by Orin Starn, Carlos Ivan Degregori, and Robin Kirk, 460–467. Durham, NC: Duke University Press.

Fuller, Norma. 2001. "The Social Constitution of Gender Identity among Peruvian Men." *Men and Masculinities* 3, no. 3: 316–331.

Fuller, Norma. 2003. "Adolescencia y riesgo: Reflexiones desde la antropología y los estudios de género." In *Varones adolescentes: Género, identidades y sexualidades en América Latina*, edited by José Olavarría, 71–84. Santiago, Chile: FLACSO.

Fuller, Norma. 2005. "Cambios y permanencias en las relaciones de género en el Perú." In *Familia y vida privada: ¿Transformaciones, tensiones, resistencias y nuevos sentidos?*, edited by Teresa Valdés Echeñique and Ximena Valdés, 107–129. Santiago, Chile: FLACSO.

Gandolfo, Daniella. 2009. *The City at Its Limits: Taboo, Transgression, and Urban Renewal in Lima*. Chicago: University of Chicago Press.

García, María Elena. 2005. *Making Indigenous Citizens: Identity, Development, and Multicultural Activism in Peru*. Stanford, CA: Stanford University Press.

Geertz, Clifford. 1986. "Experiences, Authoring Selves." In *The Anthropology of Experience*, edited by Victor Turner and Edward M Bruner, 373–380. Urbana: University of Illinois Press.

Ghertner, D. Asher. 2015. *Rule by Aesthetics: World-Class City Making in Delhi*. Oxford, England: Oxford University Press.

Gilbert, Alan, ed. 1996. *The Mega-City in Latin America*. Tokyo: United Nations University Press.

Gilbert, Alan. 2002. "On the Mystery of Capital and the Myths of Hernando de Soto: What Difference Does Legal Title Make?" *International Development Planning Review* 24, no. 1: 1–19.

Gilbert, Alan. 2007. "The Return of the Slum: Does Language Matter?" *International Journal of Urban and Regional Research* 31, no. 4: 697–713. https://doi.org/10.1111/j.1468-2427.2007.00754.x.

Goldstein, Daniel M. 2004. *The Spectacular City: Violence and Performance in Urban Bolivia*. Latin America Otherwise. Durham, NC: Duke University Press.

Golte, Jürgen, and Norma Adams. 1990. *Los caballos de Troya de los invasores: Estrategias campesinas en la conquista de la gran Lima*. 2nd ed. Lima: Instituto de Estudios Peruanos.

Goodale, Mark. 2008. "Legalities and Illegalities." In *A Companion to Latin American Anthropology*, edited by Deborah Poole, 214–229. Malden, MA: Blackwell.

Goode, Judith. 2010. "How Urban Ethnography Counters Myths about the Poor." In *Urban Life: Readings in the Anthropology of the City*, 5th ed., edited by George Gmelch, Robert V. Kemper and Walter P. Zenner, 279–295. Long Grove, IL: Waveland.

Goody, Jack. 1986. *The Logic of Writing and the Organization of Society*. Cambridge, England: Cambridge University Press.

Gordillo, Gaston. 2006. "The Crucible of Citizenship: ID-Paper Fetishism in the Argentinean Chaco." *American Ethnologist* 33, no. 2: 162–176.

Gramsci, Antonio. 1971. *Selections from the Prison Notebooks of Antonio Gramsci*. Translated by Geoffrey Nowell-Smith and Quintin Hoare. New York: International.

Green, Maia. 2006. "Representing Poverty and Attacking Representations: Perspectives on Poverty from Social Anthropology." *Journal of Development Studies* 42, no. 7: 1108–1129.

Greenhalgh, Susan. 2003. "Planned Births, Unplanned Persons: 'Population' in the Making of Chinese Modernity." *American Ethnologist* 30, no. 2: 196–215.

Gupta, Akhil. 2011. "National Poverty and Global Poverty in the Age of Neoliberalism

(Pauvreté nationale et pauvreté mondiale dans l'âge du néolibéralisme)." *Cahiers d'Études Africaines* 51, nos. 202–203: 1–10.

Gupta, Akhil. 2012. *Red Tape: Bureaucracy, Structural Violence, and Poverty in India.* Durham, NC: Duke University Press.

Gupta, Akhil, and James Ferguson. 1997. *Anthropological Locations: Boundaries and Grounds of a Field Science.* Berkeley: University of California Press.

Guyer, Jane I., Naveeda Khan, and Juan Obarrio, with Caroline Bledsoe, Julie Chu, Souleymane Bachir Diagne, Keith Hart, et al. 2010. "Introduction: Number as Inventive Frontier." *Anthropological Theory* 10, no 1–2: 36–61. https://doi.org/10.1177/1463499610365388.

Han, Clara. 2012. *Life in Debt: Times of Care and Violence in Neoliberal Chile.* Berkeley: University of California Press.

Harris, Olivia. 1980. "The Power of Signs: Gender, Culture, and the Wild in the Bolivian Andes." In *Nature, Culture, and Gender*, edited by Carol MacCormack and Marilyn Strathern, 70–94. Cambridge England: Cambridge University Press.

Harris, Olivia. 2008. "Alterities: Kinship and Gender." In *A Companion to Latin American Anthropology*, edited by Deborah Poole, 276–302. Malden, MA: Blackwell.

Harvey, Penelope. 1994. "Domestic Violence in the Peruvian Andes." In *Sex and Violence: Issues in Representation and Experience*, edited by Penelope Harvey and Peter Gow, 66–89. London: Routledge.

Haya de la Torre, Victor Raúl. 2005 [1931]. "The Apra." In *The Peru Reader: History, Culture, and Politics*, edited by Orin Starn, Carlos Ivan Degregori, and Robin Kirk, 253–258. Durham, NC: Duke University Press.

Hetherington, Kregg. 2011. *Guerrilla Auditors: The Politics of Transparency in Neoliberal Paraguay.* Durham, NC: Duke University Press.

Hetherington, Kregg. 2018. "Comment to Residency Counts and Housing Rights: Conflicting Enactments of Property in Lima's Central Margins." *Current Anthropology* 59, no. 6: 705–706.

Hickey, Sam. 2010. "The Government of Chronic Poverty: From Exclusion to Citizenship?" *Journal of Development Studies* 46, no. 7: 1139–1155.

Hirsch, Jennifer S. 2003. *A Courtship after Marriage: Sexuality and Love in Mexican Transnational Families.* Berkeley: University of California Press.

Hirsch, Jennifer S., and Holly Wardlow. 2006. *Modern Loves: The Anthropology of Romantic Courtship and Companionate Marriage.* Ann Arbor: University of Michigan Press.

Holland, Alisha C. 2016. "Forbearance." *American Political Science Review* 110, no. 2: 232–246.

Holston, James. 2007. "Citizenship in Disjunctive Democracies." In *Citizenship in Latin America*, edited by Joseph S. Tulchin and Meg Ruthenburg, 75–94. Boulder, CO: Lynne Reinner.

Holston, James. 2008. *Insurgent Citizenship: Disjunctions of Democracy and Modernity in Brazil.* In-Formation Series. Princeton, NJ: Princeton University Press.

Huayhua, Margarita. 2014. "Racism and Social Interaction in a Southern Peruvian

Combi." *Ethnic and Racial Studies* 37, no. 13: 2399–2417. https://doi.org/10.1080/01419870.2013.809129.

Hull, Matthew S. 2012. "Documents and Bureaucracy." *Annual Review of Anthropology* 41: 251–267.

INEI (Instituto Nacional de Estadística e Informática). 2001. "Estadísticas vitales en Lima metropolitana: 1999–2000." Lima: INEI.

INEI (Instituto Nacional de Estadística e Informática). 2007. "Censos nacionales: XI de población y VI de vivienda—cédula censal." Lima: INEI.

INEI (Instituto Nacional de Estadística e Informática). 2010. "Encuesta nacional de hogares 2010 condiciones de vida y pobreza—cuestionario." Lima: INEI.

INEI (Instituto Nacional de Estadística e Informática). 2011. "Ficha técnica encuesta nacional de hogares sobre condiciones de vida y pobreza, ENAHO 2011." Lima: INEI.

INEI (Instituto Nacional de Estadística e Informática). 2012. "Condiciones de Vida en el Perú." No. 2, June. Lima: INEI. https://www.inei.gob.pe/media/MenuRecursivo/boletines/12996.pdf.

INEI (Instituto Nacional de Estadística e Informática). 2017. "Censos nacionales 2017: XII de Población, VII de Vivienda y III de Comunidades indígenas." Lima: INEI.

Irigoyen, Marina, Teresa Chipoco, and Alberto Cheng. 1988. *Planificación con el pueblo: Una estrategia de gestión municipal Ate-Vitarte Programa Urbano del Centro IDEAS*. Lima: Programa Urbano del Centro IDEAS.

Jeganathan, Pradeep. 2004. "Checkpoint: Anthropology, Identity, and the State." In *Anthropology in the Margins of the State*, edited by Veena Das and Deborah Poole, 67–80.

Johnson-Hanks, Jennifer. 2002. "On the Limits of Life Stages in Ethnography: Toward a Theory of Vital Conjunctures." *American Anthropologist* 104, no. 3: 865–880.

Kabeer, Naila. 1994. *Reversed Realities: Gender Hierarchies in Development Thought*. London: Verso.

Kafka, Ben. 2009. "Paperwork: The State of the Discipline." *Book History* 12, no. 1: 340–353.

Kanbur, Ravi, and Paul Shaffer. 2007. "Epistemology, Normative Theory, and Poverty Analysis: Implications for Q-Squared in Practice." *World Development* 35, no. 2: 183–196. https://doi.org/10.1016/j.worlddev.2005.10.016.

Kar, Sohini. 2018. *Financializing Poverty: Labor and Risk in Indian Microfinance*. Stanford, CA: Stanford University Press.

Kay, Bruce H. 1996. "'Fujipopulism' and the Liberal State in Peru, 1990–1995." *Journal of Interamerican Studies and World Affairs* 38, no. 4: 55–98.

Kertzer, David I., and Tom Fricke, eds. 1997. *Anthropological Demography: Toward a New Synthesis*. Population and Development Series. Chicago: University of Chicago Press.

Kleinman, Arthur, and Joan Kleinman. 1996. "The Appeal of Experience, the Dismay of Images: Cultural Appropriations of Suffering in Our Times." *Daedalus* 125, no. 1: 1–23.

Kreager, Philip. 1986. "Demographic Regimes as Cultural Systems." In *The State of Population Theory: Forward from Malthus*, edited by R. Schofield and David Coleman, 131–155. Oxford, England: Blackwell.

Kuznesof, Elizabeth Anne. 2005. "The House, the Street, Global Society: Latin American Families and Childhood in the Twenty-First Century." *Journal of Social History* 38, no. 4: 859–872.

Lambek, Michael. 2013. "Kinship, Modernity, and the Immodern." In *Vital Relations: Modernity and the Persistent Life of Kinship*, edited by Susan McKinnon and Fenella Cannell, 241–260. Santa Fe, NM: SAR Press. https://muse.jhu.edu/pub/257/monograph/book/35840.

Laplante, Lisa J., and Kimberly Theidon. 2008. "Claiming Citizenship: Collective Reparations in Post-TRC Peru." *Anthropology News* 49, no. 1: 36.

Lazar, Sian. 2005. "Citizens despite the State: Everyday Corruption and Local Politics in El Alto, Bolivia." In *Corruption: Anthropological Perspectives*, edited by Dieter Haller and Cris Shore, 212–228. London: Pluto. https://doi.org/10.2307/j.ctt18fs7ts.

Lazar, Sian. 2008. *El Alto, Rebel City: Self and Citizenship in Andean Bolivia*. Durham, NC: Duke University Press.

Leinaweaver, Jessaca B. 2007. "On Moving Children: The Social Implications of Andean Child Circulation." *American Ethnologist* 34, no. 1: 163–180.

Leinaweaver, Jessaca B. 2008. *The Circulation of Children: Kinship, Adoption, and Morality in Andean Peru*. Latin America Otherwise. Durham, NC: Duke University Press.

Leinaweaver, Jessaca B. 2009. "Raising the Roof in the Transnational Andes: Building Houses, Forging Kinship." *Journal of the Royal Anthropological Institute* 15, no. 4: 777–796.

Leinaweaver, Jessaca B., and Linda J. Seligmann. 2009. "Introduction: Cultural and Political Economies of Adoption in Latin America." *Journal of Latin American and Caribbean Anthropology* 14, no. 1: 1–19.

Lewis, Oscar. 1966. "The Culture of Poverty." *Scientific American* 215, no. 4: 19–25.

Li, Tania Murray. 2005. "Beyond 'the State' and Failed Schemes." *American Anthropologist* 107, no. 3: 383–394.

Lind, Amy. 2009. "Governing Intimacy, Struggling for Sexual Rights: Challenging Heteronormativity in the Global Development Industry." *Development* 52, no. 1: 34–42.

Lloyd, Peter. 1980. *The Young Towns of Lima: Aspects of Urbanization in Peru*. Cambridge, England: Cambridge University Press.

Lobo, Susan. 1982. *A House of My Own: Social Organization in the Squatter Settlements of Lima, Peru*. Tucson: University of Arizona Press.

LP Pasión por el Derecho. 2020. "Jurisprudencia actualizada y relevante del delito de omisión a la asistencia familiar." Blog post, October 8. https://lpderecho.pe/jurisprudencia-actualizada-relevante-delito-omision-prestacion-alimentos/.

Málaga, Iana. 2010. "¿Por qué el programa del Vaso de Leche no gotea a los más necesitados?" *El Comercio* (Lima), September 5.

Malinowski, Bronislaw. 2014 [1922]. *Argonauts of the Western Pacific: An Account of Native Enterprise and Adventure in the Archipelagoes of Melanesian New Guinea.* Oxon, England: Routledge.

Mangin, William, and John C. Turner. 1968. "The Barriada Movement." *Progressive Architecture* 49, no. 5: 154–162.

Mannarelli, María Emma. 1999. *Limpias y modernas: Género, higiene y cultura en la Lima del novecientos.* Lima: Flora Tristán.

Matos Mar, José. 1984. *Desborde popular y crisis del estado: El nuevo rostro del Perú en la década de 1980.* Lima: Instituto de Estudios Peruanos.

Mayer, Enrique. 1991. "Peru in Deep Trouble: Mario Vargas Llosa's 'Inquest in the Andes' Reexamined." *Cultural Anthropology* 6, no. 4: 466–504.

Mazzarella, William. 2004. "Culture, Globalization, Media." *Annual Review of Anthropology* 33: 345–367.

Mazzarella, William. 2006. "Internet X-Ray: E-Governance, Transparency, and the Politics of Immediation in India." *Public Culture* 18, no. 3: 473–505.

McFarlane, Colin, and Michael Waibel. 2016. *Urban Informalities: Reflections on the Formal and Informal.* London: Routledge.

McKinnon, Susan, and Fenella Cannell, eds. 2013. *Vital Relations: Modernity and the Persistent Life of Kinship.* 2013. Santa Fe, NM: SAR Press. https://muse.jhu.edu/pub/257/monograph/book/35840.

Meltzer, Judy. 2013. "Shifting Imaginaries of 'Good Citizens': Governing Citizens in 20th Century Peru." PhD diss., Carleton University.

Merry, Sally Engle. 1992. "Anthropology, Law, and Transnational Processes." *Annual Review of Anthropology* 21: 357–379.

Merry, Sally Engle. 2011. "Measuring the World." *Current Anthropology* 52, no. S3: S83–S95.

Merry, Sally Engle. 2016. *The Seductions of Quantification: Measuring Human Rights, Gender Violence, and Sex Trafficking.* Chicago: University of Chicago Press.

Milanich, Nara. 2002. "Historical Perspectives on Illegitimacy and Illegitimates in Latin America." In *Minor Omissions: Children in Latin American History and Society*, edited by Tobias Hecht, 72–101. Madison: University of Wisconsin Press.

Millar, Kathleen M. 2018. *Reclaiming the Discarded: Life and Labor on Rio's Garbage Dump.* Durham, NC: Duke University Press.

Milton, Cynthia E. 2007. *The Many Meanings of Poverty: Colonialism, Social Compacts, and Assistance in Eighteenth-Century Ecuador.* Stanford, CA: Stanford University Press.

MIMDES (Ministerio de la Mujer y Desarollo Social). 2007. "INABIF 26 años al servicio del bienestar familiar." Lima: MIMDES.

Mosse, David. 2013. "The Anthropology of International Development." *Annual Review of Anthropology* 42: 227–246. https://doi.org/10.1146/annurev-anthro-092412-155553.

Murphy, Edward. 2015. *For a Proper Home: Housing Rights in the Margins of Urban Chile, 1960–2010.* Pittsburgh, PA: University of Pittsburgh Press.

Nader, Laura. 1994. "Comparative Consciousness." In *Assessing Cultural Anthropology*, edited by Robert Borofsky, 84–93. New York: McGraw-Hill.

Nading, Alexander M. 2014. *Mosquito Trails: Ecology, Health, and the Politics of Entanglement*. Oakland: University of California Press.

Nelson, Diane M. 2019. "The Gender of the Number." Review of *The Seductions of Quantification* by Sally Engle Merry. *American Anthropologist* 121, no. 1: 266–268. https://doi.org/10.1111/aman.13177.

Ong, Aihwa, and Stephen J. Collier. 2005. *Global Assemblages: Technology, Politics, and Ethics as Anthropological Problems*. Malden, MA: Blackwell.

Orlove, Benjamin S. 1985. "The History of the Andes: A Brief Overview." *Mountain Research and Development* 5, no. 1: 45–60. https://doi.org/10.2307/3673222.

Parker, David S. 1998. "Civilizing the City of Kings: Hygiene and Housing in Lima, Peru." In *Cities of Hope: People, Protests, and Progress in Urbanizing Latin America, 1870–1930*, edited by Ronn Pineo and James Baer, 153–178. Boulder, CO: Westview.

Parró, Alberto Arca. 1942. "Census of Peru, 1940." *Geographical Review* 32, no 1: 1–20.

Patico, Jennifer. 2010. "From Modern Loves to Universal Passions: Ethnographies of Love, Marriage, and Globalization." *Identities* 17, no. 4: 372–386. https://doi.org/10.1080/1070289X.2010.492306.

Peattie, Lisa R. 1992. "Aesthetic Politics: Shantytown or New Vernacular?" *Traditional Dwellings and Settlements Review* 3, no. 2: 23–32.

Pereyra, Omar. 2004. "Del barrio y del crimen: El fantasma de la criminalidad en Nuevo Pachacútec." *Anthropologica* 22, no. 22: 93–117.

Ponce Alegre, Ana. 2007. "*Madres que crían solas a sus hijos." XXVI Congreso de la Asociación Latinoamericana de Sociología. Guadalajara, Mexico. https://cdsa.aacademica.org/000-066/619.

Poole, Deborah. 2004. "Between Threat and Guarantee: Justice and Community in the Margins in the Peruvian State." In *Anthropology in the Margins of the State*, edited by Veena Das and Deborah Poole, 35–66.

Poole, Deborah, and Gerardo Rénique. 1992. *Peru: Time of Fear*. London: Latin American Bureau.

Portes, Alejandro, and Bryan R. Roberts. 2005. "The Free-Market City: Latin American Urbanization in the Years of the Neoliberal Experiment." *Studies in Comparative International Development* 40, no. 1: 43–82.

Povinelli, Elizabeth A. 2002. "Notes on Gridlock: Genealogy, Intimacy, Sexuality." *Public Culture* 14, no. 1: 215–238.

Povinelli, Elizabeth A. 2006. *The Empire of Love: Toward a Theory of Intimacy, Genealogy, and Carnality*. Durham, NC: Duke University Press.

Pribilsky, Jason. 2007. *La Chulla Vida: Gender, Migration, and the Family in Andean Ecuador and New York City*. Syracuse, NY: Syracuse University Press.

Price, Richard. 1965. "Trial Marriage in the Andes." *Ethnology* 4, no. 3: 310–322.

Radcliffe-Brown, A. R. 1950. Preface to *African Political Systems*, edited by Edward Evan Evans-Pritchard and Meyer Fortes, xi–xxiii. London: Oxford University Press.

Radcliffe-Brown, A. R. 1952. "The Study of Kinship Systems." In *Structure and Function in Primitive Society: Essays and Addresses*, 49–89. Glencoe, IL: Free Press.

RENIEC (Registro Nacional de Identificación y Estado Civil). 2005. "Plan Nacional de Restitución de la Identidad: Documentando a las personas indocumentadas 2005–2009." Registro No. 2005—4491. Lima: RENIEC. http://bvs.minsa.gob.pe/local/contenido/6601.PDF.

Rénique, Gerardo. 2009. "Blood at the Blockade: Peru's Indigenous Uprising." *NACLA* 8. https://nacla.org/news/blood-blockade-perus-indigenous-uprising.

Riles, Annelise. 1998. "Infinity within the Brackets." *American Ethnologist* 25, no. 3: 378–398.

Riles, Annelise. 2006. "Introduction: In Response." In *Documents: Artifacts of Modern Knowledge*, edited by Annelise Riles, 1–41. Ann Arbor: University of Michigan Press.

Rist, Gilbert. 2008. *The History of Development: From Western Origins to Global Faith.* Translated by Patrick Camiller. 3rd ed. London: Zed.

Roberts, Kenneth M. 1995. "Neoliberalism and the Transformation of Populism in Latin America: The Peruvian Case." *World Politics* 48, no. 1: 82–116.

Roberts, Kenneth M. 1998. *Deepening Democracy? The Modern Left and Social Movements in Chile and Peru.* Stanford, CA: Stanford University Press.

Rojas, Christian, Lely Solari, Cesar Herrera, Eduardo Sanchez, Geoffrey Young, Cesar Bonilla, Rocio Hurtado, et al. 2008. "Challenges of Diagnosis and Management of Tuberculosis and HIV Coinfection in Resource-Limited Settings: A Case Report from Lima, Peru." *Journal of the International Association of Physicians in AIDS Care (JIAPAC)* 7, no. 5: 232–237. https://doi.org/10.1177/1545109708325468.

Ronsbo, Henrik. 2008. "Hybridity and Change: Gamonales, Montoneros and Young Politicos in South-Central Peru." *Bulletin of Latin American Research* 27, no. 1: 83–101.

Rose-Redwood, Reuben, and Anton Tantner. 2012. "Introduction: Governmentality, House Numbering and the Spatial History of the Modern City." *Urban History* 39, no. 4: 607–613.

Rostow, W. W. 1990 [1960]. *The Stages of Economic Growth: A Non-Communist Manifesto.* 3rd ed. Cambridge, England: Cambridge University Press.

Roy, Ananya. 2003. *City Requiem, Calcutta: Gender and the Politics of Poverty.* Minneapolis: University of Minnesota Press.

Roy, Ananya. 2011. "Slumdog Cities: Rethinking Subaltern Urbanism." *International Journal of Urban and Regional Research* 35, no. 2: 223–238.

Roy, Ananya, and Emma Shaw-Crane. 2015. *Territories of Poverty: Rethinking North and South.* Atlanta: University of Georgia Press.

Salazar, Gabriel. 1985. *Labradores peones y proletarios: Formación y crisis de la sociedad popular chilena del siglo XIX.* Santiago, Chile: Sur.

Scheper-Hughes, Nancy. 1992. *Death without Weeping: The Violence of Everyday Life in Brazil.* Berkeley: University of California Press.

Schuster, Caroline E. 2015. *Social Collateral: Women and Microfinance in Paraguay's Smuggling Economy.* Oakland: University of California Press.

Scott, James C. 1998. *Seeing Like a State: How Certain Schemes to Improve the Human Condition Have Failed*. New Haven, CT: Yale University Press.

Scott, James C. 2005. "Afterword to 'Moral Economies, State Spaces, and Categorical Violence.'" *American Anthropologist* 107, no. 3: 395–402.

Seligmann, Linda. 1995. *Between Reform and Revolution: Political Struggles in the Peruvian Andes, 1969–1991*. Stanford, CA: Stanford University Press.

Seligmann, Linda J. 2009. "Maternal Politics and Religious Fervor: Exchanges between an Andean Market Woman and an Ethnographer." *Ethos* 37, no. 3: 334–361.

Sen, Amartya. 1999. *Development as Freedom*. New York: Knopf.

Shah, L., H. Choi, F. Krapp, C. Zamudio, C. Seas, A. Ciampi, T. Brewer, and E. Gotuzzo. 2010. Predictors of Primary Multiple Drug Resistant Tuberculosis (MDR-TB) Transmission in Lima, Peru." *International Journal of Infectious Diseases* 14, Supplement 1(0): e25–e26.

Sharma, Aradhana, and Akhil Gupta. 2006. *The Anthropology of the State: A Reader*. Malden, MA: Blackwell.

Simmel, Georg. 1965 [1908]. "The Poor." *Social Problems* 13, no. 2: 118–140.

Simone, AbdouMaliq. 2010. *City Life from Jakarta to Dakar: Movements at the Crossroads*. New York: Routledge.

Skrabut, Kristin. 2018. "Housing the Contingent Life Course: Domestic Aspiration and Extreme Poverty in Peruvian Shantytowns." *City and Society* 30, no. 1: 1–26.

Smith, Michael L. 1994. "Shining Path's Urban Strategy: Ate Vitarte." In *The Shining Path of Peru*, edited by David Scott Palmer, 145–165. New York: St. Martin's Press.

Stack, Carol B. 1974. *All Our Kin: Strategies for Survival in a Black Community*. New York: Harper and Row.

Starn, Orin. 1991. "Missing the Revolution: Anthropologists and the War in Peru." *Cultural Anthropology* 6, no. 1: 63–91.

Stengers, Isabelle. 2005. "The Cosmopolitical Proposal." In *Making Things Public: Atmospheres of Democracy*, edited by Bruno Latour and Peter Weibel, 994–1003. Cambridge, MA: MIT Press.

Stepputat, Finn. 2004. "Marching for Progress: Rituals of Citizenship, State, and Belonging in a High Andes District." *Bulletin of Latin American Research* 23, no. 2: 244–259.

Stokes, Susan C. 1995. *Cultures in Conflict: Social Movements and the State in Peru*. Berkeley: University of California Press.

Strathern, Marilyn. 2000. *Audit Cultures: Anthropological Studies in Accountability, Ethics, and the Academy*. London: Routledge.

Strathern, Marilyn. 2004. "Losing (out on) Intellectual Resources." In *Law, Anthropology, and the Constitution of the Social: Making Persons and Things*, edited by Alain Pottage and Martha Mundy, 201–233. Cambridge, England: Cambridge University Press.

Takenaka, Ayumi, and Karen A. Pren. 2010. "Leaving to Get Ahead: Assessing the Relationship between Mobility and Inequality in Peruvian Migration." *Latin American Perspectives* 37, no. 5: 29–49. https://doi.org/10.1177/0094582X10379106.

Taussig, Michael. 1984. "Culture of Terror—Space of Death. Roger Casement's Putumayo Report and the Explanation of Torture." *Comparative Studies in Society and History* 26, no. 3: 467–497.

Thomas, Todne. 2016. "Strangers, Friends, and Kin: Negotiated Recognition in Ethnographic Relationships." *Anthropology and Humanism* 41, no. 1: 66–85.

Thornton, Arland. 2001. "The Developmental Paradigm, Reading History Sideways, and Family Change." *Demography* 38, no. 4: 449–465.

Thurner, Mark. 1997. *From Two Republics to One Divided: Contradictions of Postcolonial Nationmaking in Andean Peru*. Durham, NC: Duke University Press.

Torribio, Mercedes. 2005. "Recipe for a House." In *The Peru Reader: History, Culture, Politics*, edited by Orin Starn, Carlos Ivan Degregori, and Robin Kirk, 293–295. Durham, NC: Duke University Press.

Trouillot, Michel-Rolph. 2001. "The Anthropology of the State in the Age of Globalization: Close Encounters of the Deceptive Kind." *Current Anthropology* 42, no. 1: 125–138.

Vincent, Susan. 2000. "Flexible Families: Capitalist Development and Crisis in Rural Peru." *Journal of Comparative Family Studies* 31, no. 2: 155–170.

Van Vleet, K. E. 2008. *Performing Kinship: Narrative, Gender, and the Intimacies of Power in the Andes*. Austin: University of Texas Press.

Van Vleet, Krista E. 2019. *Hierarchies of Care: Girls, Motherhood, and Inequality in Peru*. Urbana: University of Illinois Press.

Vargas Llosa, Mario. 1996. *La utopía arcáica: José María Arguedas y las ficciones del indigenismo*. Mexico City: Fondo de Cultura Económica.

Velasco, Juan. 2005 [1969]. "The Master Will No Longer Feed Off Your Poverty." In *The Peru Reader: History, Culture, and Politics*, edited by Orin Starn, Carlos Ivan Degregori, and Robin Kirk, 279–284. Durham, NC: Duke University Press.

Verran, Helen. 2010. "Number as an Inventive Frontier in Knowing and Working Australia's Water Resources." *Anthropological Theory* 10, no. 1–2: 171–178.

Wacquant, Loïc. 2007. "Territorial Stigmatization in the Age of Advanced Marginality." *Thesis Eleven* 91, no. 1: 66–77. https://doi.org/10.1177/0725513607082003.

Wacquant, Loïc. 2008. *Urban Outcasts: A Comparative Sociology of Advanced Marginality*. Malden, MA: Polity.

Wade, Peter. 2008. "Race in Latin America." In *A Companion to Latin American Anthropology*, edited by Deborah Poole, 177–193. Malden, MA: Blackwell.

Walker, Charles. 1999. *Smoldering Ashes: Cuzco and the Creation of Republican Peru, 1780–1840*. Latin America Otherwise. Durham, NC: Duke University Press.

Watkins-Hayes, Celeste, and Elyse Kovalsky. 2016. "The Discourse of Deservingness." In *The Oxford Handbook of the Social Science of Poverty*, edited by David Brady and Linda M. Burton, 193–220. New York: Oxford University Press.

Webb, Richard, Diether Beuermann, and Carla Revilla. 2006. *La construcción del derecho de propiedad: El caso de los asentamientos humanos en Perú*. Lima: Colegio de Notarios de Lima.

Weber, Max. 1968. *Economy and Society: An Outline of Interpretive Sociology*. New York: Bedminster.

Weber, Max. 2006. "Bureaucracy." In *The Anthropology of the State: A Reader*, edited by Aradhana Sharma and Akhil Gupta, 49–71. Malden, MA: Blackwell.

Weinstein, Liza. 2014. *The Durable Slum: Dharavi and the Right to Stay Put in Globalizing Mumbai*. Minneapolis: University of Minnesota Press.

Weismantel, Mary. 1995. "Making Kin: Kinship Theory and Zumbagua Adoptions." *American Ethnologist* 22, no. 4: 685–704. https://doi.org/10.1525/ae.1995.22.4.02a00010.

Weismantel, Mary J. 2001. *Cholas and Pishtacos: Stories of Race and Sex in the Andes*. Women in Culture and Society. Chicago: University of Chicago Press.

Weismantel, Mary, and Mary Elena Wilhoit. 2019. "Kinship in the Andes." In *The Cambridge Handbook of Kinship*, edited by Sandra Bamford, 179–210. Cambridge Handbooks in Anthropology. Cambridge, England: Cambridge University Press. https://doi.org/10.1017/9781139644938.008.

Wilhoit, Mary Elena. 2017. "'Un Favorzote': Gender and Reciprocity in the Andes." *Journal of Latin American and Caribbean Anthropology* 22, no. 3: 438–458.

Wilson, William J. 1987. *The Truly Disadvantaged: The Inner City, the Underclass, and Public Policy*. Chicago: University of Chicago Press.

Wise, Carol. 1994. "The Politics of Peruvian Economic Reform: Overcoming the Legacies of State-Led Development." *Journal of Interamerican Studies and World Affairs* 36, no. 1: 75–125.

Wolf, Eric R. 1966. "Kinship, Friendship, and Patron-Client Relations in Complex Societies." In *The Social Anthropology of Complex Societies*, edited by Michael P. Banton, 1–22. London: Tavistock.

Wolf, Eric R. 1982. *Europe and the People without History*. Berkeley: University of California Press.

World Bank. 2000. *World Development Report 2000–2001: Attacking Poverty*. New York: Oxford University Press.

World Bank. 2020. "Poverty Headcount Ratio at National Poverty Lines (% of Population)—Peru." Poverty and Inequality Platform. https://data.worldbank.org/indicator/SI.POV.NAHC?locations=PE.

Yudice, George. 1991. "Testimonio and postmodernism." *Latin American Perspectives* 18, no. 3: 15–31.

Zarate, Andrea, and Nicholas Casey. 2019. "How a Political Crisis Seized Peru: Boom Times, Corruption, and Chaos at the Top." *New York Times*, October 3. https://www.nytimes.com/2019/10/03/world/americas/peru-corruption-economy.html.

Zhang, Li. 2001. *Strangers in the City: Reconfigurations of Space, Power, and Social Networks within China's Floating Population*. Stanford, CA: Stanford University Press.

Index

Kolibri 360 GmbH
Ferdinand-Jühlke-Straße 7
99095 Erfurt, Deutschland
produktsicherheit@kolibri360.de